IMAGES
of America

Arlington Park Racetrack

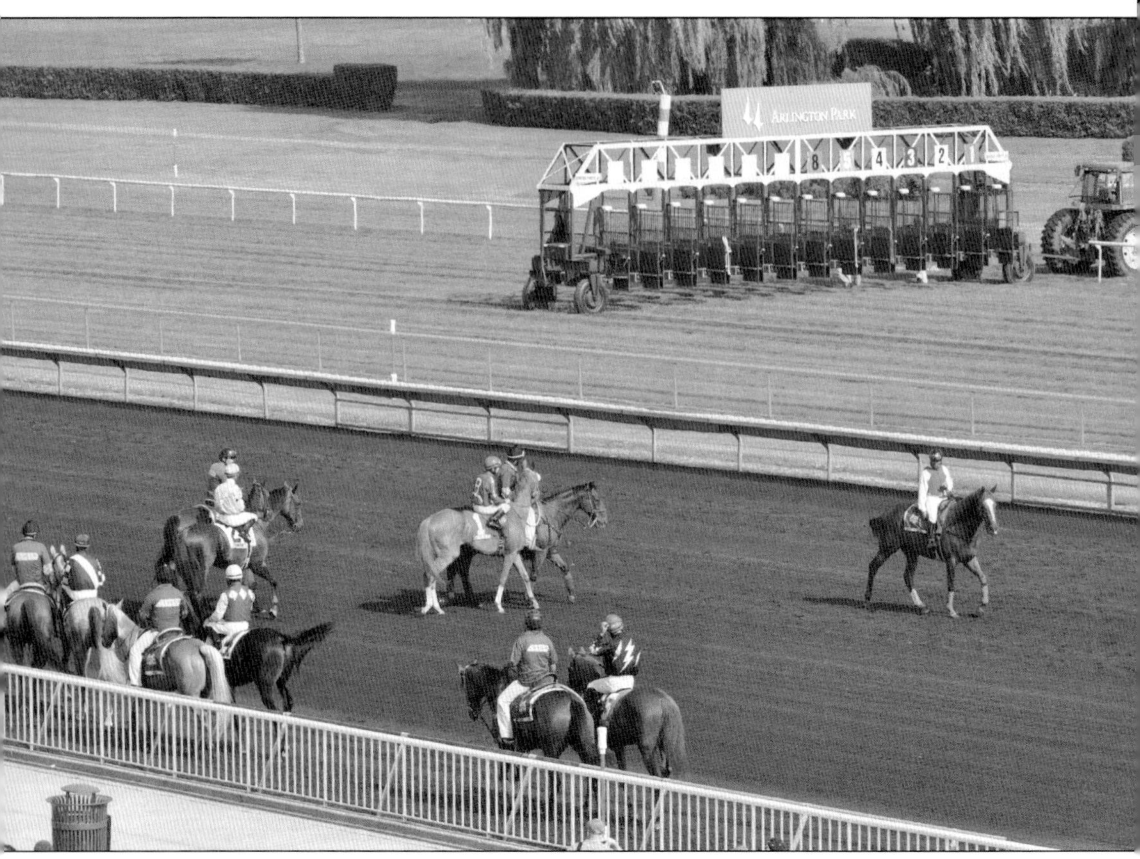

Few racetracks can rival the magnificent stature of Arlington Park. Some of the greatest Thoroughbreds in horse racing history have set hoof over the Arlington dirt and turf courses during the nine decades of its existence along with their teams of trainers, owners, jockeys, and breeders. This book chronicles some of the extraordinary horses and people who have graced Arlington over the years, spotlighting their efforts and accomplishments. (Author's collection.)

On the Cover: A full field of Thoroughbreds round the final turn of the Arlington Park racetrack turf course. A perennial favorite with horse racing fans on both the national and international stages, Arlington has a storied history that has seen it survive multiple ownerships and overcome a devastating fire, only to rise from the ashes to become one of the world's most spectacular racing venues. (Courtesy of Arlington Park.)

IMAGES
of America

ARLINGTON PARK RACETRACK

Kimberly A. Rinker

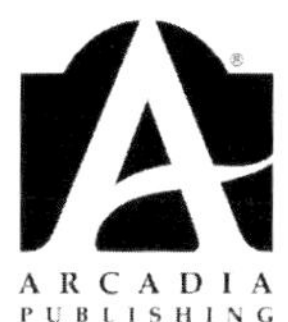

Copyright © 2018 by Kimberly A. Rinker
ISBN 978-1-4671-2879-7

Published by Arcadia Publishing
Charleston, South Carolina

Printed in the United States of America

Library of Congress Control Number: 2017957478

For all general information, please contact Arcadia Publishing:
Telephone 843-853-2070
Fax 843-853-0044
E-mail sales@arcadiapublishing.com
For customer service and orders:
Toll-Free 1-888-313-2665

Visit us on the Internet at www.arcadiapublishing.com

This book is dedicated to the memory of Speed Minister

Contents

ACKNOWLEDGMENTS

The author thanks the following individuals and organizations for supplying photographs and personal recollections that aided in the preparation of this book: Eddie Arroyo, Dr. Bill Cassidy, Renee Catalano, Joan Colby, Jimmy Divito, Moira Fanning, Joe Lindeman, and the Arlington Park and Midwest Outdoors staffs. The author also expresses her thanks to the numerous horses and personalities involved in racing at Arlington over the decades who have made the research for and writing of this book so engaging.

Introduction

Arlington Park's storied history is interwoven with the village of Arlington Heights, which was birthed via William H. Dunton, an early settler whose farm first occupied the area in 1836. The New York native and his family filed a homestead claim for the 160 acres of land that became Arlington Heights. The Duntons' first home was built there in 1845 on an old Indian trail that later became Arlington Heights Road.

Eventually, the North Western railroad line began service throughout the area, which quickly expanded due to the growth of metropolitan Chicago. Between 1910 and 1920, Chicago's outlying suburban areas' population expanded by more than 50 percent, and the 22-mile distance between Arlington Heights and State Street became a quick, half-an-hour ride. By 1926, Arlington Heights' population had boomed to 5,000.

When Illinois reinstated gambling in 1924, H.D. "Curly" Brown headed to the Windy City, uniting Chicago financiers and well-known racehorse owners John Hertz, Otto Lehmann, Laurence Amour, and Frederick McLaughlin together into what became known as the American Jockey Club. Brown was a transplanted Californian entrepreneur who had made his mark by building tracks in places with newly legalized pari-mutuel wagering, such as Florida, Maryland, New Orleans, and Havana, Cuba.

In 1927, Arlington Park began its foray into Illinois and national horse racing history, sprouting from 1,001 acres of land after Brown's American Jockey Club melded together a $3.6 million investment of that patch of prairieland. The new racetrack was hailed as "operating for the sake of sport and not for profit" by local racing aristocracy.

The original plans of Arlington Park called for polo fields, golf courses, riding paths, tennis courts, and a host of other athletic activities to be built as a complement to the racing facility. An 18,000-seat grandstand and a double-oval track were planned—featuring both dirt and turf courses—with stabling for 1,600 horses.

"My intention is to build for this city the most beautiful track in America," Brown is quoted as saying in a 1927 *Chicago Tribune* feature. "Every effort will be made to make the new plant not only the most accommodating from a physical standpoint, but the most scenic. Arlington Park will be a meeting place for society, wealth, industry, and the masses at its opening ceremonies."

When Arlington opened for its initial meeting on a chilly Thursday, October 13, 1927, afternoon, more than 30,000 fans came from the nearby suburbs, riding the Chicago & North Western line from downtown to watch jockey Joe Bollero steer Luxembourg to win the very first race ever contested over its dirt oval. As well, the Chicago Day Handicap was contested, with Chicago mayor William Hale Thompson attending as Ruane, a 19-1 longshot, captured the feature.

The following day, the Associated Press reported that "Arlington is one of the most pretentious (tracks) in America, with quarters so gorgeous that the plant looked like a hotel."

Because of a successful meeting, two more were scheduled for 1928, and during the interim the track's parking lots were completed.

Soon, however, Brown's larcenist nature got the best of him, and he was found to be skimming money from Arlington's coffers, causing dissent among his colleagues, who soon sent him scurrying back to California. Historians offer that Brown absconded with more than half a million of the racetrack's assets before he was discovered, while Arlington had lost just over $100,000.

Chicago gangsters attempted to take over, with little success, from the American Jockey Club members in 1929, and the following season the track was sold to Washington Park owner and real estate developer Benjamin Lindheimer and John Allen of Brinks & Company for $1.6 million. Lindheimer created a year-round racing platform in Chicago—coordinating racing dates between his two tracks. He also began implementing updates to both tracks and installed banked turns over Arlington's turf course, the first track in North America to feature these.

Arlington became known as the "racetrack of firsts," as it was the first to install an electric totalizator (in 1933), the first photo finish camera (1933), and the first electric starting gate (1940).

Arlington shut its doors from 1943 to 1946, due to World War II, but upon reopening hosted some of the greatest horses of the day, including the mighty Citation. When Lindheimer died in 1960, his daughter Marjorie Everett took over the reins and worked tirelessly to attract the nation's top horses, riders, and trainers to Arlington. She implemented the richest race ever at the time—the $357,250 Arlington-Washington Futurity—in 1962, but was ousted in 1971, when she was allegedly involved in a scheme to bribe Illinois governor Otto Kerner for choice racing dates.

In 1969, Gulf & Western Industries merged with Chicago Thoroughbred Enterprises (Arlington's parent company), and former FBI agent John Loome replaced Everett as the new general manger. Madison Square Garden then purchased Arlington in 1971.

In 1973, Arlington hosted a special race for three-year-olds—the Arlington Invitational, bringing Triple Crown winner Secretariat to the track. The chestnut colt's appearance caused a sensation, boosting attendance and handle when he appeared at Arlington that summer. A turf race named in his honor was later created.

In 1981, Arlington Park hosted the inaugural Arlington Million—the world's first million-dollar Thoroughbred race—making John Henry a national hero. In the mid-1980s, Richard Duchossois bought out partners Joe Joyce, Sheldon Robbins, and Ralph Ross to become Arlington's sole proprietor. Duchossois envisioned a newer, greater Arlington, but then tragedy struck in late July 1985, when an electrical malfunction caused a five-alarm fire that destroyed the grandstand and clubhouse. Duchossois's crew worked night and day, clearing countless piles of debris, until finally, three weeks later, on August 25, more than 35,000 patrons seated in temporary stands watched the "Miracle Million" run as scheduled.

Arlington Park was subsequently rebuilt and reopened in 1989, emerging as the magnificent facility it is today. In another "first," Arlington became the only Illinois racetrack to hold the prestigious Breeders' Cup Championships, in 2002.

Today, Arlington Park stands as symbol of pride throughout the community of Arlington Heights—which now lies in both Cook and Lake Counties, and boasts an area of 16,639 acres and 76,024 residents—the highest population density of an incorporated American village.

One

Curly's Vision 1927–1969

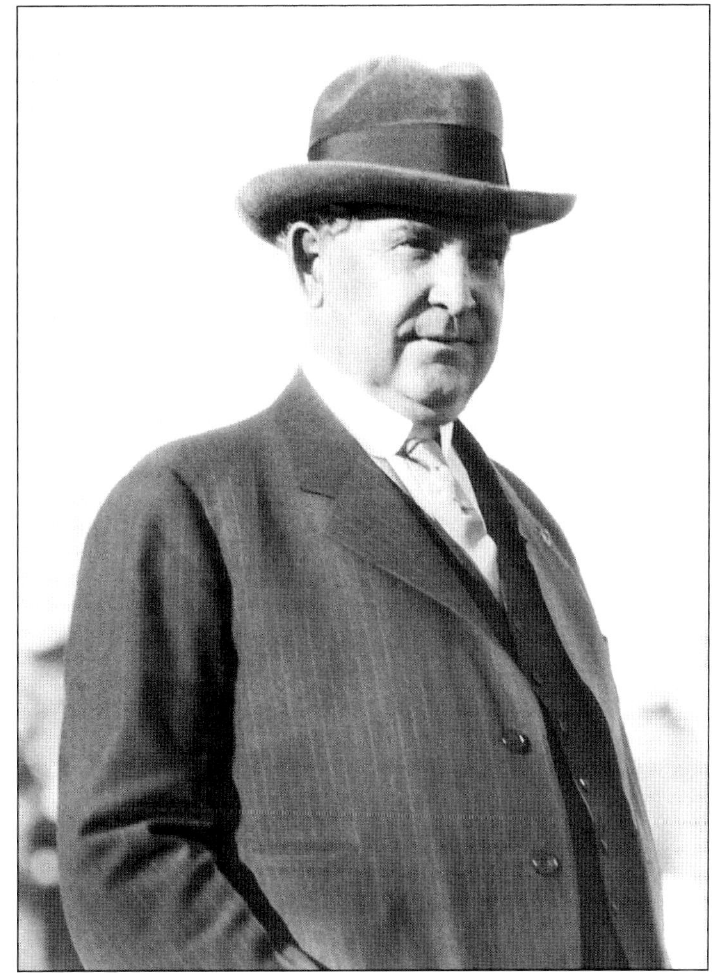

Harry D. "Curly" Brown was a self-made businessman and visionary. Born March 19, 1863, Brown built tracks in Maryland, Florida, New Orleans, and Cuba before purchasing 1,001 acres northwest of Chicago once pari-mutuel wagering was implemented in the Prairie State. On June 27, 1927, he broke dirt in the ground near the Chicago and North Western Railroad lines and began the process of building Arlington Park. (Courtesy of Arlington Park.)

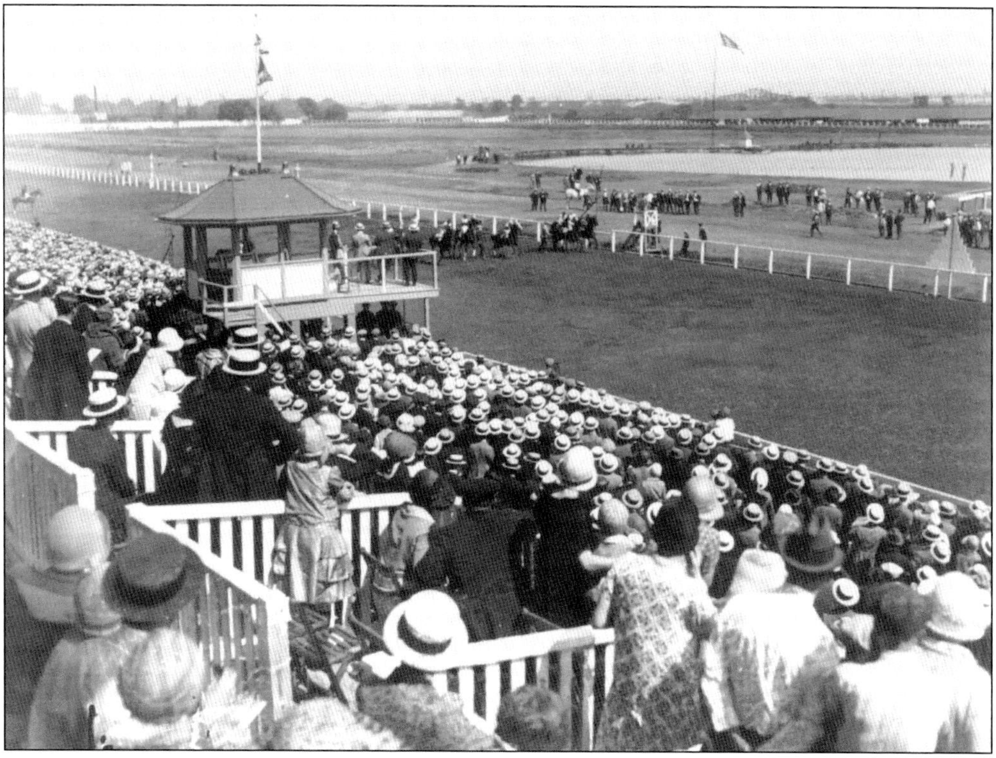

When Arlington Park opened on October 13, 1927, more than 20,000 fans witnessed jockey Joe Bollero—a 16-year-old apprentice—win the very first race with trainer Frank Rector's Luxembourg, a three-year-old stallion he steered to victory in 1:19 over six furlongs on a muddy track, returning $2.92 as the favorite. Starter Lester Dean raised the tape long before modern-day starting gates were in fashion, as Arlington Heights welcomed in the new one-and-one-eighth-mile track with an inside one-mile turf course. Arlington Park dignitaries included Charles McCulloch, chairman of the board; Otto Lehman, president; and John D. Hertz, chairman. Steeplechase races were held on a limited basis throughout the decades, as the course was changed to dirt and then back to grass. A second, seven-and-a-half-furlong, inside turf course was added in 1967. (Courtesy of Arlington Park.)

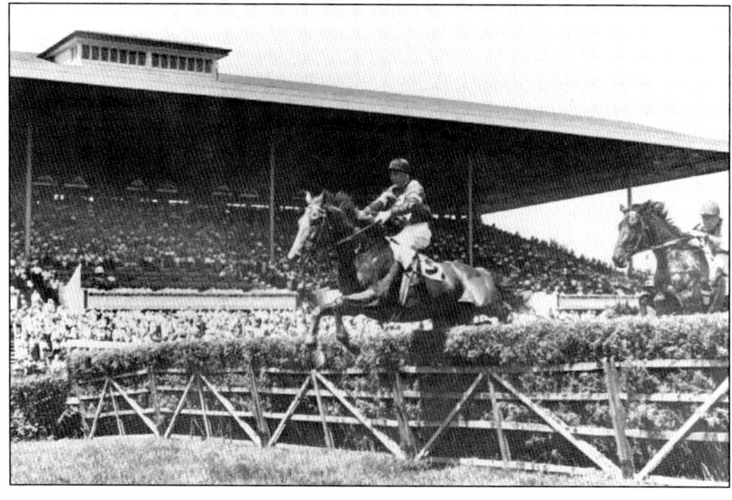

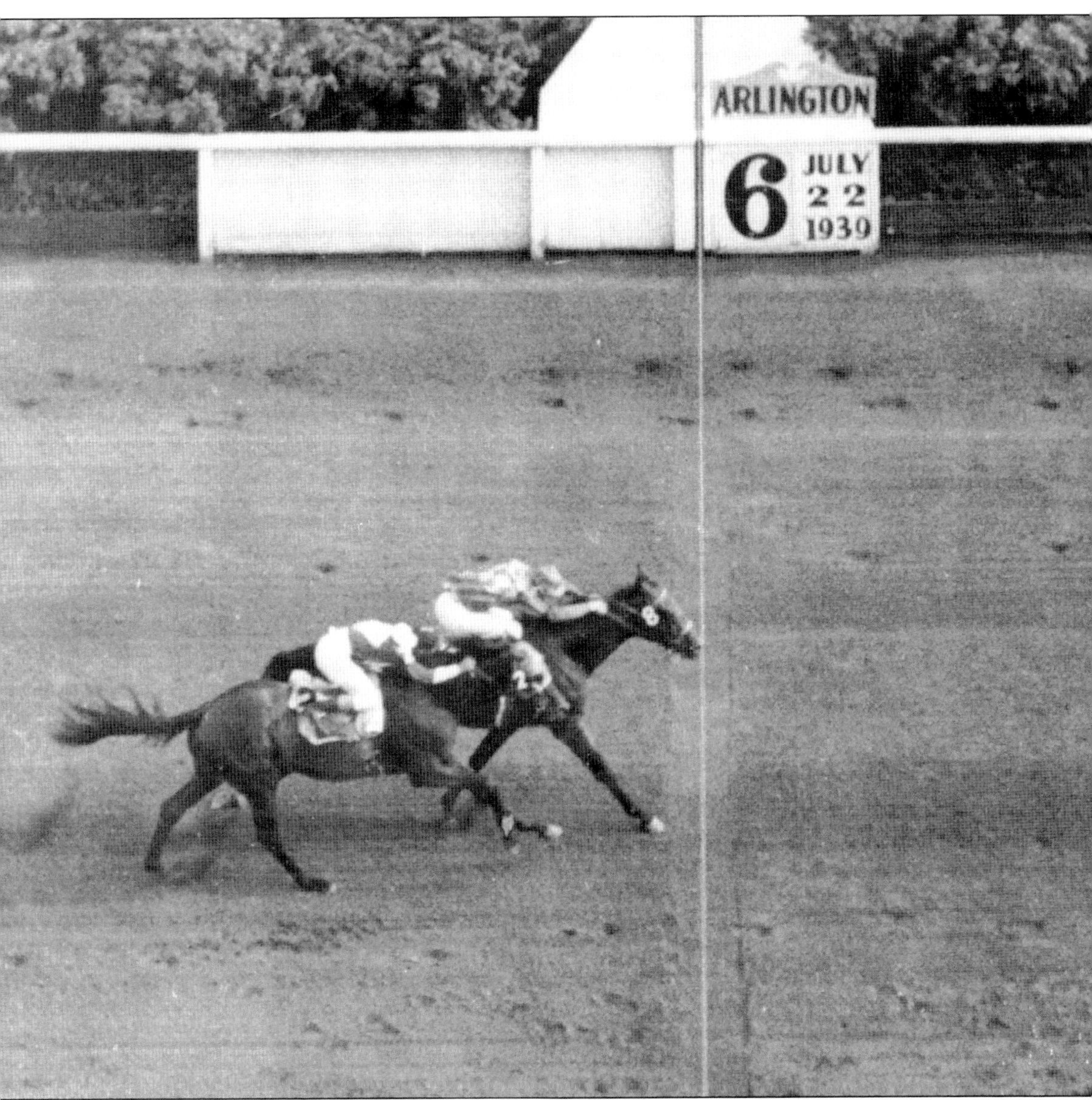

In 1929, the American National Jockey Club was reorganized, sporting $500,000 in purses for the Arlington meeting, of which $147,000 was added for stakes. On July 13, 1929, more than 50,000 people attended the $50,000 Arlington Classic for three-year-olds and up. The 14-horse field included Kentucky Derby, American Derby, Withers, Belmont, Kentucky Oaks, Illinois Oaks, and Preakness winners. Blue Larkspur won that first edition of the Classic by five lengths and was named 1929 Champion Three-Year-Old Colt and Horse of the Year. In 1936, Arlington became the first racetrack in the Windy City to install a photo finish camera, known as the "Eye in the Sky." The advent of such cameras was an attempt to protect the betting public and to determine, without a doubt, the race winner when the finish was close. (Author's collection.)

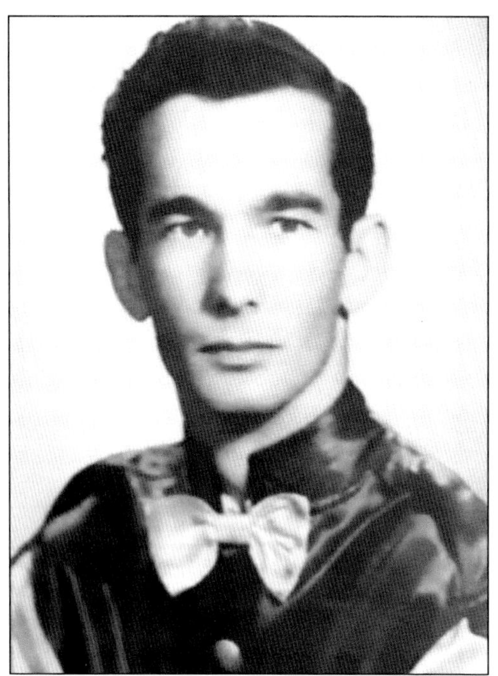

William Lee Shoemaker was born August 19, 1931 in Fabens, Texas. Known as "Willie" or "the Shoe," he became one of the greatest jockeys of all time. Shoemaker scored 8,833 career victories aboard some of racing's greatest equine athletes in a career that spanned six decades and won the Arlington Handicap four times, as well as other major stakes at the Illinois oval. (Courtesy of Arlington Park.)

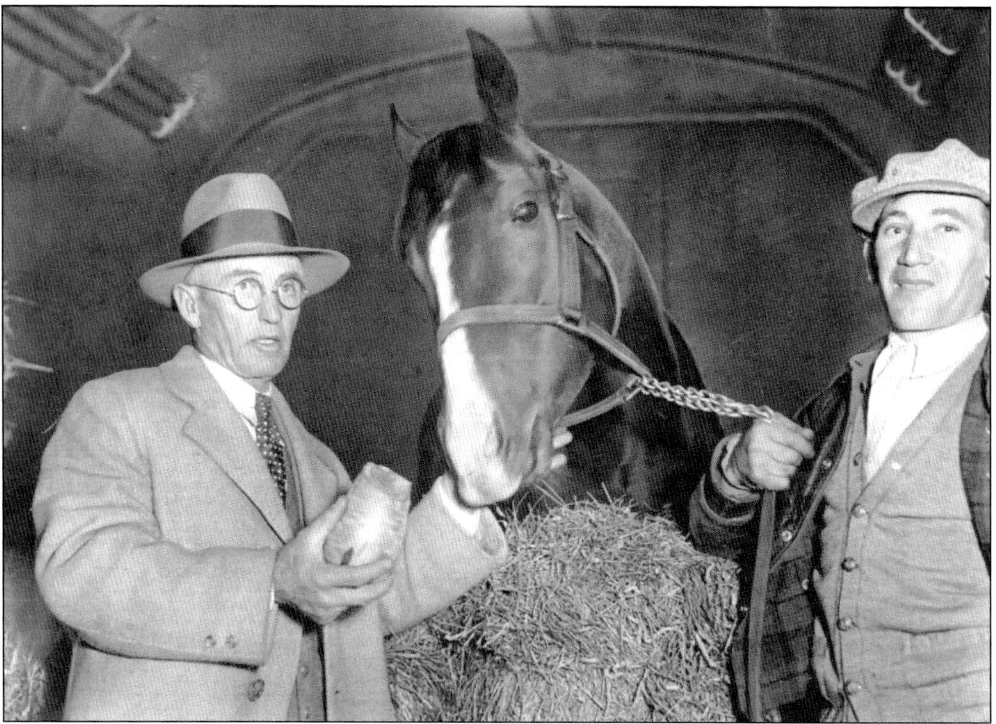

Triple Crown winner Gallant Fox was foaled March 23, 1927, at Claiborne Farm in Paris, Kentucky, and was owned by William Woodward Sr. and trained by James E. "Sunny Jim" Fitzsimmons. After sweeping the Kentucky Derby, Preakness, and Belmont Stakes, Gallant Fox came to Arlington in 1930 in a first-class train car. He is shown here eating a sweet potato with his connections. (Courtesy of Arlington Park.)

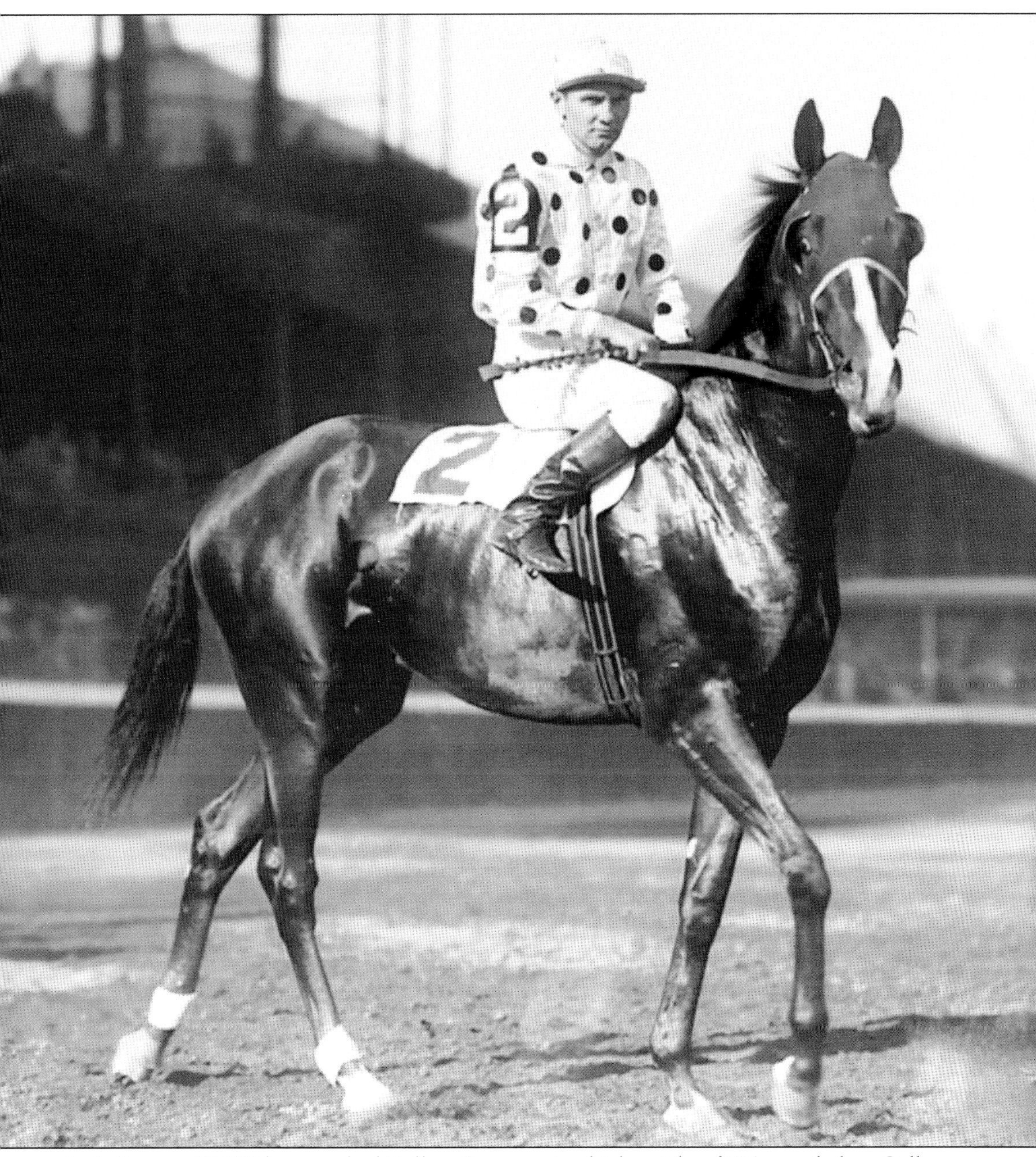

At Arlington, 60,000 fans watched Gallant Fox, carrying high weight of 126 pounds, best Gallant Knight by a neck in the Arlington Classic. Jockey Earle Sande came out of retirement specifically to ride Gallant Fox, who scored 11 career wins, 3 seconds, and 2 thirds from 17 career starts. He was the first horse to earn more than $300,000 in a single season. Gallant Fox became a successful sire, died on November 13, 1954, and was buried at Claiborne Farm in Lexington, Kentucky. He was inducted into the National Museum of Racing and Hall of Fame in 1957 and is ranked 28th in *Blood Horse* magazine's Top 100 US Thoroughbred Champions of the 20th Century. (Courtesy of Arlington Park.)

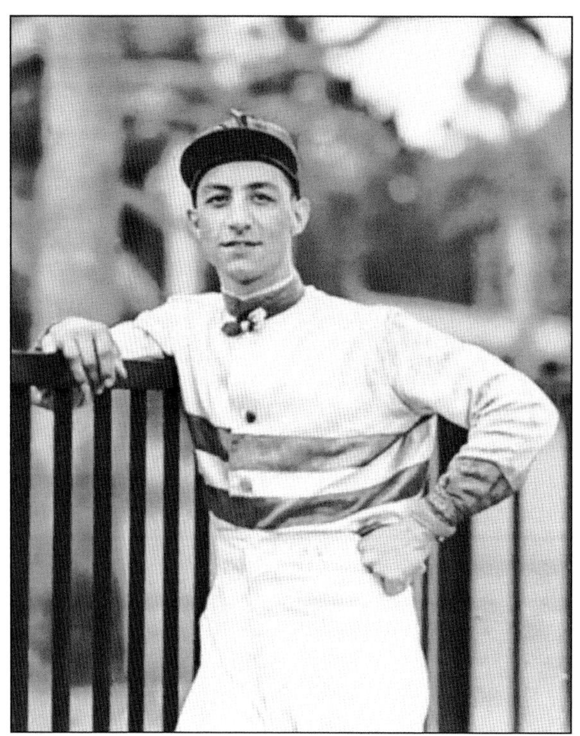

George Edward "Eddie" Arcaro was one of the most successful riders of all time and the first jockey to win five Kentucky Derbys. Born February 19, 1916, in Cincinnati, Ohio, Arcaro won 4,779 during his career, which began in 1932, and earned $30,039,543. He retired from riding in 1962 and was inducted into the National Museum of Racing and Hall of Fame in 1958. (Courtesy of Arlington Park.)

Citation, shown here in an early morning gallop, was foaled April 11, 1945, and was the first horse in history to earn $1 million. Because of his tendency to run off with his exercise rider, a special bit was created to help slow him down, and was coined the "Citation bit," which is still used by trainers today to control unruly horses. (Courtesy of Arlington Park.)

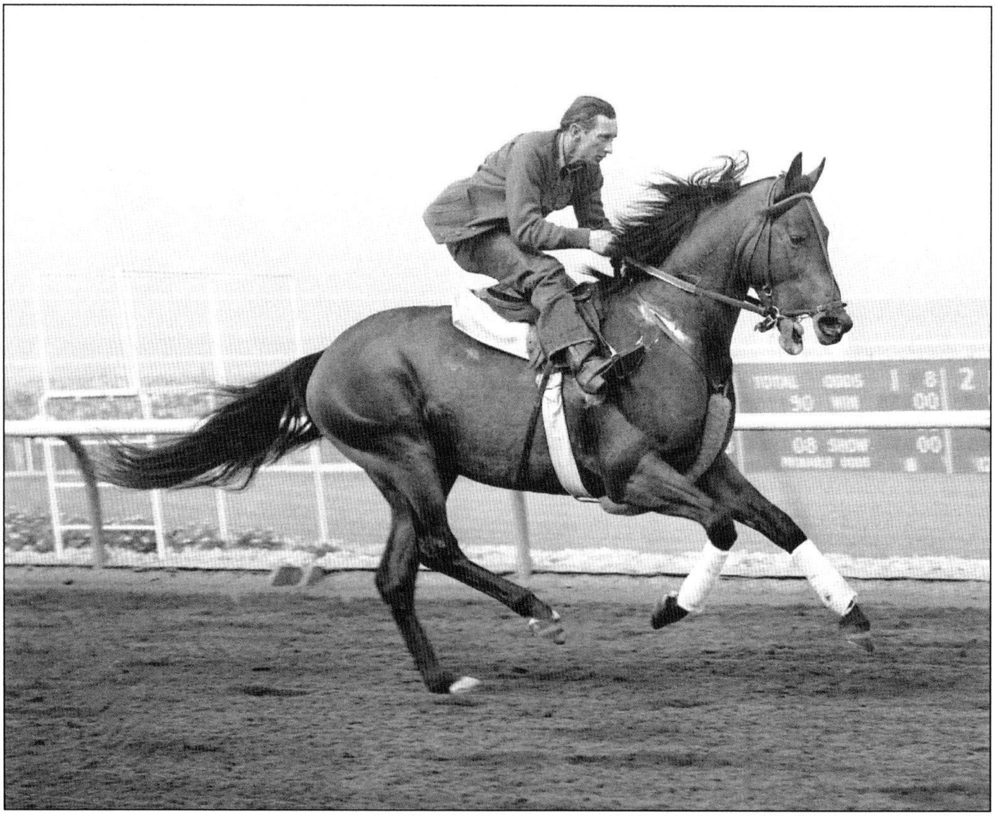

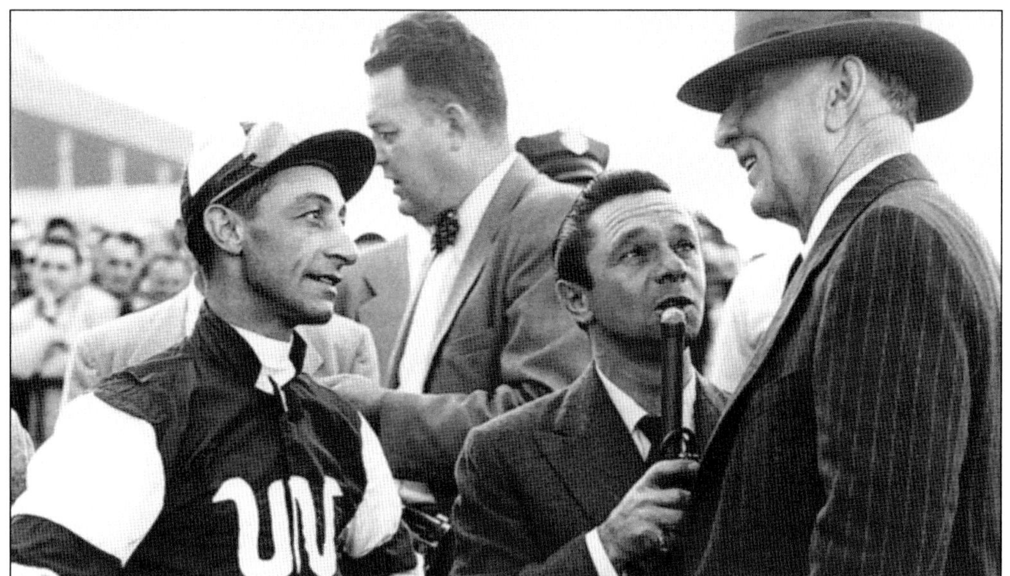

Jockey Eddie Arcaro is seen with Hall of Fame trainer Max Hirsch (July 12, 1880–April 3, 1969). Hirsch conditioned horses for the King Ranch Stable for most of his career, as well as for the Vanderbilt and Hancock families. He won the Arlington Classic three times—in 1932, 1941, and 1947—and trained Assault to win the 1946 Triple Crown. (Courtesy of Arlington Park.)

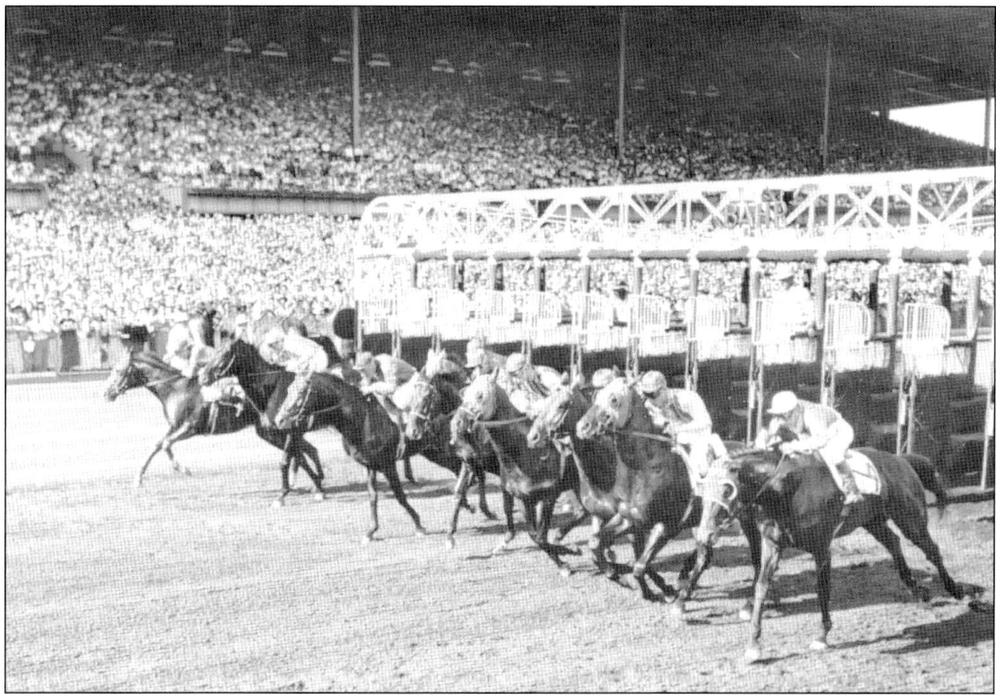

Citation, sixth from the right, is pictured at the start of the 1948 Stars & Stripes Handicap at Arlington Park. The son of Bull Lea was the eighth Triple Crown winner (1948) and one of three North American Thoroughbreds to win at least 16 consecutive stakes races—along with champions Cigar and Zenyatta. Citation earned $1,085,760 from 32 wins, 10 seconds, and 2 thirds in 45 starts. (Courtesy of Arlington Park.)

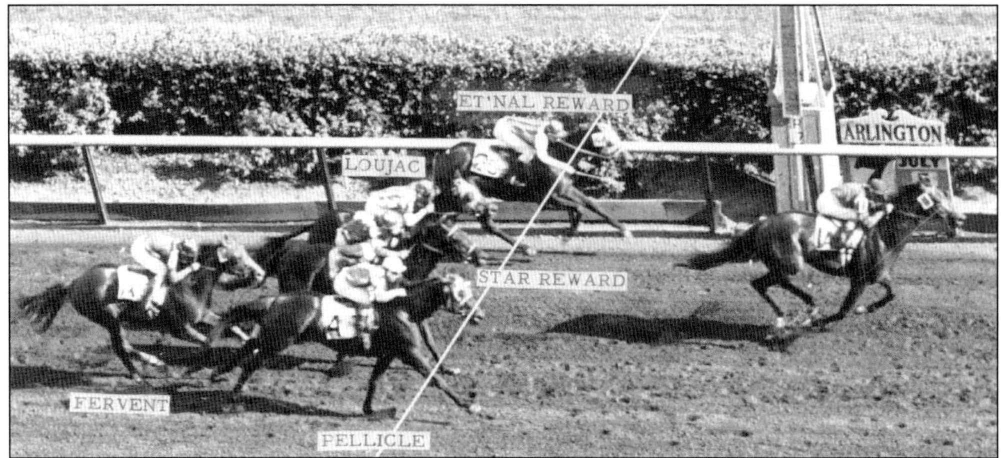

Citation is shown here winning the 1948 Stars & Stripes Handicap at Arlington over Eternal Reward and Pellicle in 1:49.20 for the nine-furlong contest. He was trained by Hall of Famers Ben and Jimmy Jones and originally was ridden by Al Snider, then by Eddie Arcaro, and later by Steve Brooks. Citation was bred and owned by the famed Calumet Farm. (Courtesy of Arlington Park.)

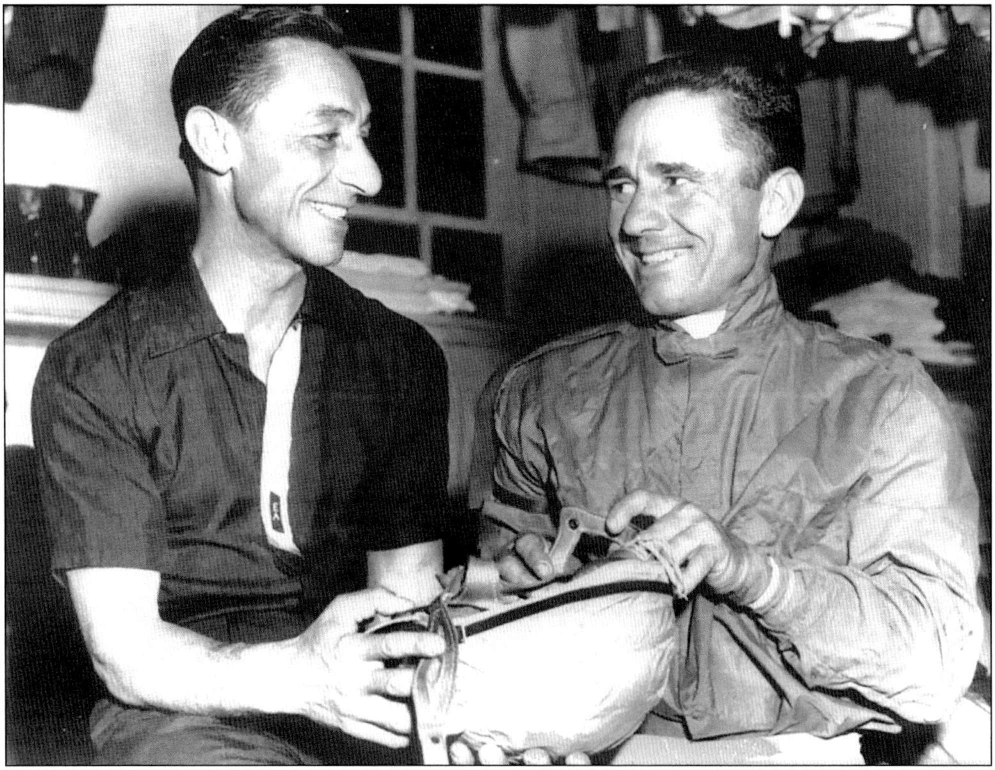

Eddie Arcaro (left) and Johnny Longden (right) share a laugh. Longden (February 14, 1907–February 14, 2003) was born in England and emigrated to Canada, becoming one of North America's top jockeys. Nicknamed the "Pumper" because of his aggressive riding style, Longden won the 1943 Triple Crown aboard Count Fleet, and was inducted into the National Museum of Racing and Hall of Fame in 1958. (Courtesy of Arlington Park.)

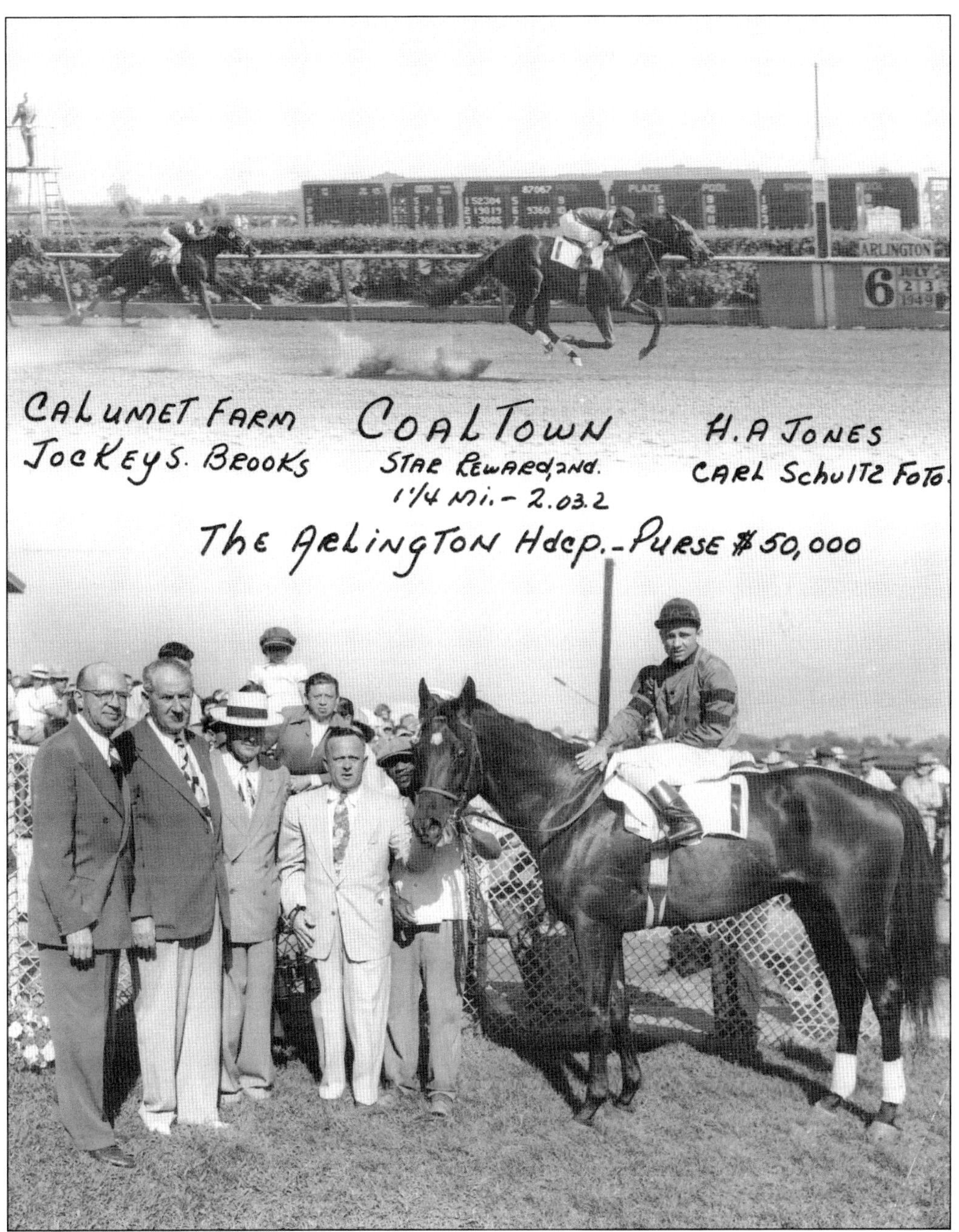

Coaltown was a stablemate to Citation and a top horse in his own right. He finished second to Citation in the 1948 Kentucky Derby and was named 1948's Champion Sprinter. He is shown winning the $50,000 Arlington Handicap in 1949 for trainer Ben Jones and owner Calumet Farm, with Steve Brooks in the saddle, timed in 2:03.2 for the one-and-one-quarter-mile event. He also won the Stars & Stripes that same year and later retired with $415,675 in career earnings from 23 wins, 6 seconds, and 3 thirds from 39 starts. He began his stallion career at Calumet in 1952 with limited success and was exported to France in 1955, where he remained until his death in 1965 at age 20. Coaltown was inducted into the National Museum of Racing and Hall of Fame in 1983. (Author's collection.)

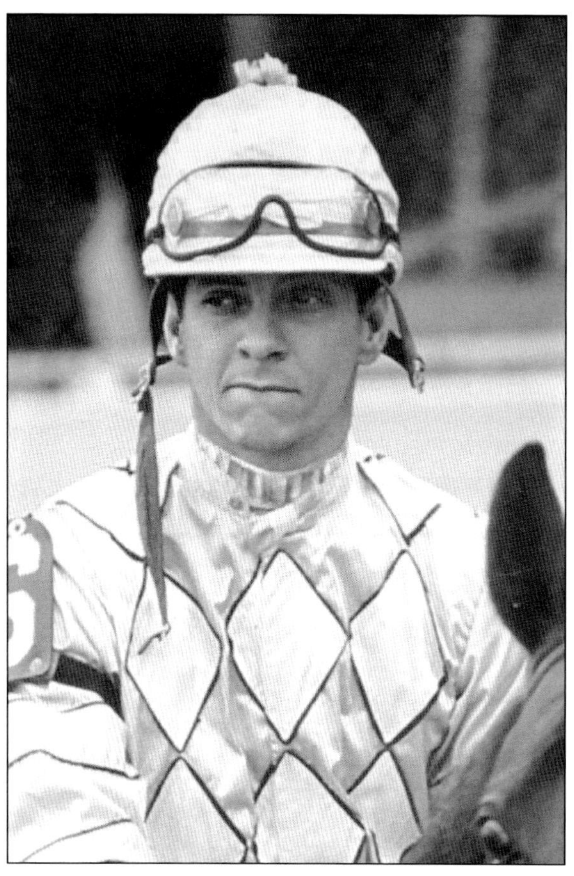

Hall of Fame jockey Bill Hartack was the leading American rider from 1955 to 1957 and again in 1960 and was Arlington's leading money-winning jockey in 1956 and 1957. He was the first jockey to earn $3 million a year, won five Kentucky Derbies, and scored his 3,000th victory at Arlington on July 7, 1962, astride Big Steve. Hartack later became a Chicago-based steward upon his retirement from riding. (Author's collection.)

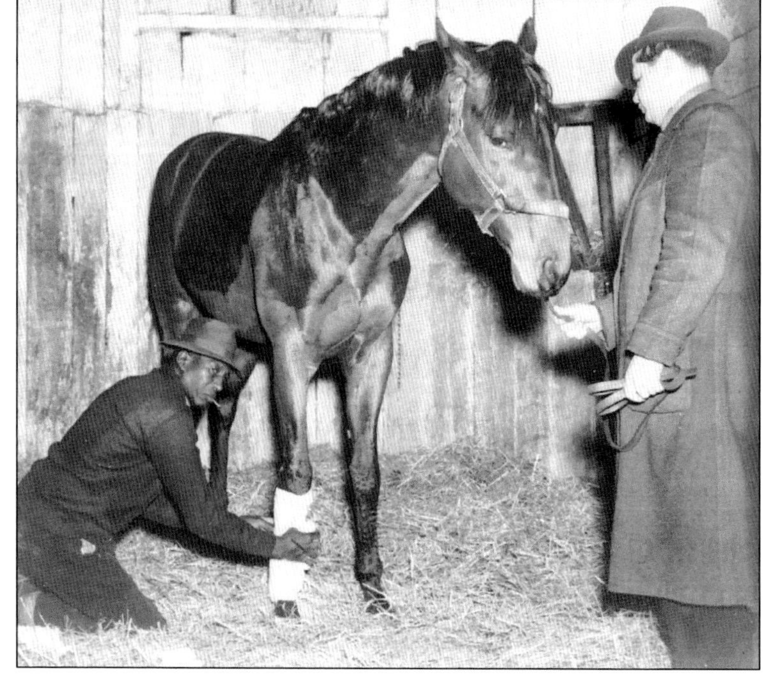

A horse stands quietly in his stall at Arlington Park while a caretaker bandages a front leg. Horses wear bandages for support and protection both on and off the racetrack. Here, the caretaker bandages a horse's leg after a workout. Many trainers like to have their horses wear standing, or stall, bandages while relaxing in their stalls to support leg tendons and ligaments. (Courtesy of Midwest Outdoors.)

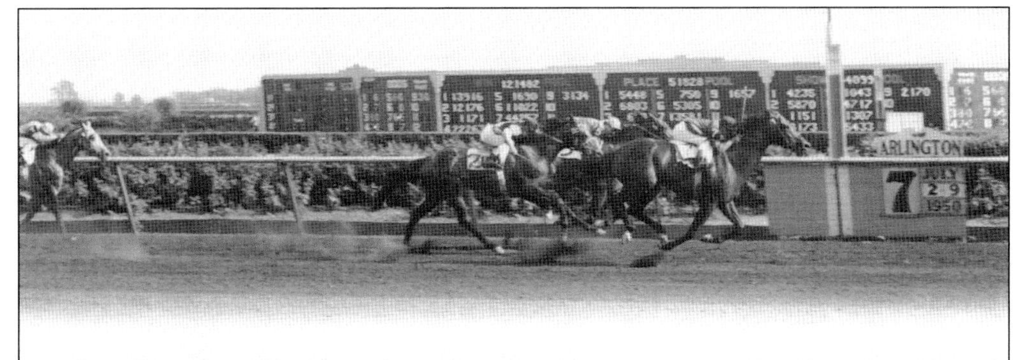

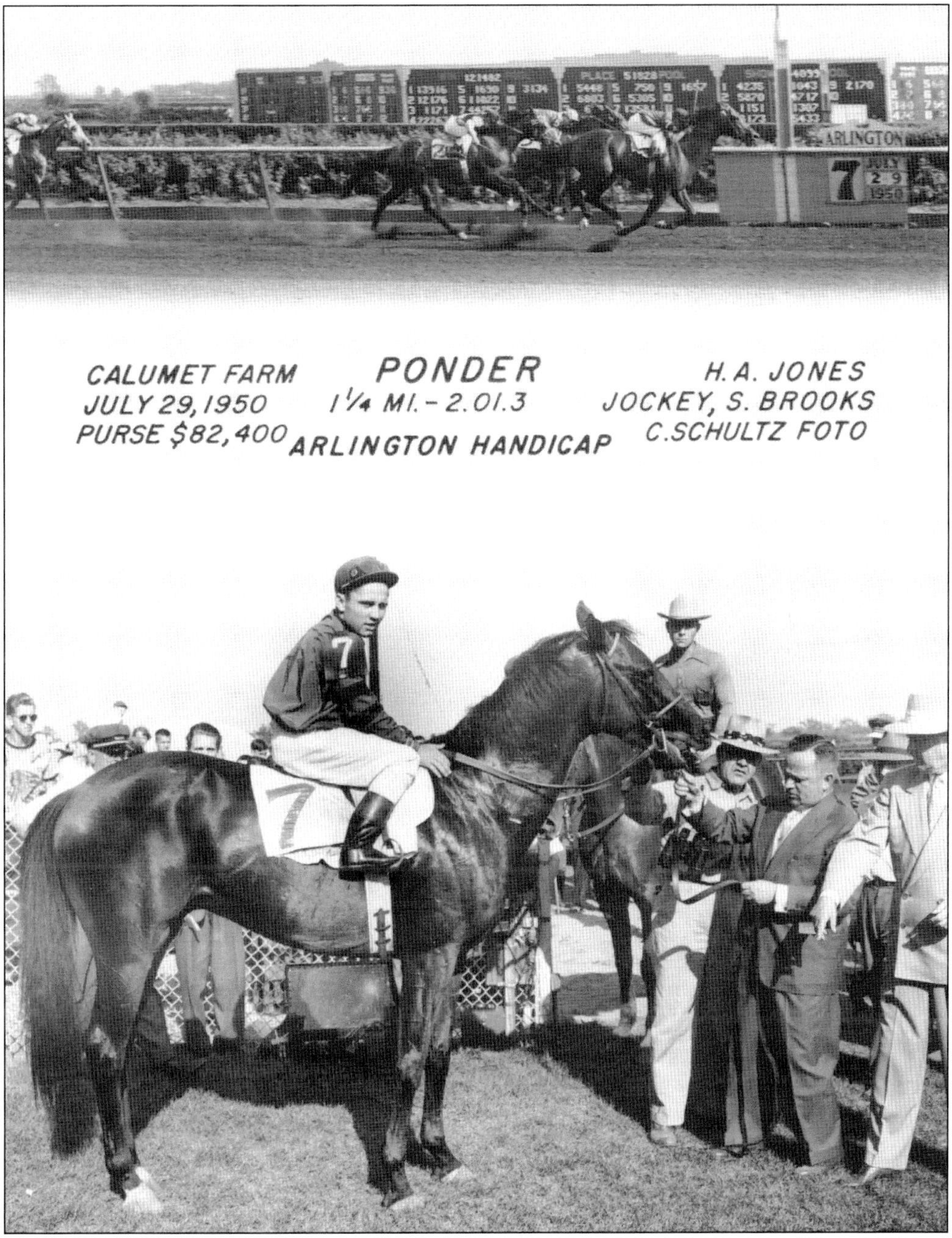

CALUMET FARM PONDER H.A. JONES
JULY 29, 1950 1¼ MI. - 2.01.3 JOCKEY, S. BROOKS
PURSE $82,400 ARLINGTON HANDICAP C.SCHULTZ FOTO

Another stablemate of the great Citation was Ponder, who was foaled April 14, 1946—bred and owned by historic Calumet Farm—and earned $541,275 under the watchful eye of trainer H.A. "Ben" Jones. Ponder is shown here winning the $82,400 Arlington Handicap on July 29, 1950, for jockey Steve Brooks. Ponder's sire, Pensive, won the 1944 Kentucky Derby, and Ponder followed in his father's hoofprints, winning the 1949 Kentucky Derby, and later sired 1956 Kentucky Derby winner Needles. Ponder also captured the 1949 Arlington Classic and retired with $542,275 in career earnings from 14 wins, 7 seconds, and 4 thirds in 41 lifetime starts. He died October 10, 1958. (Author's collection.)

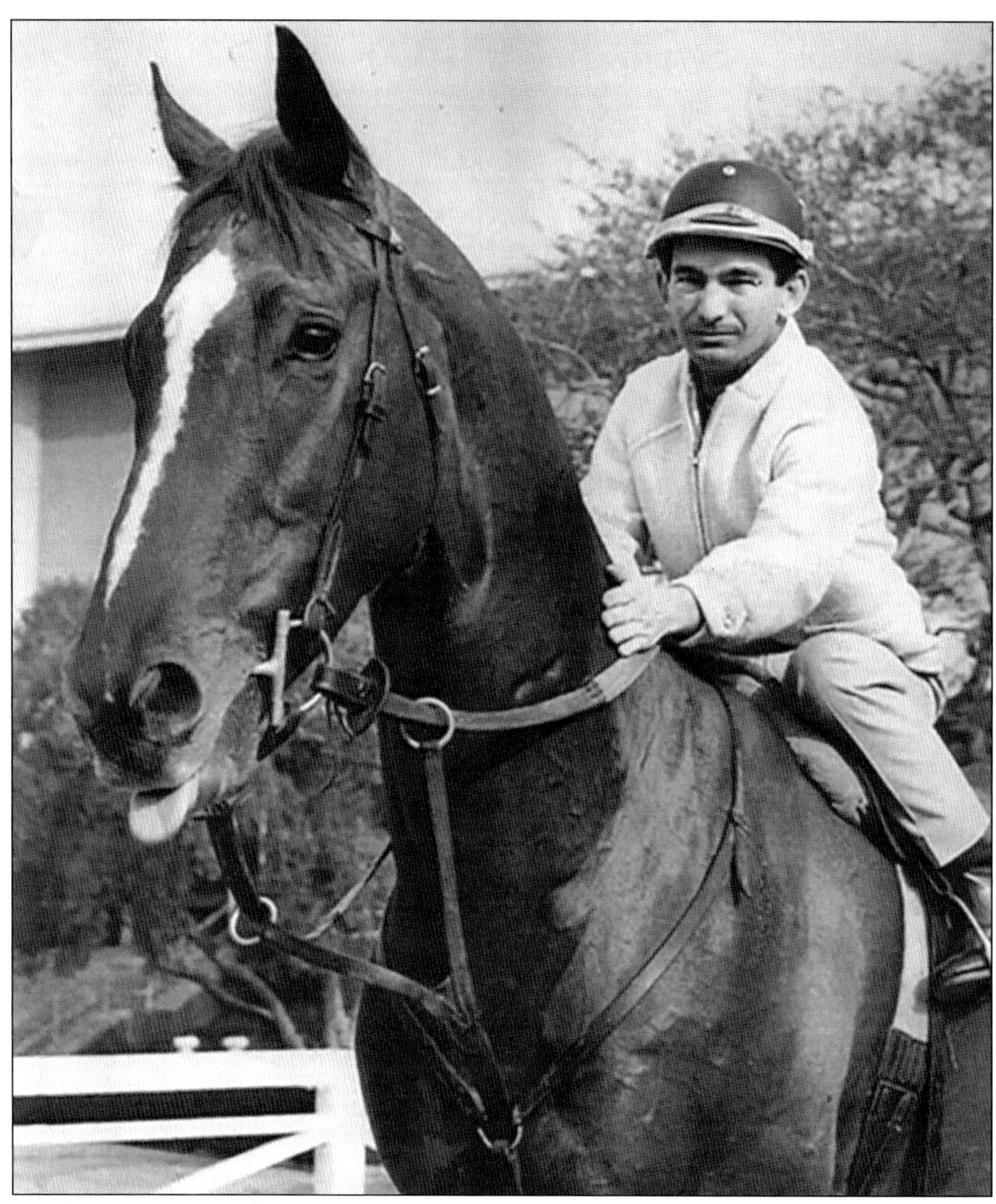

Candy Spots was a graded stakes winning son by Argentine stallion Nigromante–Candy Dish, by Khaled, who earned $824,718 from 12 wins, 5 seconds, and 1 third in 22 lifetime starts. The striking chestnut stallion, who was foaled in California on April 14, 1960, was named for the unusual white and black markings that were splattered intermittently along his hind legs and rump. Candy Spots was one of the top juvenile colts of 1962 and was undefeated going into the 1963 Kentucky Derby, where he finished third to the winning Chateaugay. Bred and owned by Rex Ellsworth, and trained throughout most of his career by Meshach A. Tenney, Candy Spots was ridden by Bill Shoemaker to victory in the richest race ever run up until that time—the $357,250 Arlington Park Futurity. (Author's collection.)

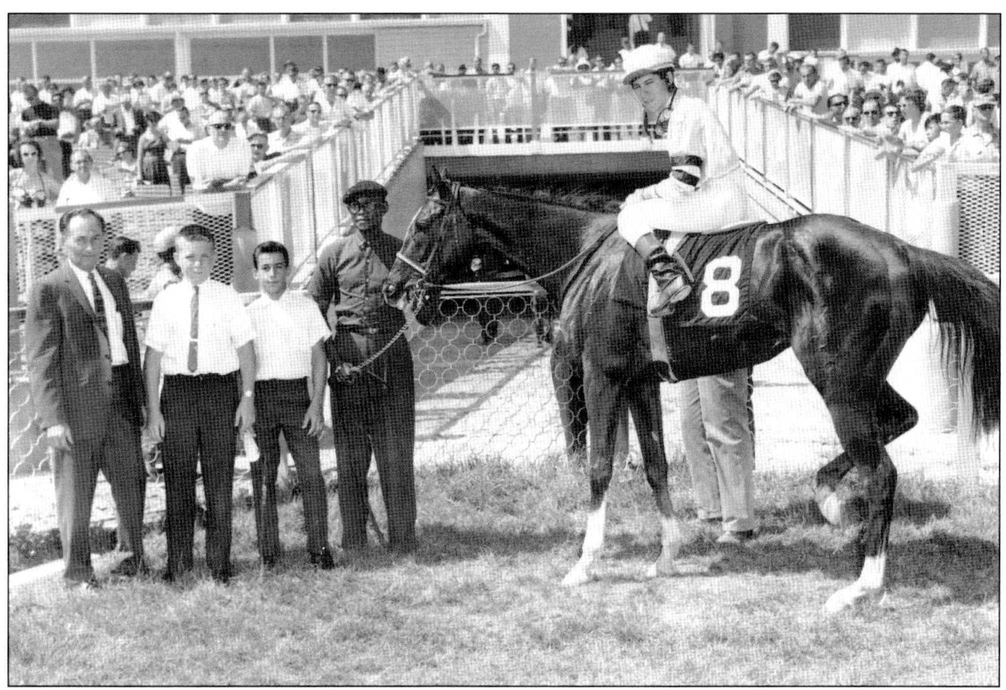

A packed crowd watches as Always Alive gets his photograph taken in the Arlington winner's circle on June 27, 1964, after capturing the third race. Owned by the North Star Ranch, Always Alive covered the one-mile test over the dirt in 1:37.2 for rider E. Dewey Keller and trainer N.J. Moran, besting rivals Mad Genius, second, and Always Mine, third. (Kuprion Photo, courtesy of James Divito.)

By the 1960s, racehorses rarely traveled by train anymore, with owners and trainers preferring to ship horses via commercial van services, such as the one shown in this photograph arriving at Arlington Park. Today, the four-to-five-day journey by train from California to New York has been replaced by a five-hour flight aboard a cargo plane designed especially for horses. (Courtesy of Midwest Outdoors.)

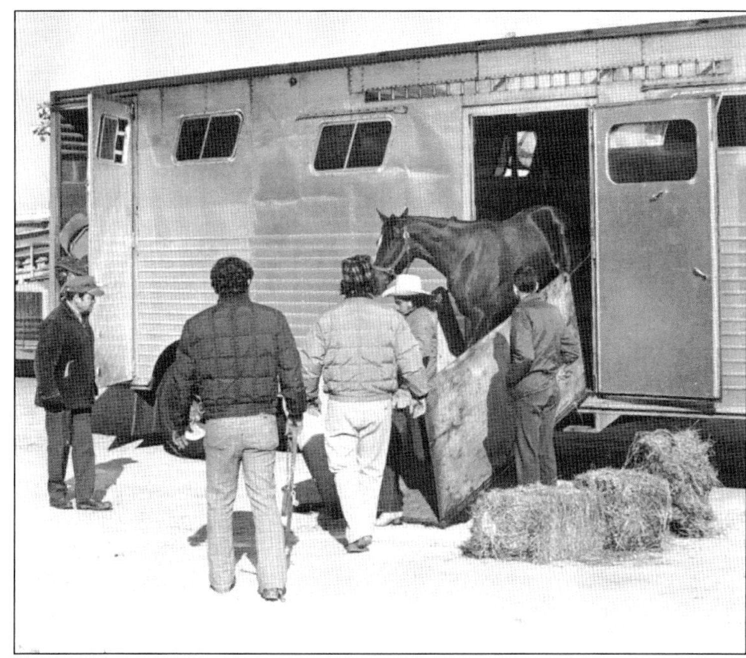

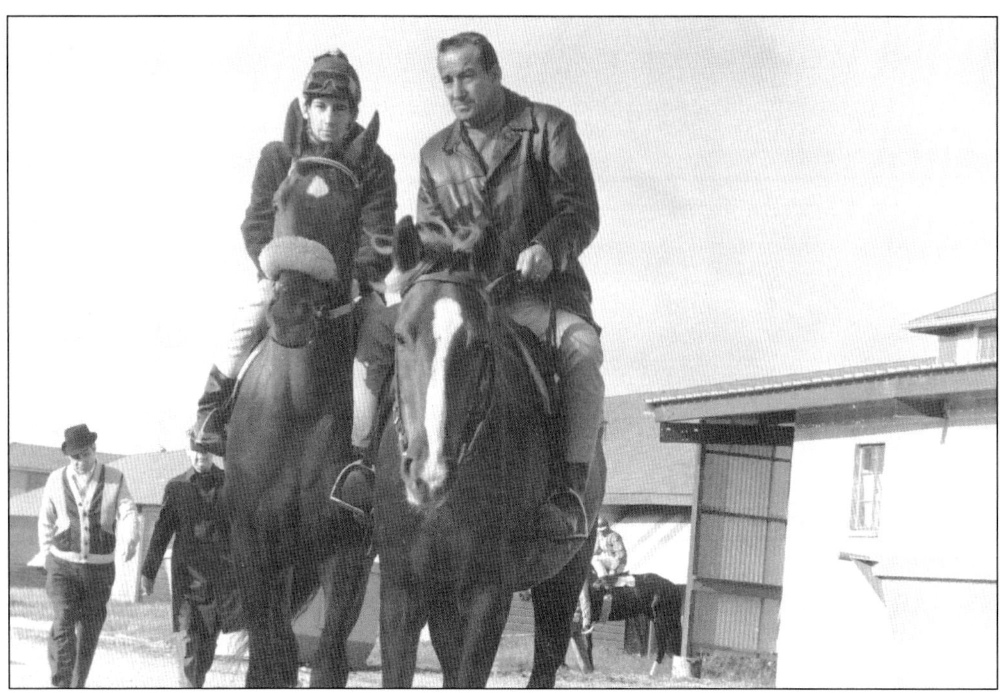

Racing has always been a family-based sport, with many trainers or jockeys following in the footsteps of their fathers and mothers. The image above shows 18-year-old James Divito being led to the Arlington track for a morning workout aboard Vee Jack, by his father, trainer Pete Divito. Vee Jack was a 1964 foal by Admiral Vee, who captured the 1966 Southern Illinois Juvenile Stakes. The elder Divito was a successful trainer who had first plied his wares on the West Coast before coming to Chicago, conditioning the winners of over $1 million for comedians Laurel and Hardy and candy heiress Helen Brach, among others. The photograph below shows the young Divito on his way to the starting gate for the first time with Vee Jack at Arlington on June 24, 1968. The pair finished third. (Courtesy of James Divito.)

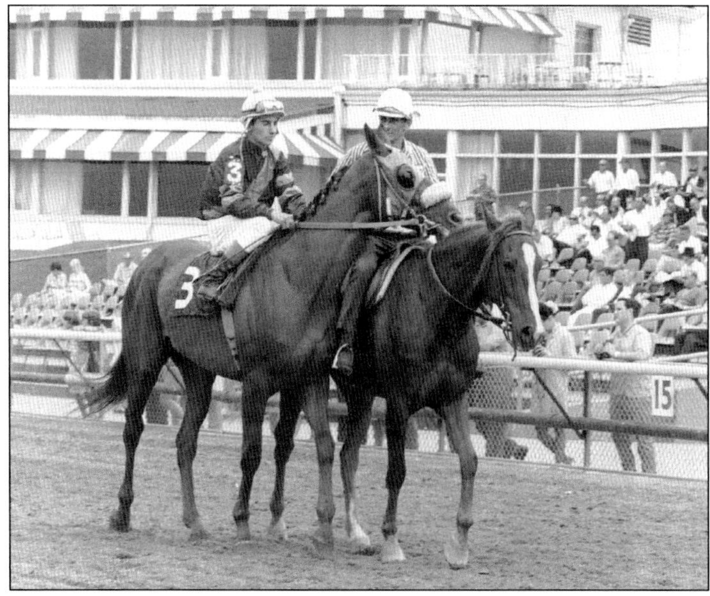

The Florida-bred Dr. Fager was foaled April 6, 1964, on owner William. L. McKnight's Tartan Farm. Named for the brain surgeon (Dr. Charles Fager) who had saved Hall of Fame trainer John Nerud's life after a 1965 fall from a stable pony, Dr. Fager was the son of 1951 Santa Anita Derby winner Rough n' Tumble, out of Aspidistra, who produced champion sprinter Ta Wee. Dr. Fager's victory in the $106,000 Arlington Classic with Braulio Baeza up, on June 24, 1967, saw him romp to a 10-length win despite a muddy track. He retired with 18 wins, 2 seconds, and 1 third in 22 starts, winning at distances of seven furlongs to one and a quarter miles; on dirt and grass at eight different tracks, setting or equaling three track records and establishing one world record, and earning $1,002,642. (Author's collection.)

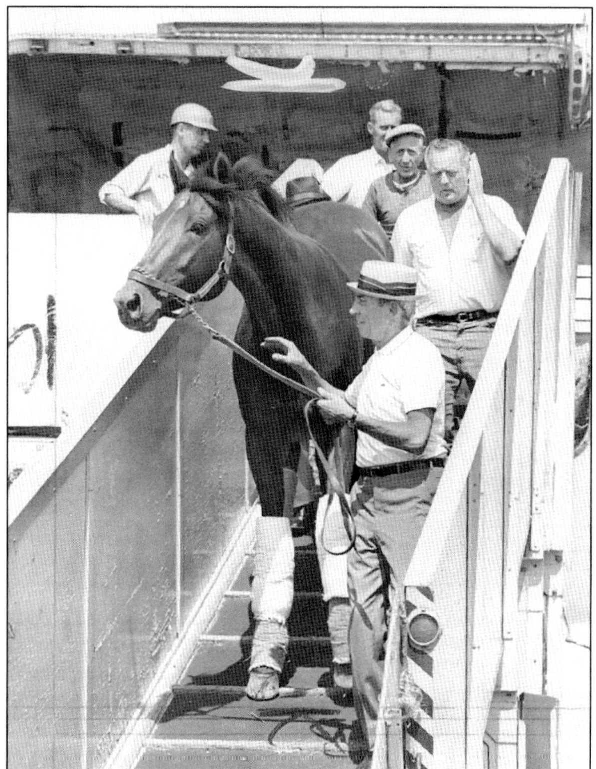

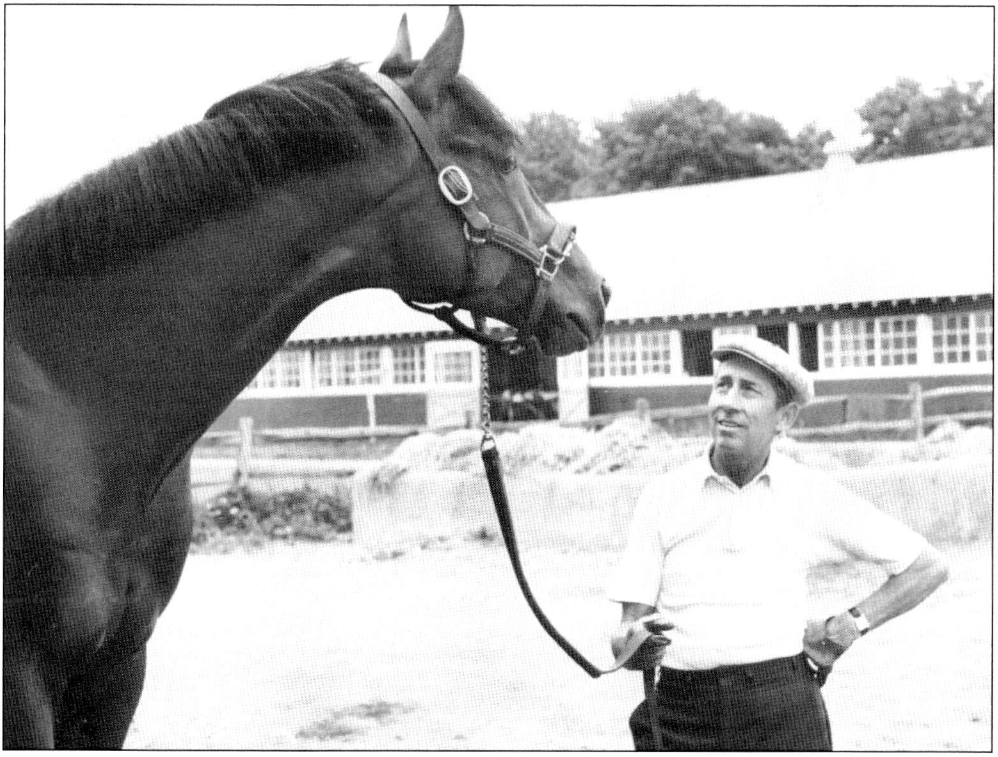

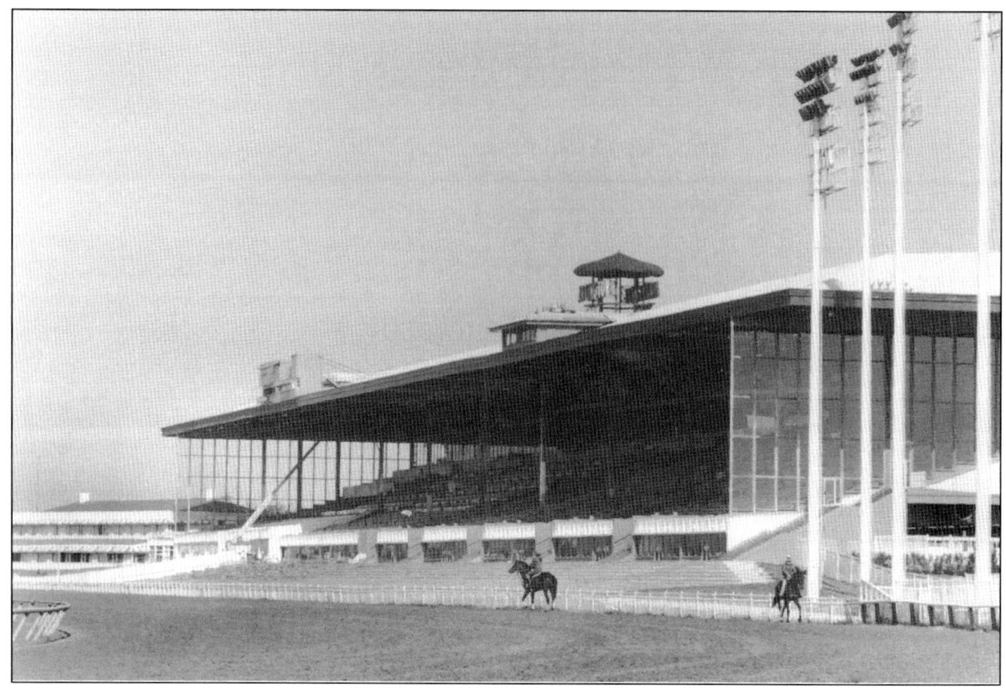

Horses work out at Arlington in 1968, the year Dr. Fager returned, this time winning the Washington Park Handicap in a world-record clocking of 1:32.1 by 10 lengths, with 134 pounds on his back, conceding 16 to 20 pounds more than his rivals. Carrying Baeza, Dr. Fager shattered Buckpasser's old record by two-fifths of a second. Dr. Fager's record would stand for three decades. (Courtesy of Midwest Outdoors.)

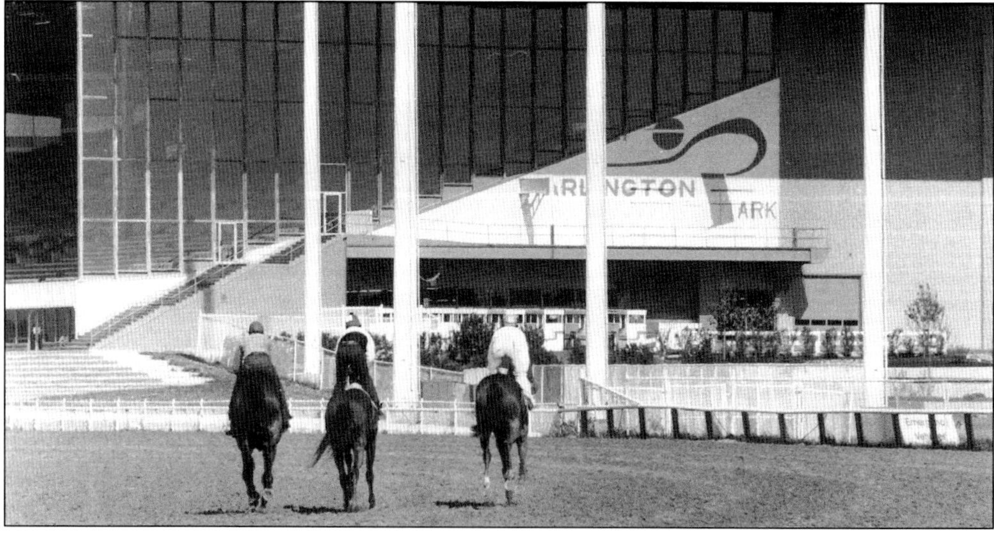

This is a close-up view of the Arlington Park grandstand entrance during the late 1960s. During those years, Arlington set many records, including for a one-day mutuel handle of $2,851,490 on Labor Day 1965, for that year's meet of $54,307,198, and for the highest attendance in 1965 of 696,804. In 1967, Gulf and Western Industries merged with Chicago Thoroughbred Enterprises, and Arlington installed the racing world's largest color, closed-circuit television network. (Courtesy of Midwest Outdoors.)

Two

An Industry Leader 1970–1979

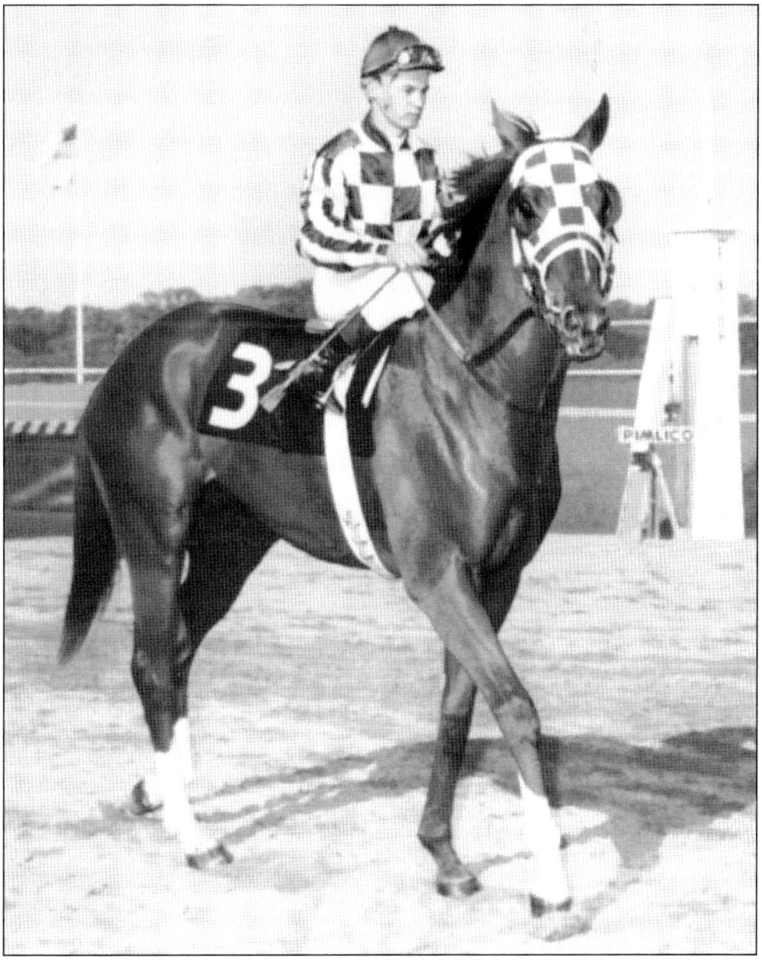

A huge crowd of 41,233 fans watched Secretariat and jockey Ron Turcotte romp to victory in the $125,000 Arlington International on June 30, 1973, returning $2.10 on a $2 ticket in his first race since capturing the Belmont Stakes en route to his Triple Crown title just three weeks earlier. (Courtesy of Moira Fanning.)

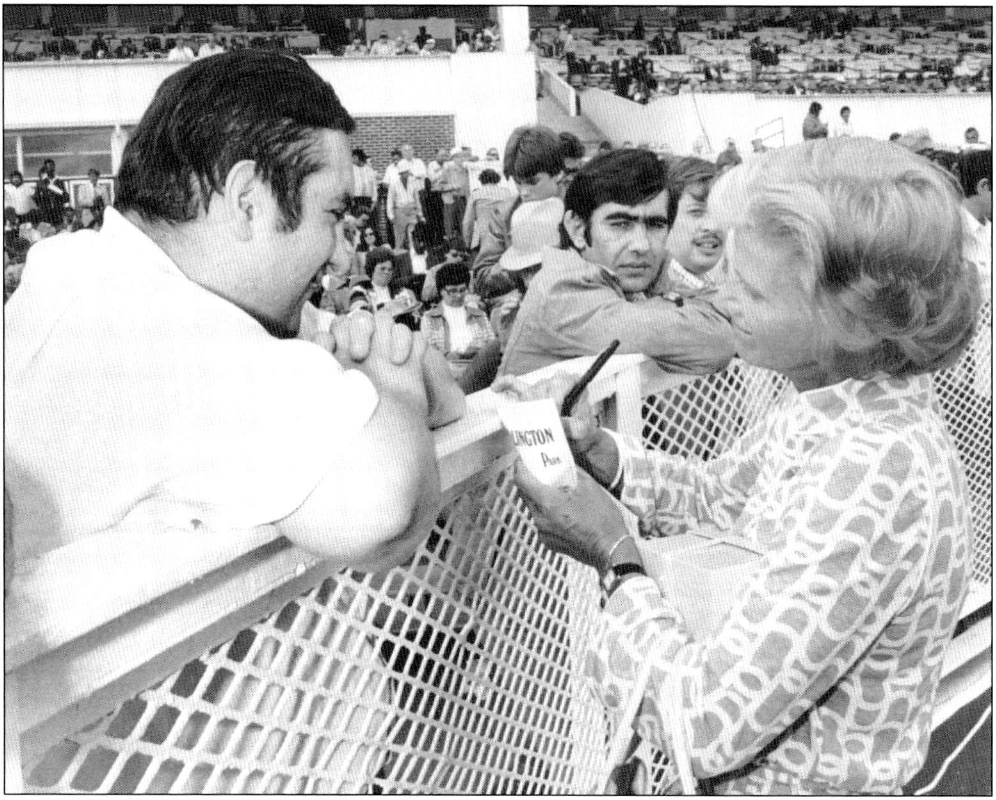

Penny Chenery signs an autograph for a fan on June 30, 1973, at Arlington Park after Secretariat captured the $125,000 Arlington International. Only three challengers broke from the gate beside the chestnut colt—Triple Crown contenders My Gallant and Our Native, and longshot Blue Chip Dan. "Big Red" was clocked in 1:47 for the one-and-one-eighth-mile test, one-fifth of a second off Damascus's track record. (Courtesy of Midwest Outdoors.)

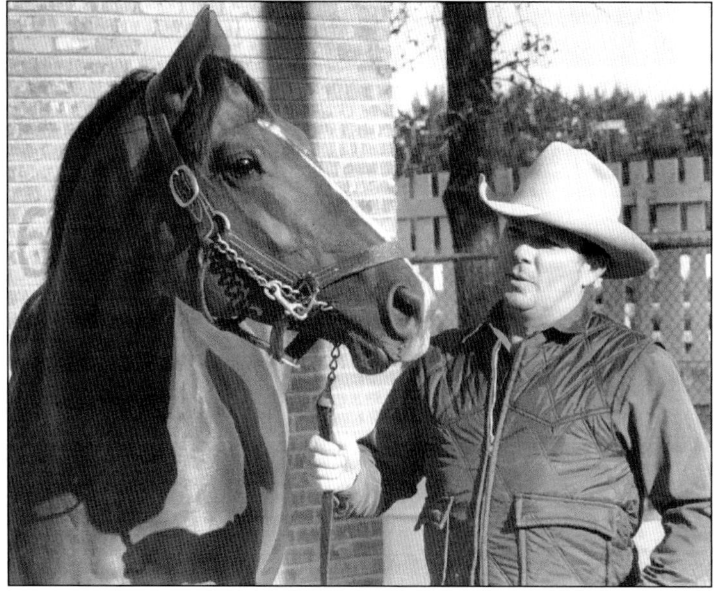

Foaled May 17, 1968, Burning On was a Kentucky-bred chestnut son by On-and-On. Bred by Daniel Scott II, this graded stakes winner was trained by Ralph Christenson and ridden to victory by Doug Richard in the 1973 edition of the Washington Park Handicap, which was contested at a mile and one-eighth at the time. In this photograph, Christenson takes the striking colt for a walk. (Courtesy of Midwest Outdoors.)

Big Dare, with Robert Breen up, is led to the starting gate. Foaled February 17, 1970, she was a multiple Chicago circuit stakes winner and a daughter of Kentucky Pride. Her first stakes triumph was in the Jet's Charm Stakes at Arlington, which she won on June 10, 1972. She went on to win 21 races, with 7 seconds and 9 thirds in 64 starts, earning $185,184 for her connections. (Courtesy of Midwest Outdoors.)

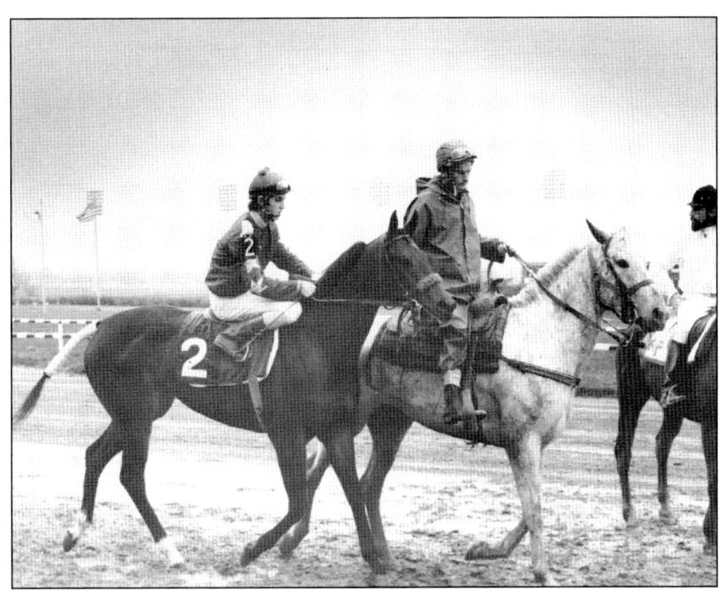

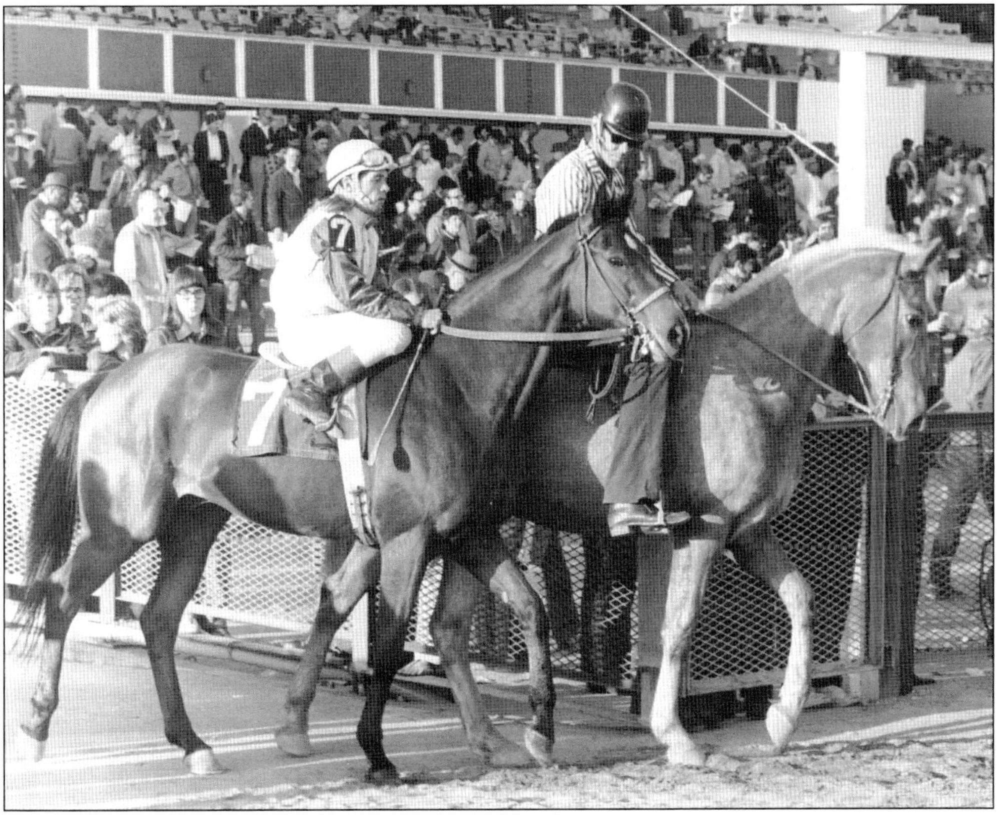

Jockey Leslie "Les" Ahrens, shown here riding Family Table to the post, was a graded stakes winning rider whose career spanned from 1968 to 1991. From 3,858 starts, Ahrens amassed $3,541,790 from 476 wins, 472 seconds, and 460 thirds. The Chicago native, who was popular with peers and fans alike, won the 1977 Illinois Derby aboard Flag Officer. He became a trainer in 1991, saddling Stalwars and Meafara, among others. (Courtesy of Midwest Outdoors.)

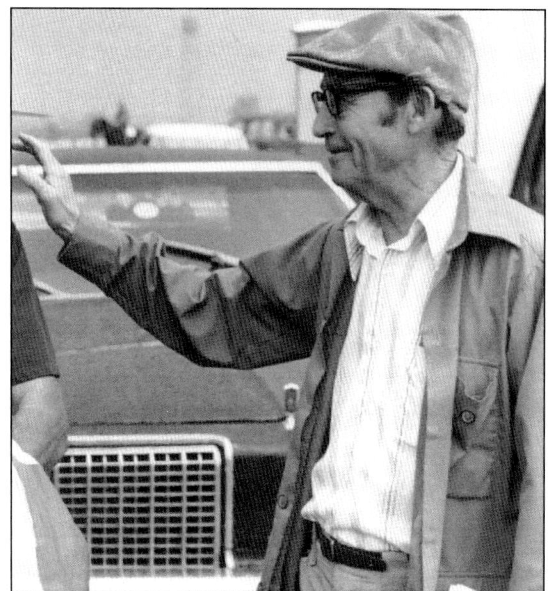

Joe Bollero—known for riding Luxembourg to win the Arlington's first race in 1927—later became a successful Chicago-based trainer. Bollero worked on the Arlington back side every season racing was contested there as a jockey or exercise rider before he turned to training in 1935. The 1969 American Derby winner Fast Hilarious and 1974 Arlington Handicap winner Buffalo Lark were among his best horses. (Courtesy of Midwest Outdoors.)

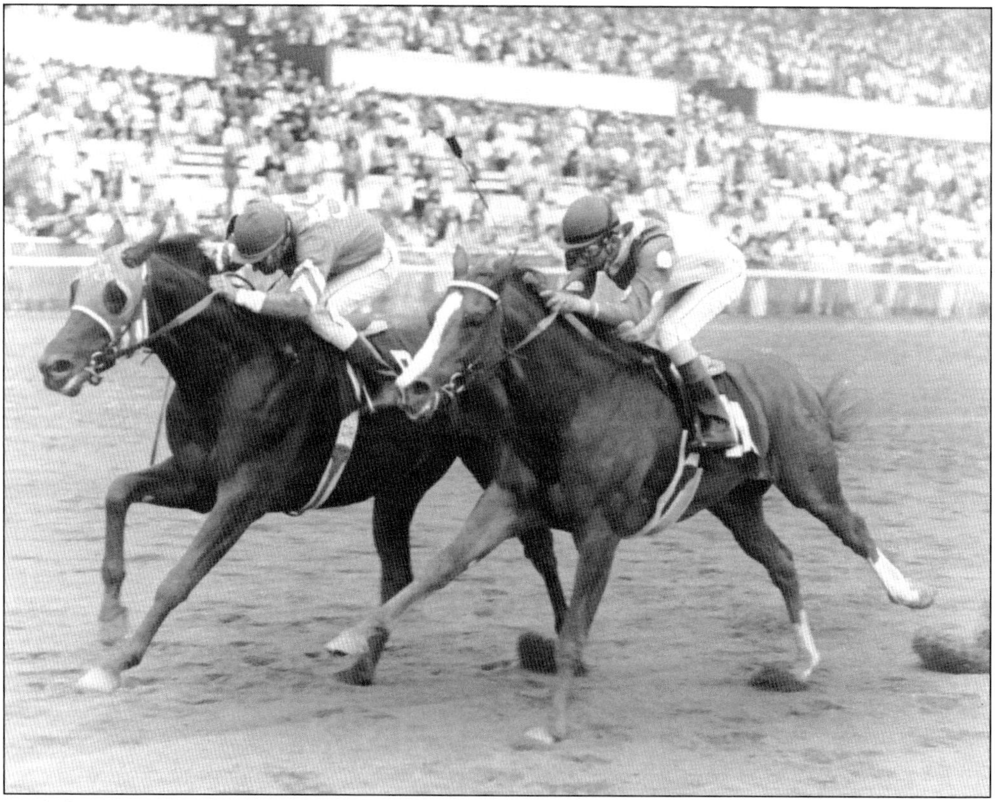

Foaled May 5, 1973, Private Thoughts (left, with hood) was a Kentucky-bred son of Pretense who earned $382,990 for Sandera Farm. Bred by R.L. Reineman, Private Thoughts was trained by Greg Sanders and won the $150,000 Arlington Classic Handicap on August 20, 1977. Ramon Perez was aboard the colt, who was clocked in 1:59.40. He retired with 11 wins, 10 seconds, and 3 thirds in 31 starts. (Courtesy of Midwest Outdoors.)

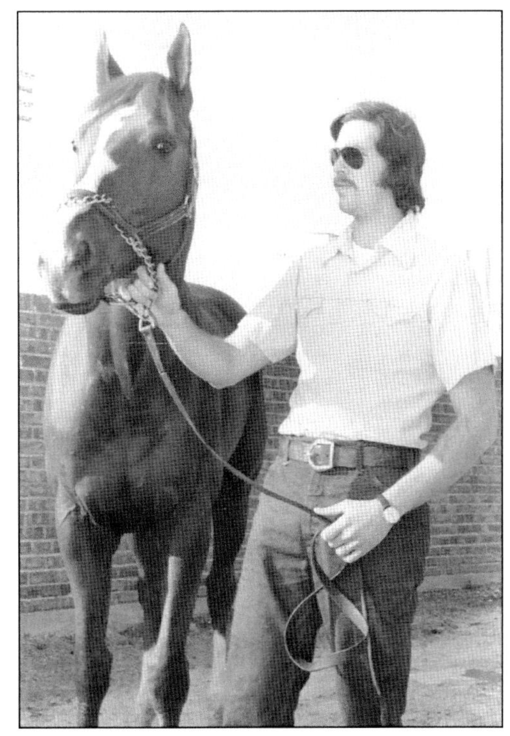

Tartar Chief, foaled March 31, 1969, was a Kentucky-bred son of Crimson Satan. Bred by the Elmendorf Farm and owned by Monticello Stable, Tartar Chief raced from 1972 to 1976 for conditioner Steve Talbert, earning $181,220 from 15 wins, 5 seconds, and 8 thirds in 45 starts. A multiple-stakes winner, Tartar Chief captured the $100,000 Sheridan Handicap (Gr. III) in 1975 at Arlington. Here, he goes for a walk with Talbert. (Courtesy of Midwest Outdoors.)

Jockey Eddie Arroyo (left) stands beside Hasty Flyer while his caretaker cleans the colt's face. Foaled March 13, 1971, Hasty Flyer was a Virginia-bred son of Misty Flight. Hasty Flyer won the 1974 Round Table Handicap (Gr. III); the 1975 Fast Hilarious Handicap and the 1975 Washington Park Handicap (Gr. III) for trainer Harry Trotsek at Arlington, earning $293,663 from 10 wins, 15 seconds, and 12 thirds in 57 starts. (Courtesy of Midwest Outdoors.)

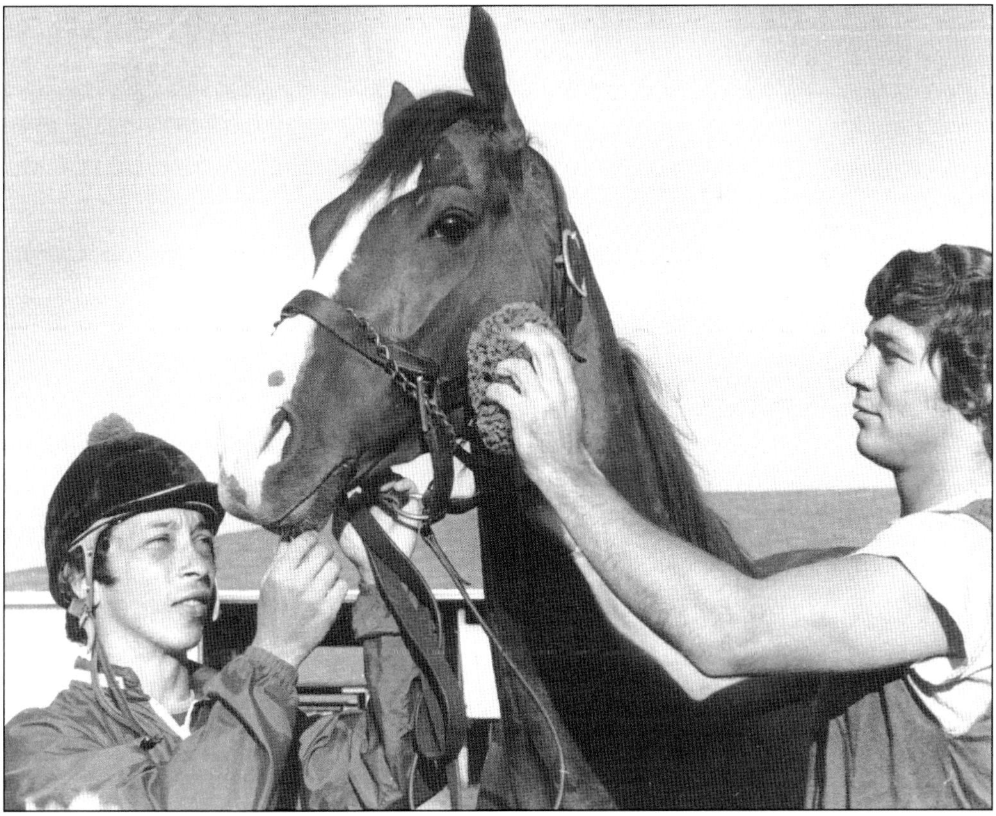

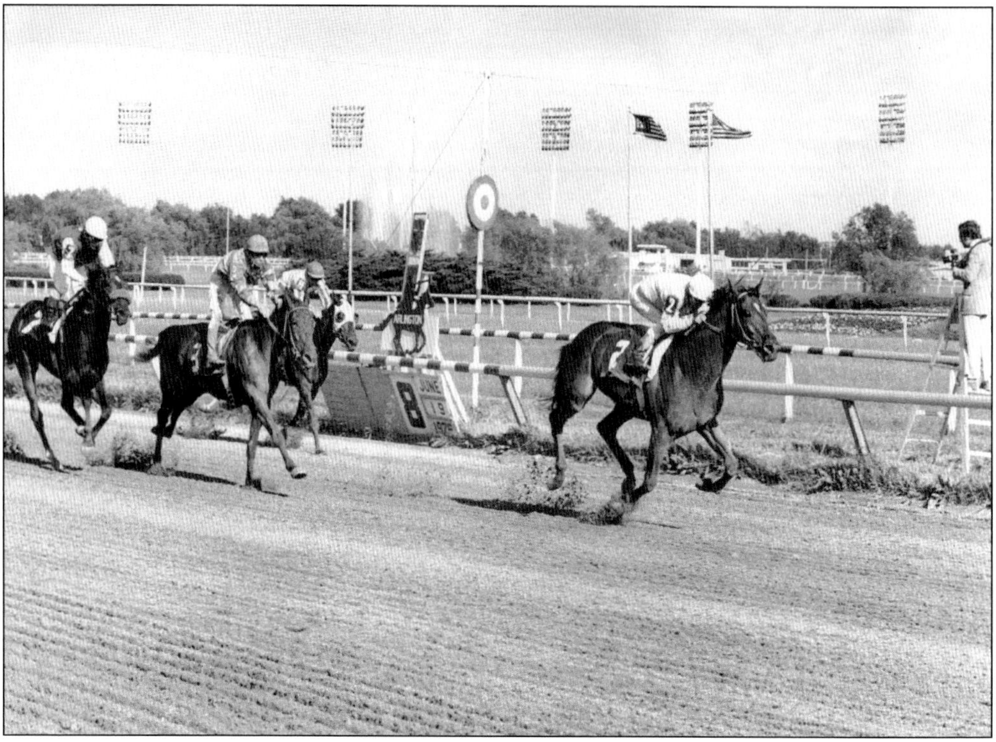

In a Trance captures the Dr. Fager Stake on June 19, 1976. The graded stakes winner was trained by H. Steward Mitchell and ridden by Danny Wright for owner Mar-Lo Stable. The bay son of Vitriolic was foaled May 8, 1973 and earned $167,732 from 10 wins, 7 seconds, and 4 thirds in 29 career starts. (Courtesy of Midwest Outdoors.)

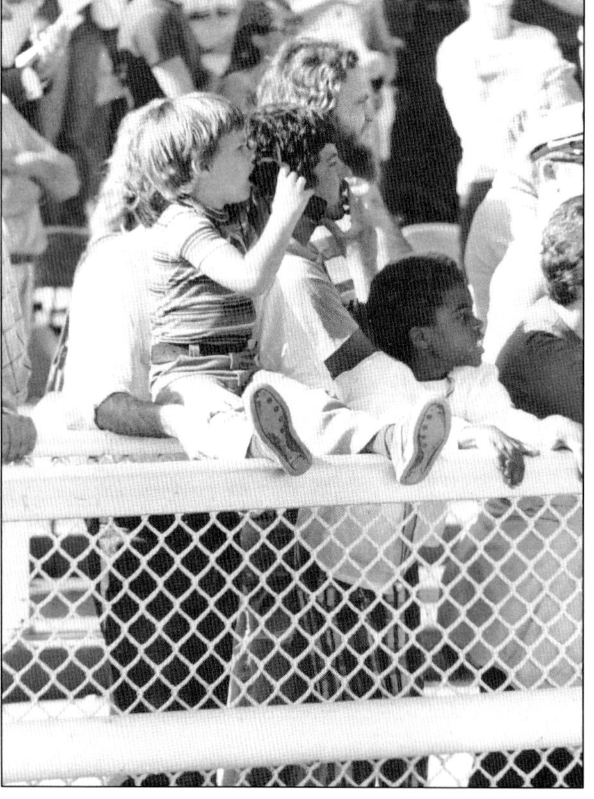

The Arlington Park fan base is wide and varied—from the $2 gambler, to the $10,000-a-wager player, to the husband and wife that bring their kids out to watch the ponies in action. Throughout the decades, Arlington has been extremely fan-friendly, inviting adults and children alike to enjoy the atmosphere and aura of one of the most beautiful racecourses in the United States. (Courtesy of Midwest Outdoors.)

Harvey Vanier was a multiple graded stakes winning trainer who conditioned 2,043 winners to $40,013,967 in purse earnings, including Grade I winners Western Playboy, Play Fellow, Safe Play, and Fortunate Moment. Other top horses include Architect, Southern Playgirl, Powerful Punch, Blue Buckaroo, Big Bobcat, Wade for Me, and Iron Courage. Born April 21, 1924, in Diller, Nebraska, Vanier was a jockey in the 1940s before becoming one of the Midwest's top trainers. He is Arlington's all-time leading stakes trainer with 37, and won 719 races there, as well as seven Arlington training titles (1987, 1989, 1993-1997). After he married Nancy Aiken-Vanier, they began breeding their own racehorses on their Fairberry Farm in Waterloo, Illinois. In the photograph at right, Harvey leads one of his star pupils off the track after a morning workout. Below, Nancy and Harvey are pictured together in their Arlington stable office. (Courtesy of Midwest Outdoors.)

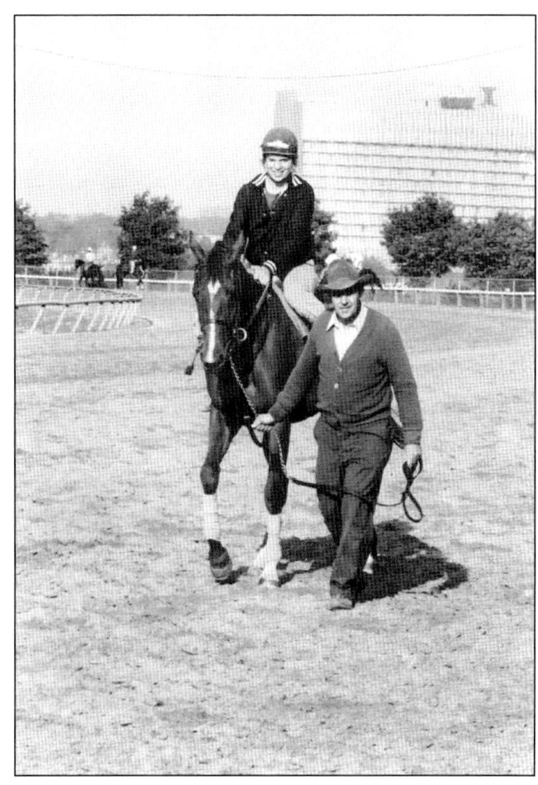

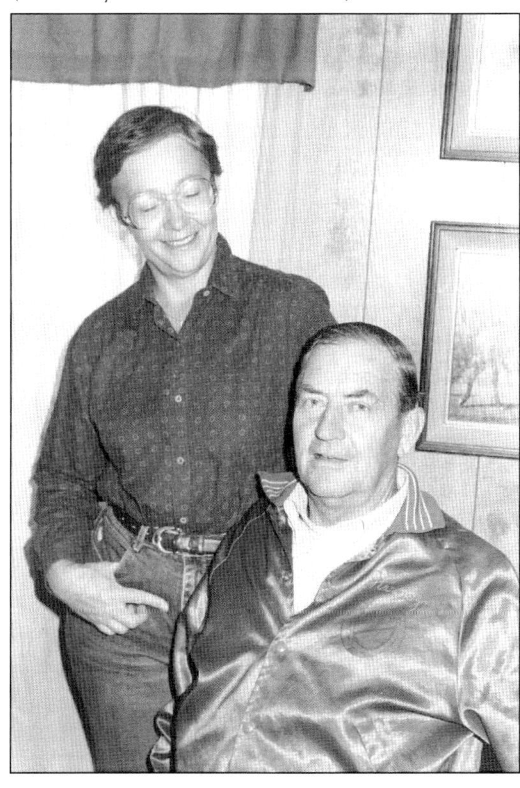

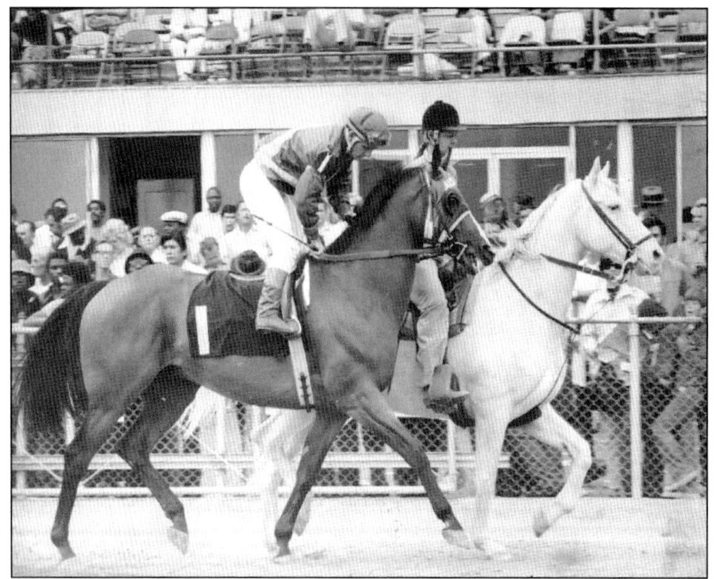

The English-bred Apollo Nine was a multiple stakes winner who earned $180,095 for the Audley Farm Stable. Foaled January 1, 1967, Apollo Nine was by the Irish stallion Skymaster and was conditioned by John Tammaro Sr. Apollo Nine won 18 of 59 starts for his connections and was ridden in most of his races by Don MacBeth. (Courtesy of Midwest Outdoors.)

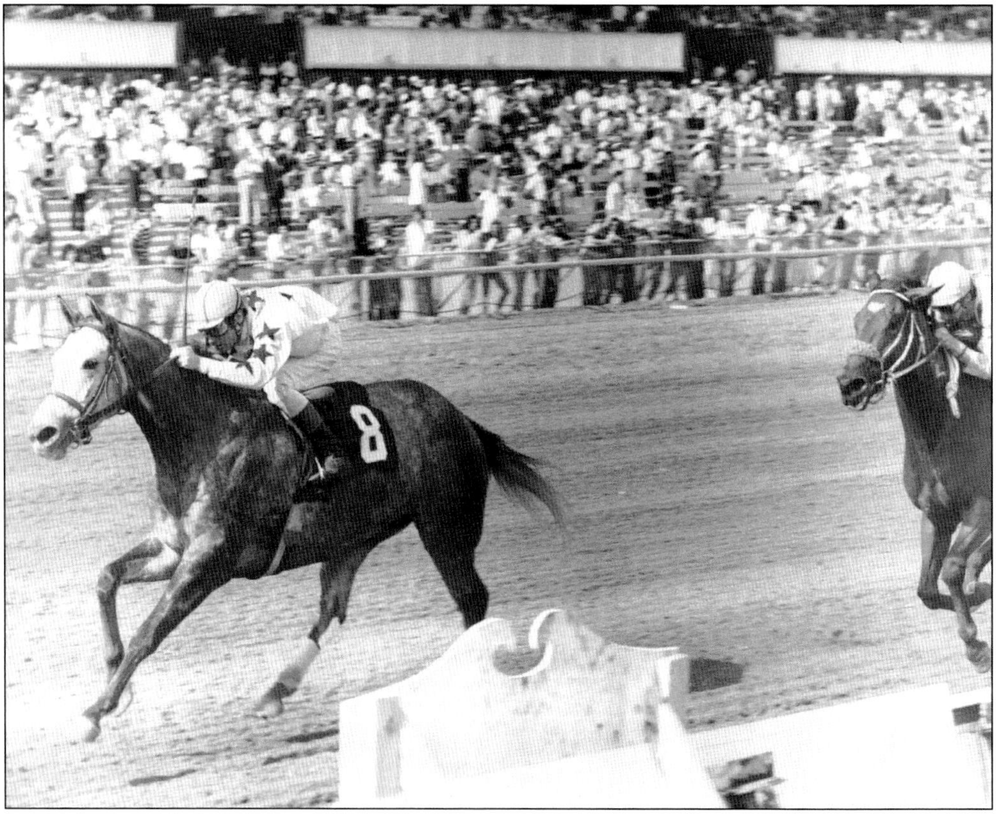

Eddie Delahoussaye, a 1993 inductee into the National Hall of Fame, rides Mighty Kitty in a June 22, 1978, allowance race at Arlington. Delahoussaye steered 6,383 winners to $195,809,734 in career earnings. Some of his top mounts include Breeders' Cup Classic winner and $2.9 million–earning AP Indy; Breeders' Cup Turf winner Prized ($1.2 million); Belmont Stakes winner and $1.7 million–earning Risen Star, and Kentucky Derby winner Gato Del Sol. (Courtesy of Midwest Outdoors.)

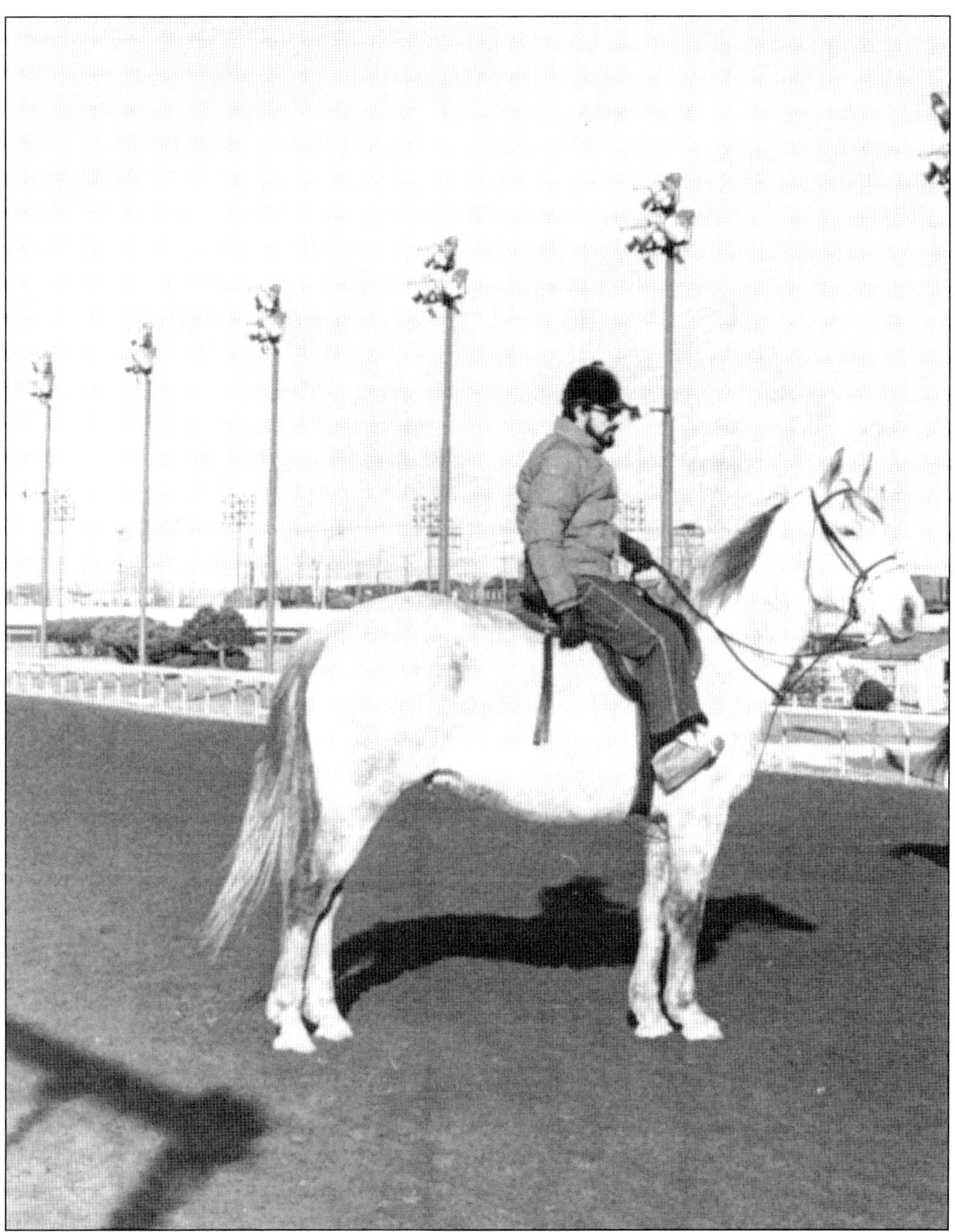

Responsible for keeping Thoroughbreds in place during pre- and postrace festivities and for catching those who unseat their riders, outrider Vince DiMeo was a mainstay on the Chicago circuit. His horses—Noname, Outrider, and Apples—were well known to Arlington fans. On June 5, 1975, DiMeo helped divert catastrophe at Arlington when attendants were unable to move the starting gate. With 12 horses thundering through the turn, DiMeo and Outrider raced to the rescue. "I realized they weren't going to be able to move the starting gate, so I had to warn the jockeys who didn't have any idea what was going to be staring them in the face in the stretch," Dimeo said at the time. "I shouted, 'The gate can't move, follow me!'" The jockeys did as DiMeo instructed and horses and riders were unscathed as a result. (Courtesy of Midwest Outdoors.)

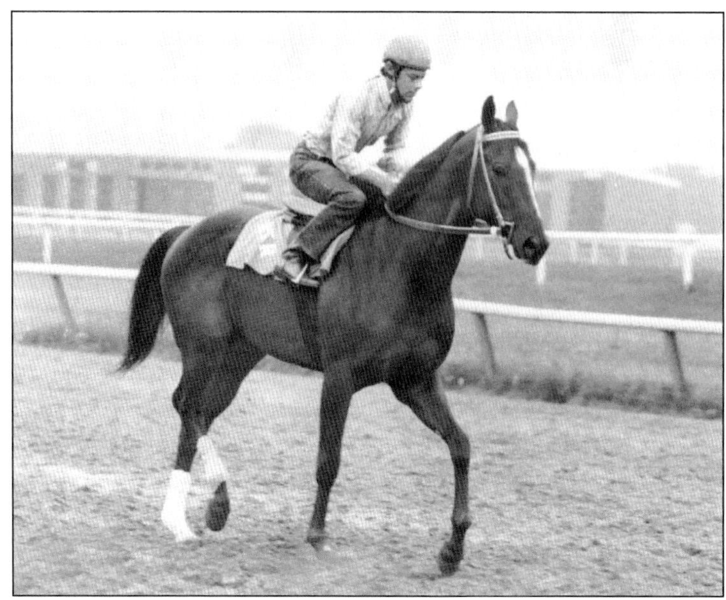

A Kentucky-bred colt by Traffic Mark foaled April 27, 1972, Honey Mark was a graded stakes winner owned by Robert and Sandy Roberts. Trained by Larry Robideaux Jr., he won 16 of his 49 career starts and $408,982, racing from 1974 through 1978. Here, exercise rider Garth Patterson takes Honey Mark for a morning stroll in 1975. (Courtesy of Midwest Outdoors.)

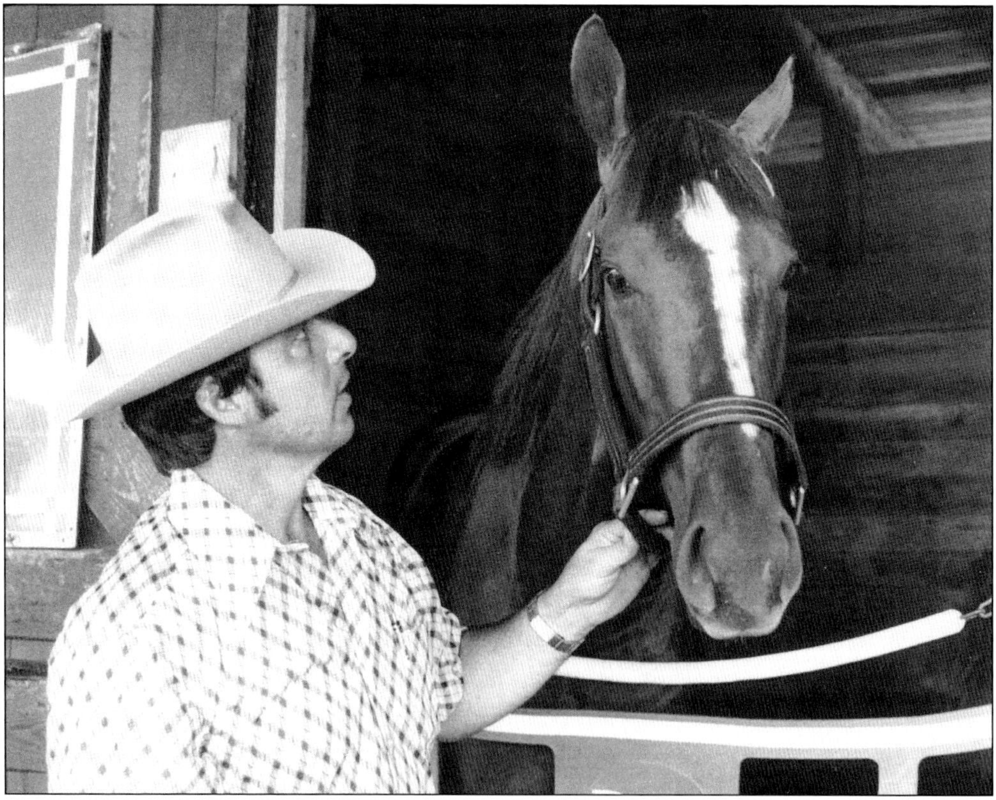

Trainer Larry Robideaux Jr. gazes admiringly at his stable star, Honey Mark. The colt captured the 1974 Hyde Park Stakes at Arlington and one month later finished a solid second in the Arch Ward Stakes. The following season, Honey Mark captured the American Derby Handicap (Gr. II) on July 5, 1975. Robideaux Jr. trained 1,963 winners to $23,569,100 in career earnings. (Courtesy of Midwest Outdoors.)

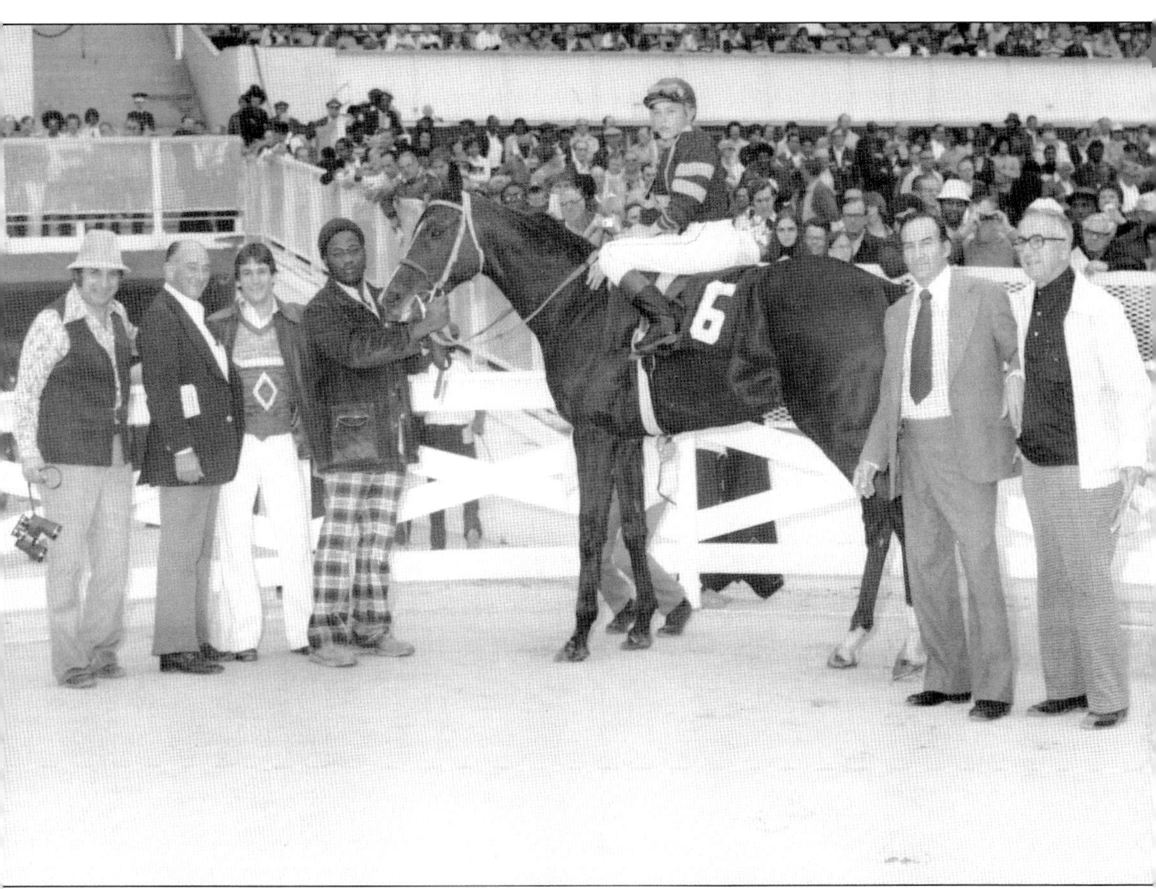

Here, a 16-year-old Steve Cauthen wins an Arlington turf race with Dabrock on September 26, 1976. Cauthen rode his first horse on May 12 that same year at Churchill Downs, finishing last on King of Swat, then had his first winner at River Downs just days later with Red Pipe. In 1977, he became the youngest jockey to win the Triple Crown, guiding Affirmed to top honors and being named Sportsman of the Year by *Sports Illustrated*. He was the last jockey to steer a Triple Crown winner until Victor Espinoza did so with American Pharoah in 2015. Cauthen was named Outstanding Apprentice Jockey of 1977 and inducted into the National Racing Museum and Hall of Fame in 1994. He later rode in England, where he won the British Jockey title three times, retiring with $13,526,857 in earnings. (Courtesy of James Divito.)

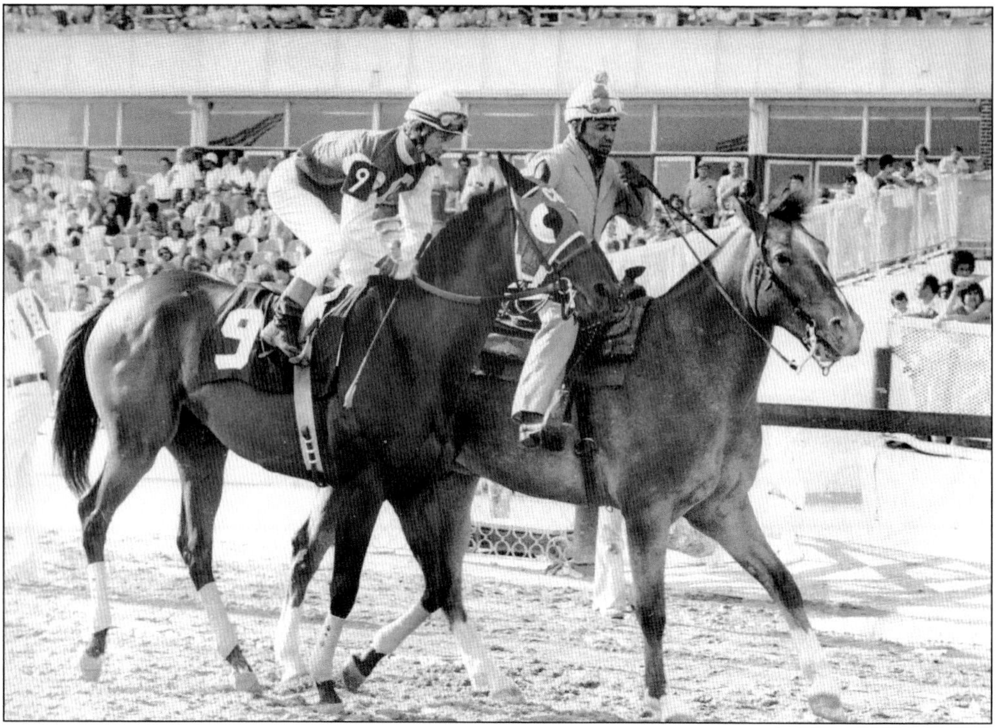

TV Vixen goes to the post for the July 24, 1976, Pucker Up Stakes (Gr. III) at Arlington. The 1973-foaled mare by T.V. Lark was owned and bred by Crimson King Farm and trained by Peter Salmen Jr. TV Vixen also won the Four Winds Stakes and the Patricia A. Stakes that same season and earned $419,314 from 20 wins in 31 starts. She later sold for $925,000 as a broodmare. (Courtesy of Midwest Outdoors.)

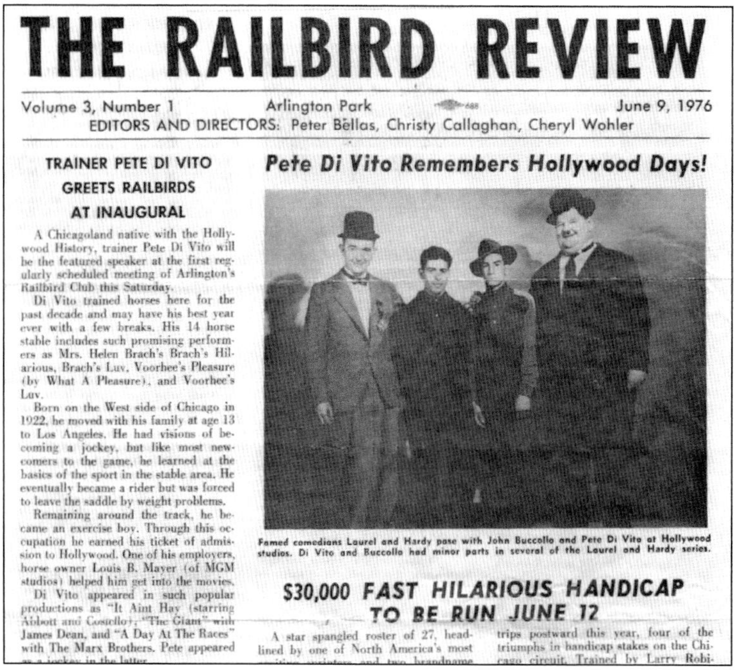

THE RAILBIRD REVIEW

Volume 3, Number 1 — Arlington Park — June 9, 1976

EDITORS AND DIRECTORS: Peter Bellas, Christy Callaghan, Cheryl Wohler

TRAINER PETE DI VITO GREETS RAILBIRDS AT INAUGURAL

A Chicagoland native with the Hollywood History, trainer Pete Di Vito will be the featured speaker at the first regularly scheduled meeting of Arlington's Railbird Club this Saturday.

Di Vito trained horses here for the past decade and may have his best year ever with a few breaks. His 14 horse stable includes such promising performers as Mrs. Helen Brach's Brach's Hilarious, Brach's Luv, Voorhee's Pleasure (by What A Pleasure), and Voorhee's Luv.

Born on the West side of Chicago in 1922, he moved with his family at age 13 to Los Angeles. He had visions of becoming a jockey, but like most newcomers to the game, he learned at the basics of the sport in the stable area. He eventually became a rider but was forced to leave the saddle by weight problems.

Remaining around the track, he became an exercise boy. Through this occupation he earned his ticket of admission to Hollywood. One of his employers, horse owner Louis B. Mayer (of MGM studios) helped him get into the movies.

Di Vito appeared in such popular productions as "It Aint Hay (starring Abbott and Costello), "The Giant" with James Dean, and "A Day At The Races" with The Marx Brothers. Pete appeared

Pete Di Vito Remembers Hollywood Days!

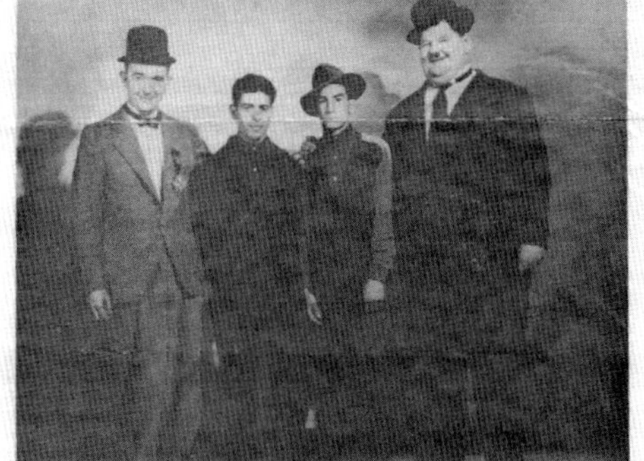

Famed comedians Laurel and Hardy pose with John Buccollo and Pete Di Vito at Hollywood studios. Di Vito and Buccollo had minor parts in several of the Laurel and Hardy series.

$30,000 FAST HILARIOUS HANDICAP TO BE RUN JUNE 12

A star spangled roster of 27, headlined by one of North America's most

trips postward this year, four of the triumphs in handicap stakes on the Chicago circuit. Trained by Larry Robi-

The *Railbird Review* was a brochure produced by Arlington Park in the 1970s featuring stories about the folks and horses stabled on the back side. This edition from June 9, 1976, spotlights trainer Pete Divito, who was set to speak about his days training for Hollywood royalty at the track's Saturday-morning Railbird Club meeting, where fans could interact with trainers and jockeys. (Courtesy of James Divito.)

Gallant Bill stands patiently whilst a caretaker cleans out his right front hoof. This 1969-foaled son of Gallant Romeo was a hard-knocking claimer who plied his wares over the Arlington Park dirt. From 63 starts racing from 1971 to 1977, he earned $76,435 with 13 wins, 6 seconds, and 9 thirds. Racehorses need to have their feet attended to daily to ensure they are sound and healthy to race. (Courtesy of Midwest Outdoors.)

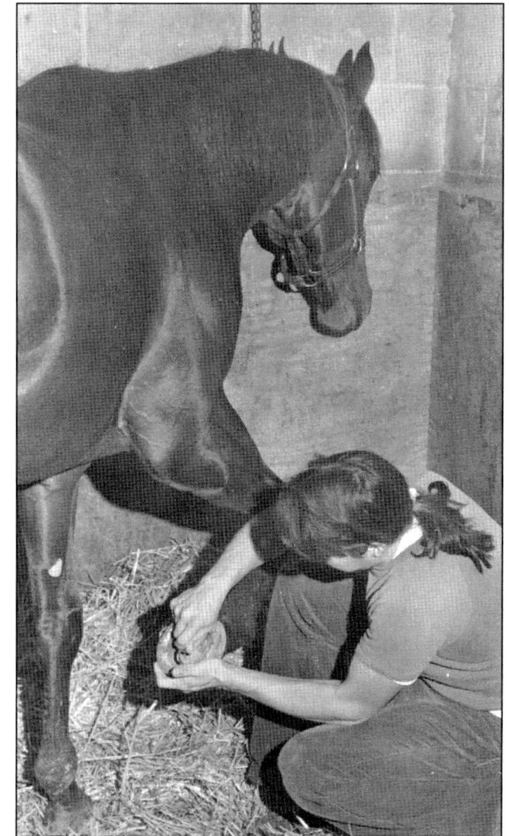

Peoria County is led back to the barn after an allowance victory at Arlington in the late 1970s. This dappled gray son of Tudor Grey won multiple allowance and handicaps at Arlington from 1976 to 1982 for owner W.R. Kelly. From 47 career starts, Peoria County earned $202,918, winning 16 times, with 8 seconds and 6 thirds. He rarely missed nabbing a purse check for his connections. (Courtesy of Midwest Outdoors.)

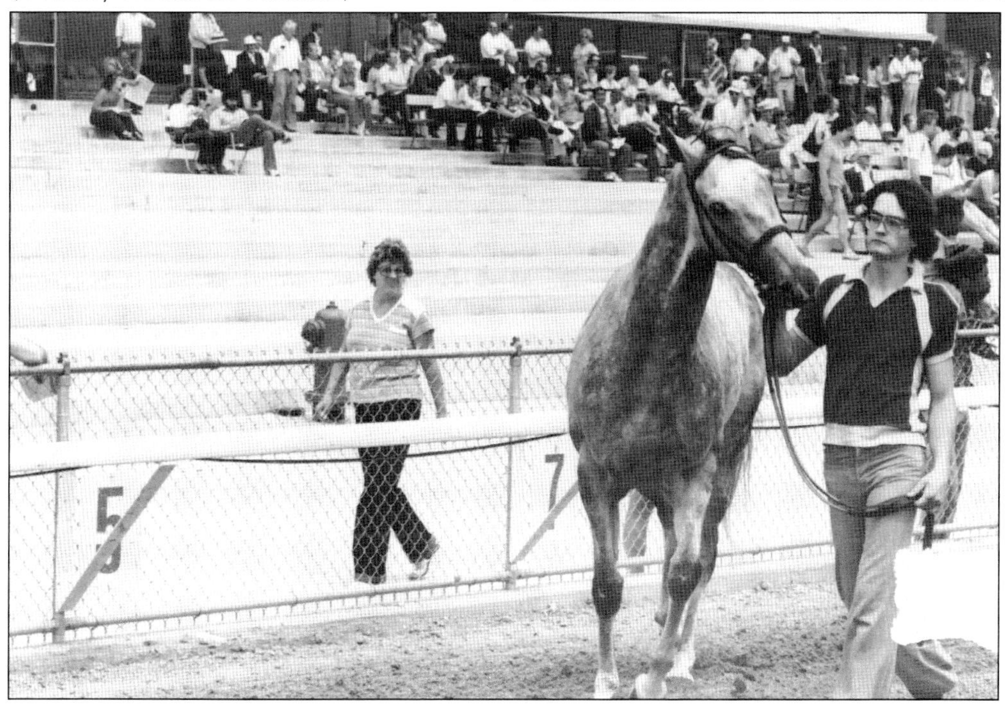

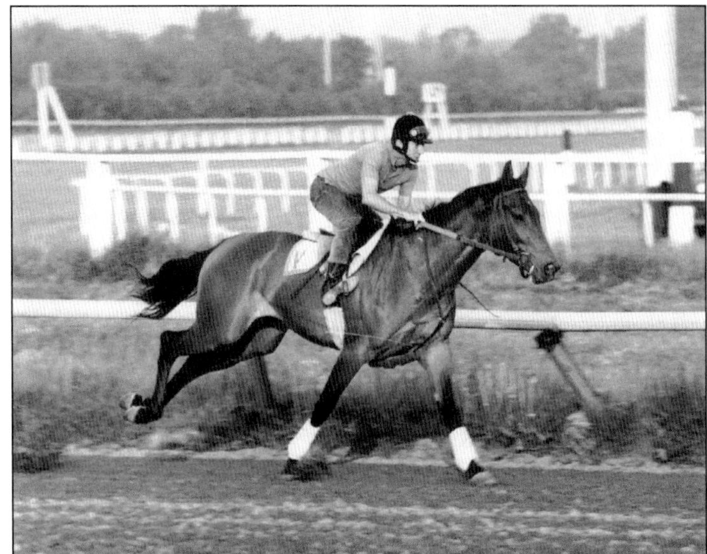

Cycylya Zee goes for a morning workout with her exercise rider aboard. She was a Maryland-bred daughter of Knightly Manner, foaled March 17, 1973. From 45 starts, she had 12 wins, 10 seconds, and 8 thirds, earning $249,022. Cycylya Zee sold for $3,000 as a yearling but later brought $210,000 as a broodmare. (Courtesy of Midwest Outdoors.)

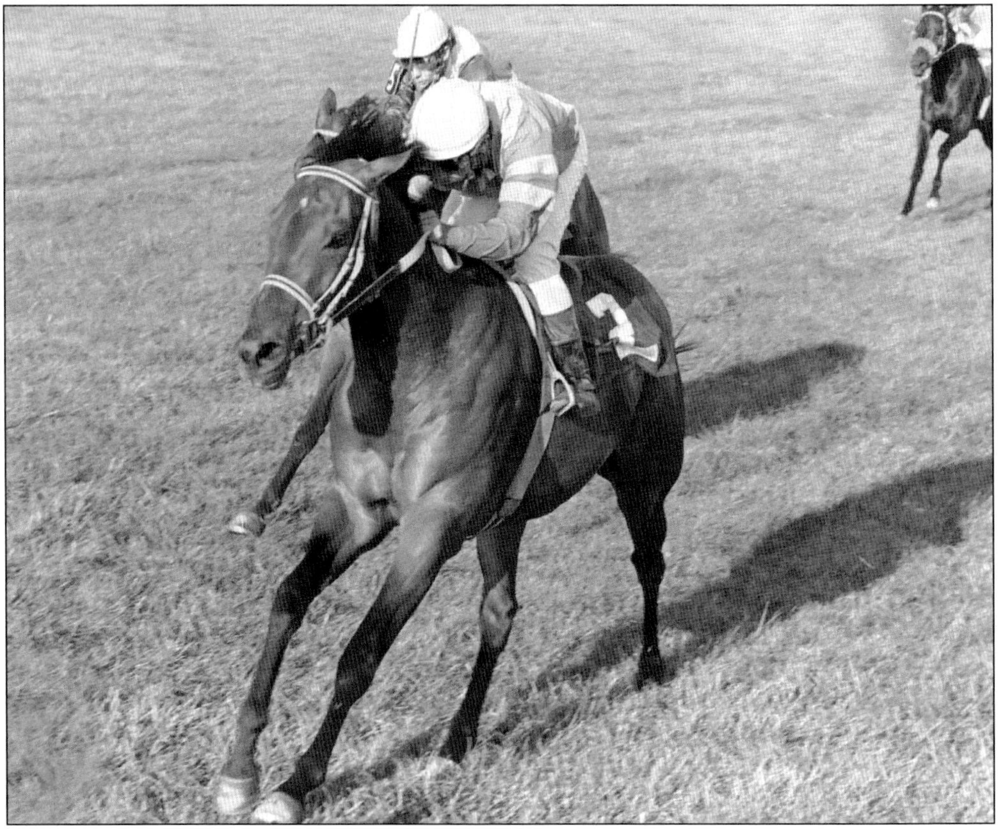

Cycylya Zee raced all over the United States—winning the Smart Deb Handicap on August 11, 1976, and the first division of the Arlington Matron Handicap (Gr. II) on September 6, 1976, with Eddie Arroyo riding for trainer Christine Janks. Nicosia won the second Matron division and was also conditioned by a female—Alice Chandler. It was unusual to have two women trainers win separate divisions of the same stake. (Courtesy of Midwest Outdoors.)

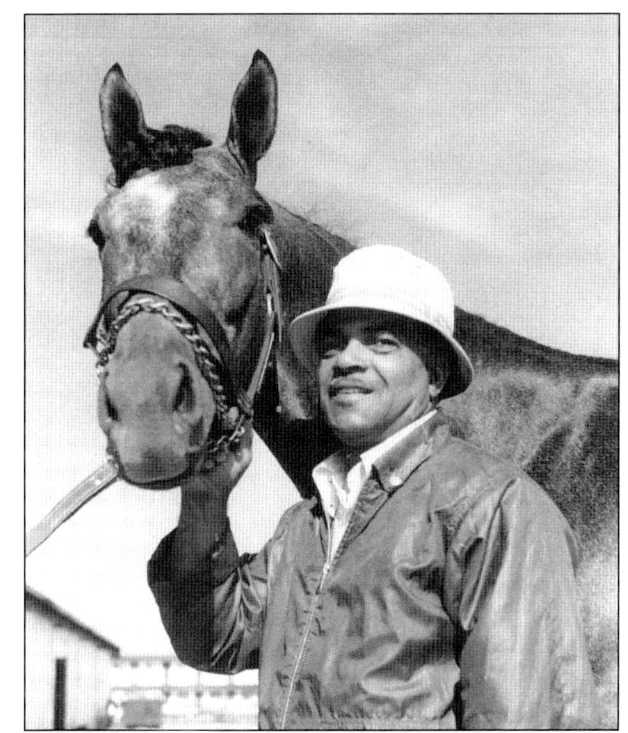

Trainer Oscar Dishman Jr. shows off his stable champion Silver Series, the Chicago Champion three-year-old of 1977. This Florida-bred, Grade I winner was foaled January 1, 1974, and went on to earn $590,902 from 29 starts, with 11 wins, 5 seconds, and 5 thirds for the Pillar Farms. Trainer Dishman Jr. also conditioned 1980 Round Table Handicap (Gr. III) winner The Messenger. (Courtesy of Midwest Outdoors.)

Silver Series captured the American Derby at Arlington Park on July 2, 1977, with Larry Snyder in the saddle for trainer Oscar Dishman Jr. This multiple graded stakes winner was bred by Dr. Archie Donaldson and was by Chieftain, out of the Summer Tan mare Cat Hat. (Courtesy of Midwest Outdoors.)

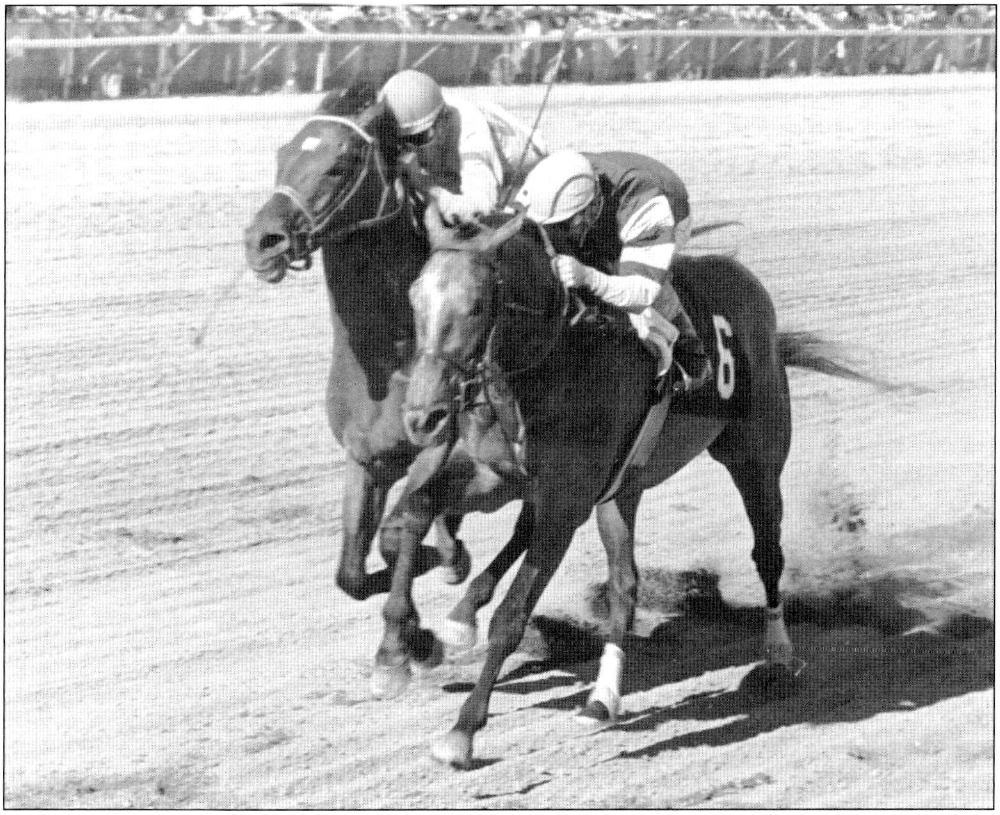

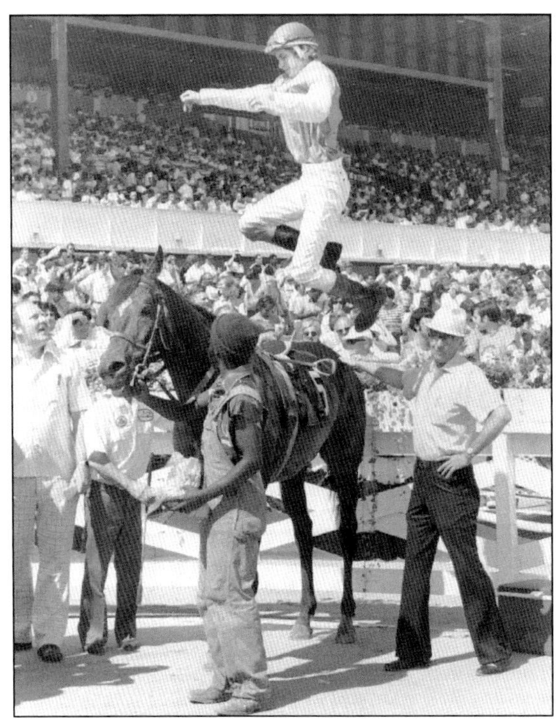

Jockey Darrell Haire jumps from the saddle after a win at Arlington Park in the late 1970s. Haire won 772 races and $7,287,059 in career earnings, riding from 1976 to 1990. His best years came in 1979, when the horses he rode earned just over $1 million, and in 1980, when he amassed $1.6 million in seasonal earnings. His best horse was the $163,104-earning Arkansas Derby winner, Temperence Hill. (Courtesy of Midwest Outdoors.)

Darrell Haire steers River Warrior (No. 2, center) to victory over Arlington's turf course on July 11, 1978 for trainer J.R. Garrard and owner G.L. May. Silver Nitrate (No. 3, far right) was a close second, while Bring the Money (No. 1, far left) was third. Haire now serves as a representative for the Jockey's Guild and was that organization's president in 2005 and 2006. (Courtesy of Midwest Outdoors.)

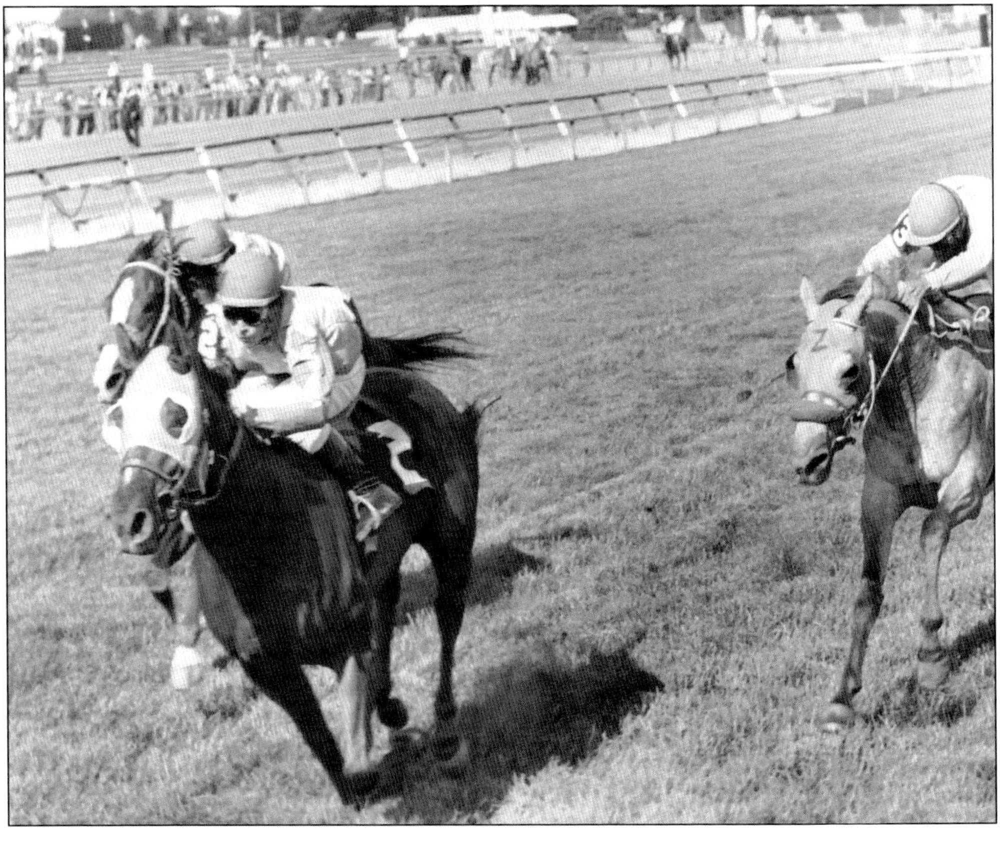

Glassy Dip gazes contentedly out of his stall at Arlington. Racing from 1976 to 1978, the Florida-bred Diplomatic Way youngster was trained by John O. Meaux for breeder/owner Donald Peltier. He was often ridden by Earlie Fires and won a pair of back-to-back allowance races at Arlington on July 23 and August 3, 1977. He retired with $118,942 in earnings from 7 wins in 42 starts. (Courtesy of Midwest Outdoors.)

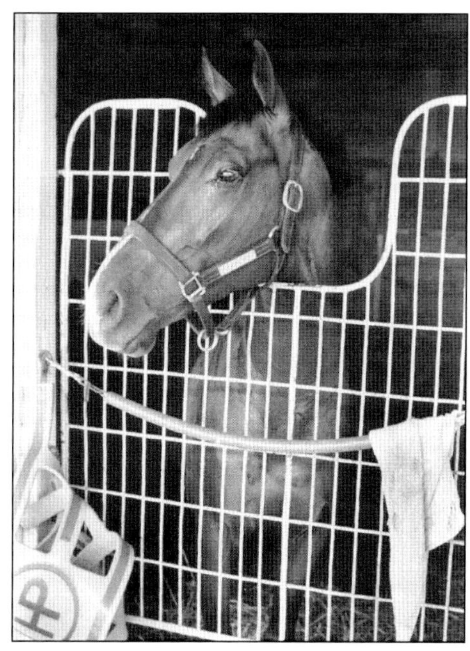

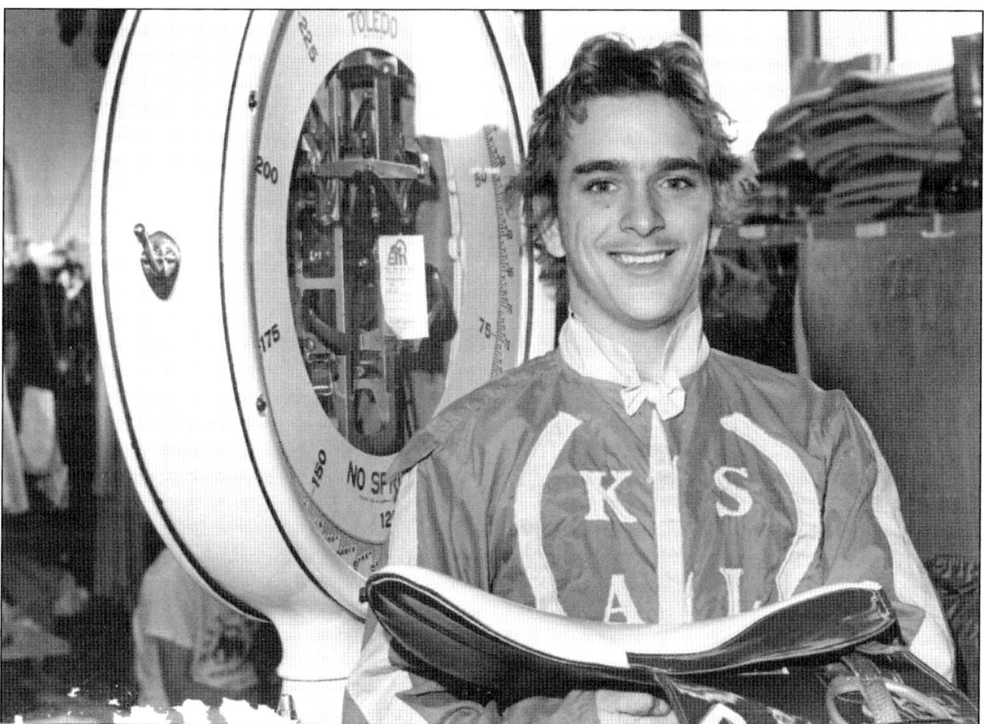

Jockey Ronnie Hirdes Jr. was an Arlington and Chicago jockey sensation, riding from 1978 to 1999. That first year, as an apprentice jockey, he amassed an impressive $1,291,665 in seasonal earnings. His top horses included the Grade II–winning Recusant ($245,646); Grade III–winning Queen Of Song ($196,083); and Grade II–winning Batonnier ($145,620), with whom he won the Illinois Derby. He retired with $13,597,266 from 1,503 winners, 1,482 seconds, and 1,566 thirds in 13,202 starts. (Courtesy of Midwest Outdoors.)

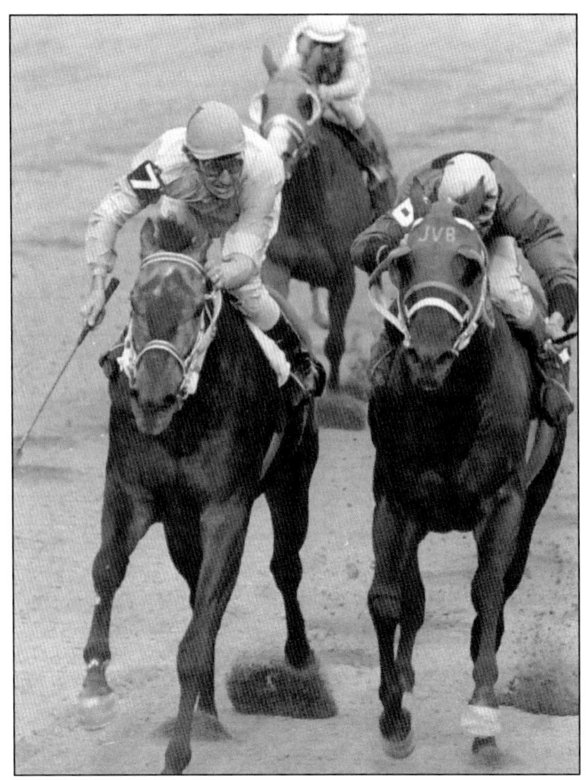

Foaled in 1974, Mr. Steel (No. 7, left) was a grey colt by Winning Hit. Trained by Edward Plesa Jr., and owned by Marion Plesa, Mr. Steel scored five straight allowance victories at Arlington in the height of summer in 1977. Hector Viera is shown here riding him to yet another triumph. Mr. Steel retired with $113,349 in career earnings from 16 wins, 9 seconds, and 4 thirds in 55 starts. (Courtesy of Midwest Outdoors.)

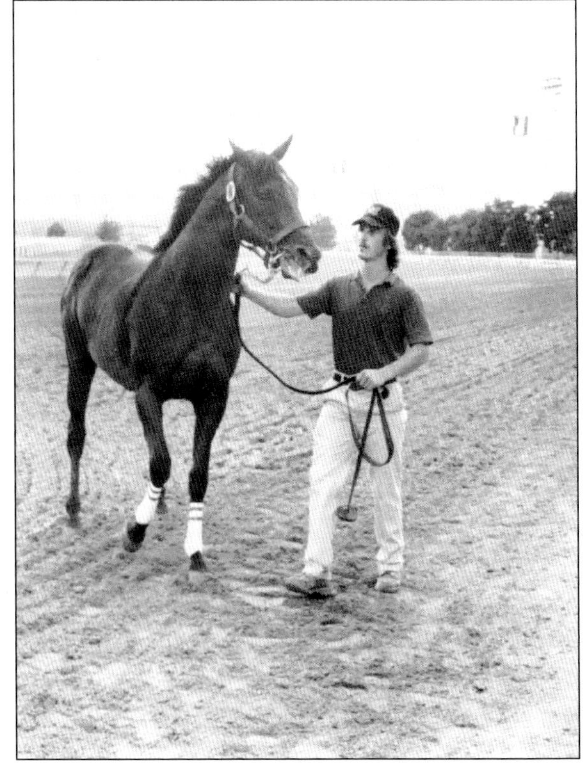

Milwaukee Avenue, shown here being led by a caretaker, was a T.V. Lark colt trained by Michael Weissman for owner/breeder Rogers Red Top Farm. Foaled March 21, 1973, Milwaukee Avenue won five straight handicaps over the Arlington dirt in 1977, and the 1979 W.H. Bishop Handicap. Racing from 1975 to 1980, Milwaukee Avenue sported 20 wins, 13 seconds, and 13 thirds in 79 starts with $384,459 upon retirement. (Courtesy of Midwest Outdoors.)

Trainer Eugene "Red" Sharp stands with Conspicuous, an Illinois-bred stakes winner by Gallant Lad. This talented distaff raced from 1977 to 1980 on the Chicago circuit and earned $111,456 from 8 wins, 4 seconds, and 10 thirds in 49 starts. She won an Arlington allowance test on June 14, 1978, for Sharp—who also trained Grade I–winner Irish Gentry. (Courtesy of Midwest Outdoors.)

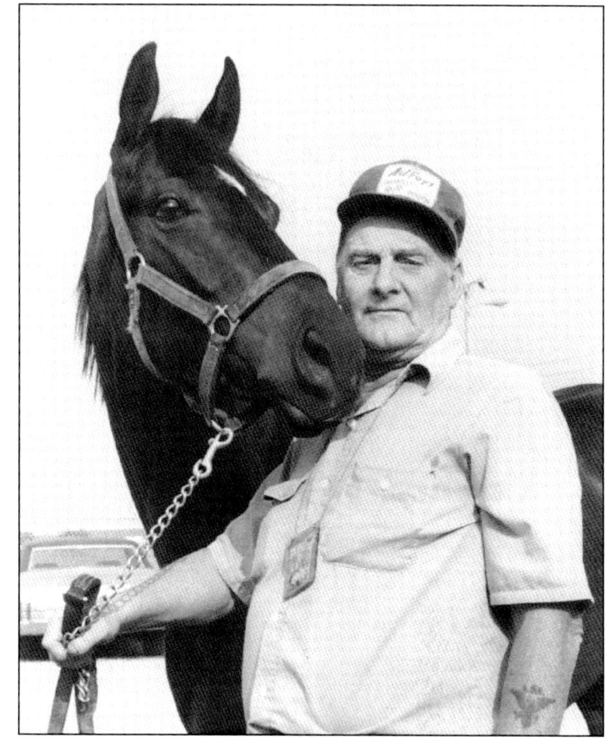

Victress Lady romps to a turf triumph for jockey Ronnie Hirdes and trainer Neil Boyce on June 23, 1978. The California-bred, Vested Power lass was owned by breeder Marlene Orrick, and covered the one-mile grass event in 1:40.2, besting rival Delayed Decision and rider Ray Sibille easily, while Solemnly Swear and jockey Carlos Silva picked up show money. (Courtesy of Midwest Outdoors.)

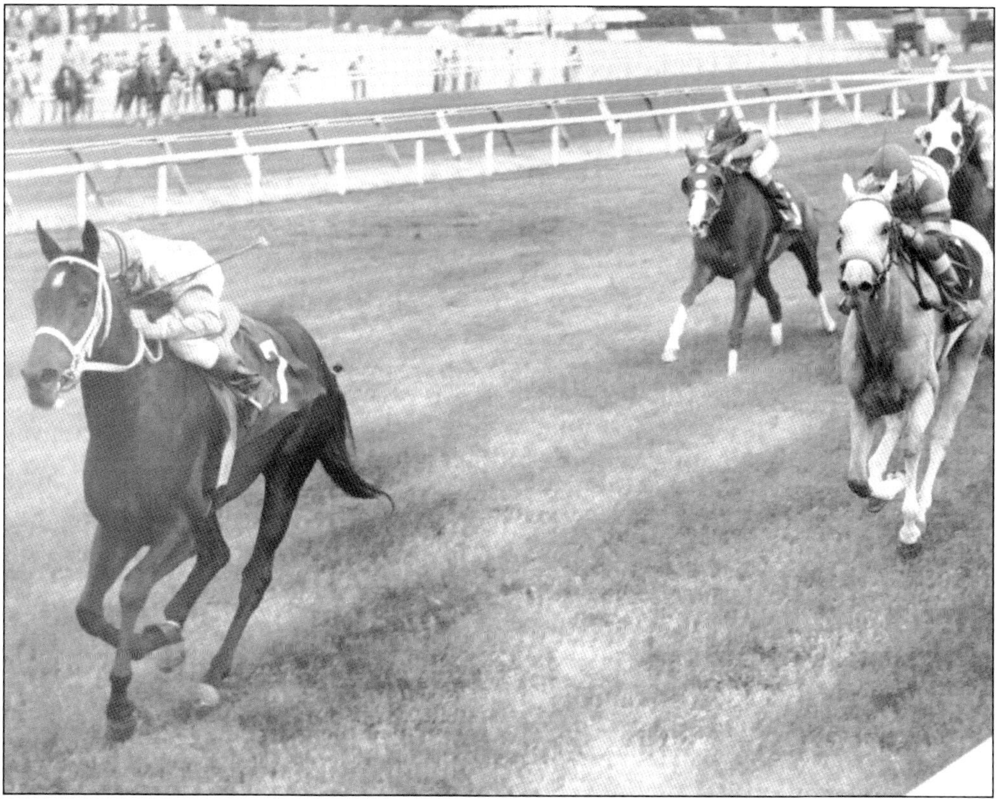

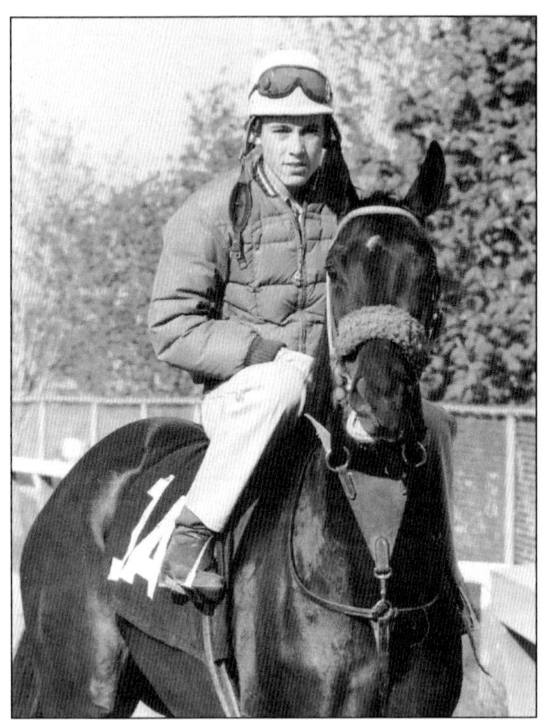

Jockey Doug Rolfe—who was the fourth-leading apprentice rider in the United States in 1978—raced through 1981, with his mounts earning $2,707,437. Some of his top horses include Thumbsucker, Off the Ground, and Raise the Blade. Here, at Arlington Park in 1978, he gets set to take a youngster through a morning workout. (Courtesy of Midwest Outdoors.)

Famed Princess wins the $20,000-added Four Wins Handicap on Arlington's opening day in 1978 with Ronnie Hirdes aboard. Drop the Pigeon was second in the six-furlong test, which was timed in 1:11.1. Famed Princess was a Florida-bred daughter by the great Nashua, and was trained by Harry Trotsek for owner E.A. Seltzer. The graded stakes–placed mare went on to earn $207,200 and later sold for $750,000 as a broodmare in foal to Fappiano. (Courtesy of Midwest Outdoors.)

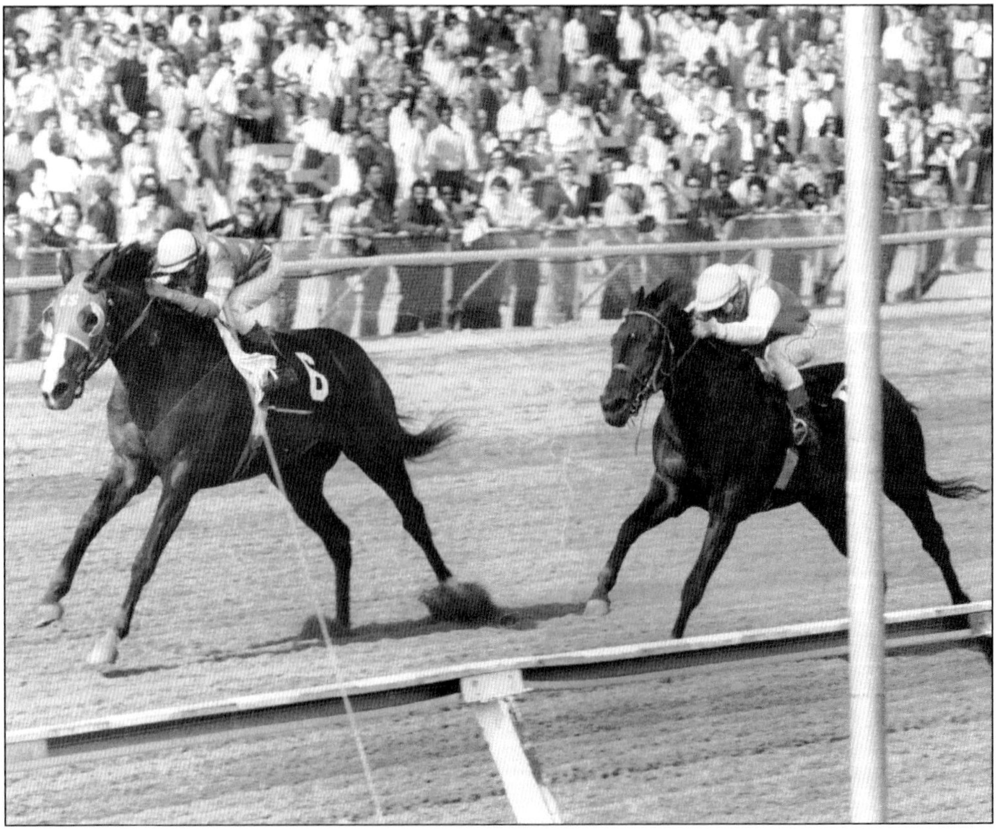

Sir Prince P—with Earlie Fires aboard—romps to a sixth consecutive triumph at Arlington. Trained by Curtis Jaynes for owner Debbie Rhone, the 1976-foaled Harbor Prince colt earned $91,260 lifetime from 15 wins, 4 seconds, and 4 thirds in 49 starts. The tough claimer and allowance winner lost the $50,000 West Virginia Derby at Waterford Park by a neck to the Illinois-bred Architect. (Courtesy of Midwest Outdoors.)

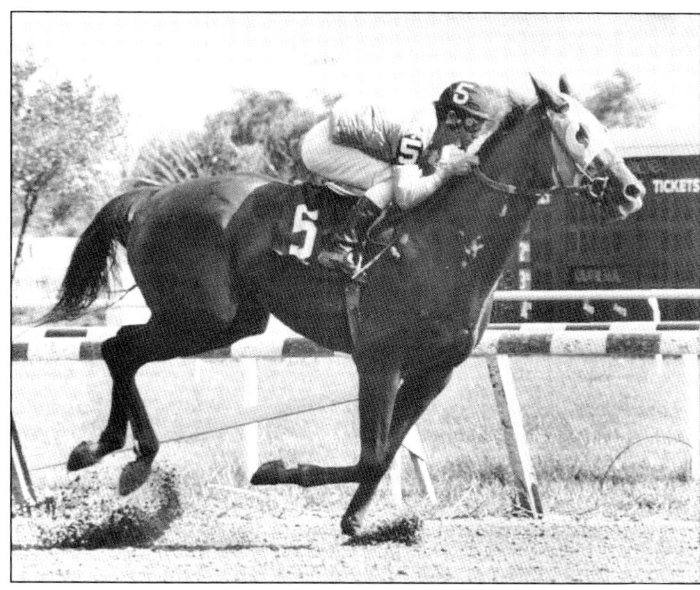

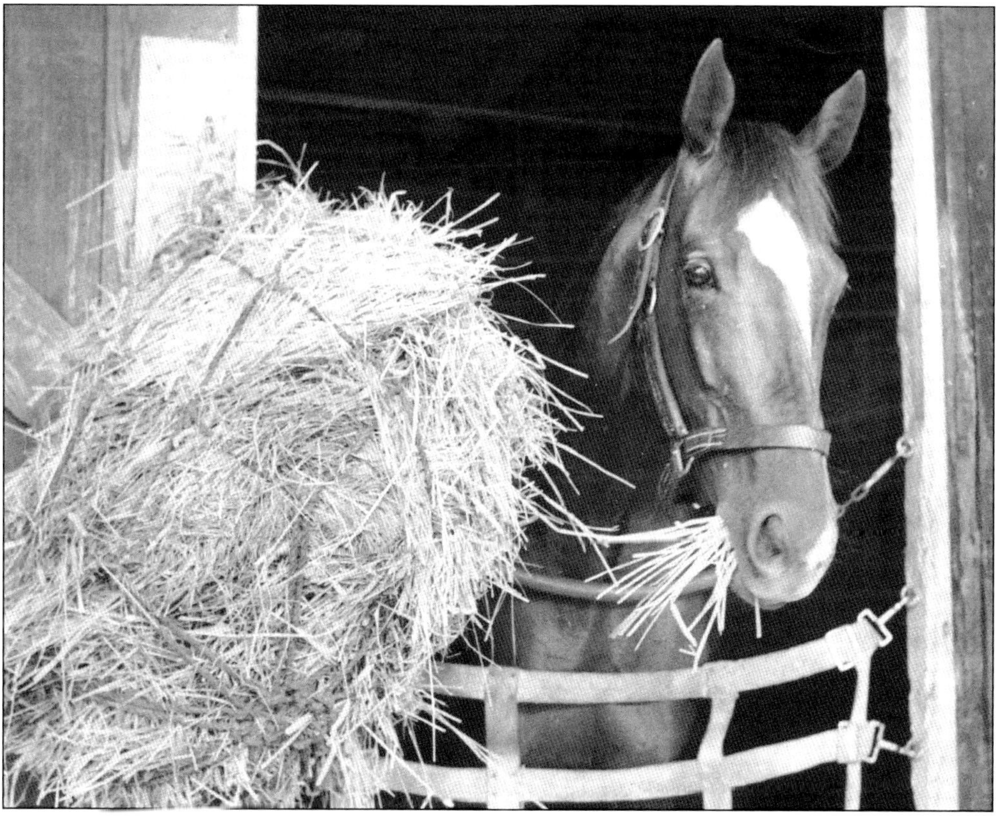

Proponent chews his hay thoughtfully in his stall at Arlington Park. The chestnut by Gallant Man was foaled February 18, 1972, and was trained by John Weipert for owner/breeder Elmendorf Farm. A multiple allowance winner, Proponent was third in the 1976 Washington Park Handicap (Gr. III) at Arlington and retired with career earnings of $147,247 from six wins in 32 starts. (Courtesy of Midwest Outdoors.)

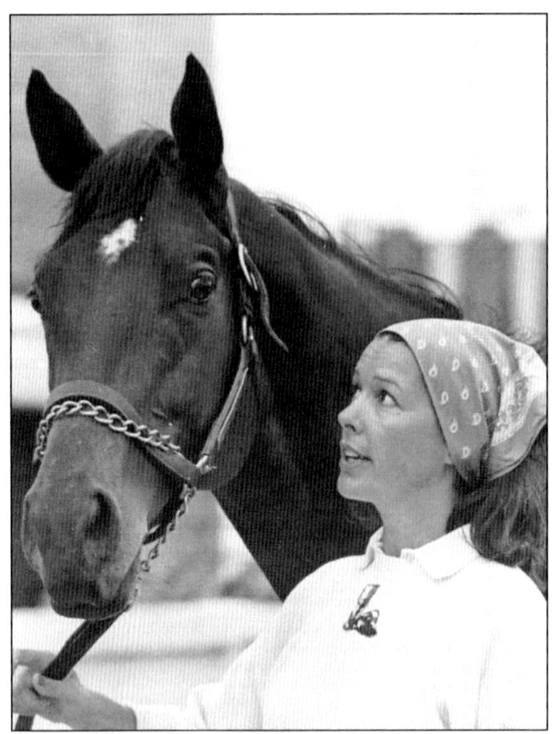

Caretaker Ginger Getz takes Blue Chip Dan for a stroll one morning at Arlington. The Kentucky-bred son by Blue Prince was foaled March 25, 1970, and saw his best season in 1973, finishing second in the Pontiac Grand Prix Stakes (Gr. II) at Arlington on June 16 of that year. He later shipped to Waterford Park, where he captured the one-and-one-eighth-mile West Virginia Derby. (Courtesy of Midwest Outdoors.)

Royal Glint strides to a four-length victory in the $127,400 Arlington Handicap (Gr. II), carrying top weight of 125 pounds before 22,130 fans on August 30, 1975. Zografos was second and Buffalo Lark third in the one-and-three-sixteenths-mile race, which was switched to the dirt oval after heavy rains drenched the turf course. Ridden by Jorge Tejeira, the five-year-old Round Table gelding was timed in 1:55.4, a track record. (Author's collection.)

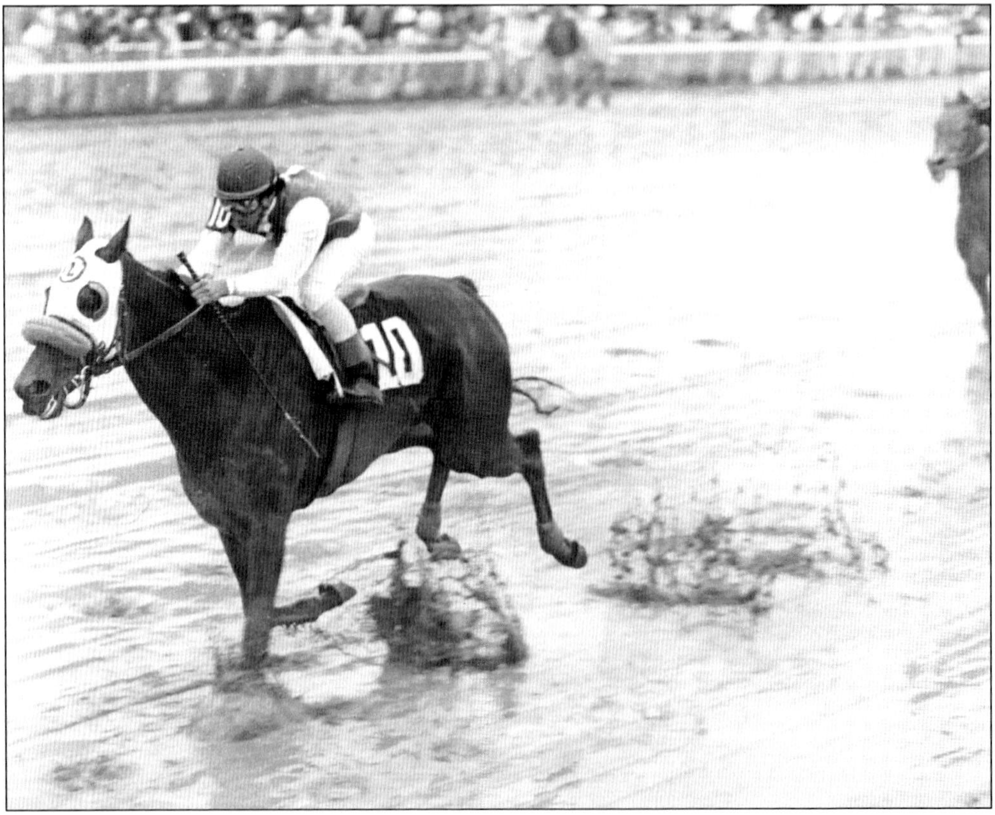

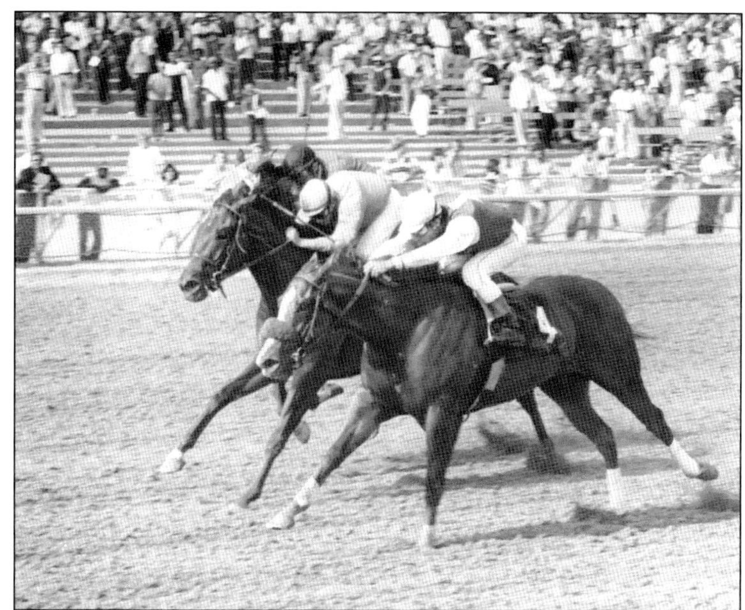

In the late 1970s, Arlington Park boasted one of the most powerful jockey colonies in North America. Here, in this dramatic, three-horse fight to the finish from 1978, Jorge Tejeira on Donawater (No. 4), out-noses top apprentice jockey Ronnie Hirdes on Little Latch (middle), while Eddie Delahoussaye guides Cheerful Princess to third, on the outside. (Courtesy of Midwest Outdoors.)

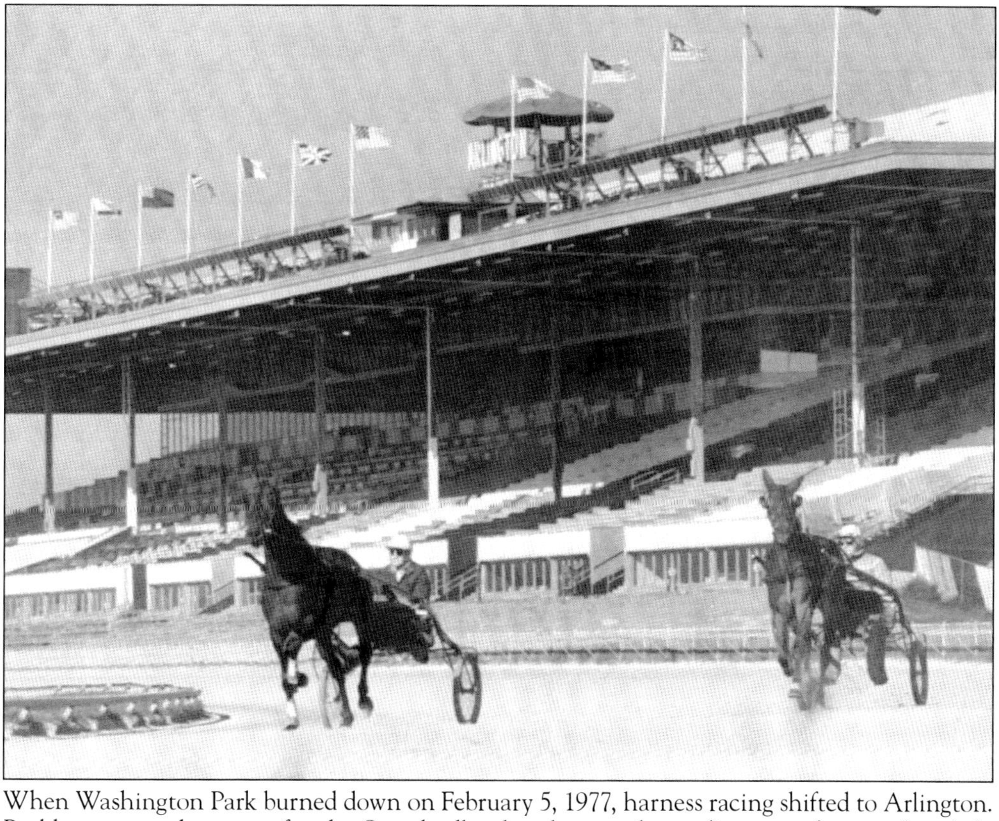

When Washington Park burned down on February 5, 1977, harness racing shifted to Arlington. Problems arose, however, for the Standardbreds, who raced at a distance of one mile, while Thoroughbred horsemen disliked changing the track surface. Harness trainers were given the option of racing at one and one-eighth miles or seventh-eighths of a mile, As a result, the trotters lasted just two years at Arlington. (Author's collection.)

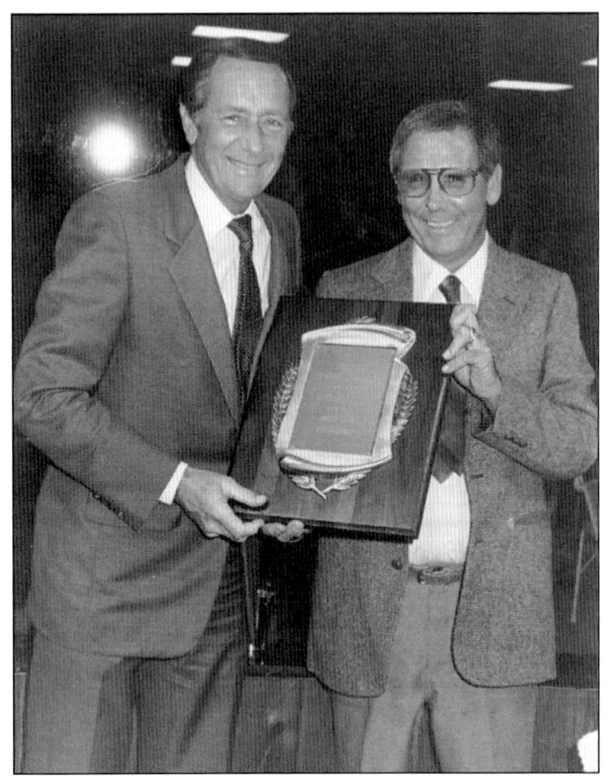

Trainer Lou Goldfine (left) is pictured with *Chicago Tribune* turf writer Elmer Polzin. Goldfine was a mainstay at Arlington and from 1964 to 2000 trained the winners of $21,247,724. From 8,838 starters, Goldfine saddled 1,352 winners, 1,227 second-place finishers, and 1,109 third-place finishers. One of his top horses was My Gallant, who faced Secretariat in the Triple Crown races, as well as Grade I–winner Wild Event and Grade II–winners Explosive Darling and Harham's Sizzler. (Courtesy of Midwest Outdoors.)

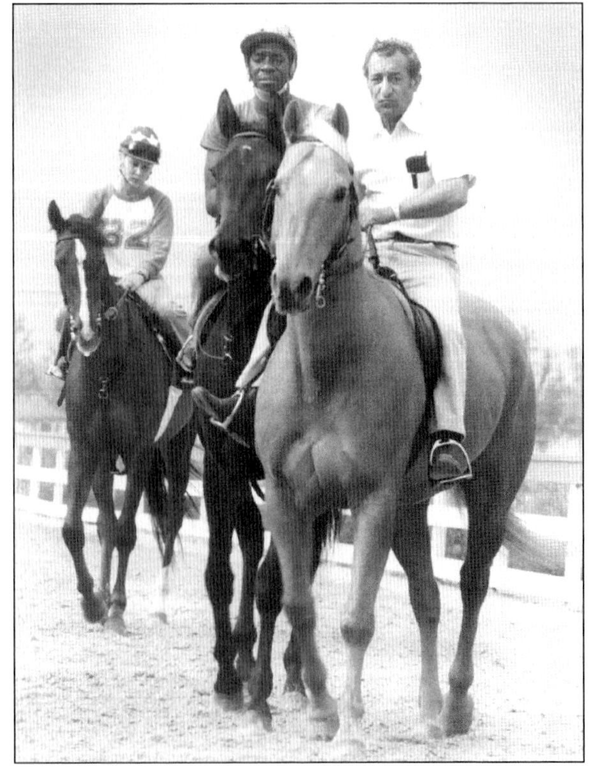

Trainer Tony Basile (right) leads a pair of his charges over Arlington's dirt track in the late 1970s. The graded stakes winning conditioner trained 329 winners from 2,661 starters to $6,336,044 during his career, which spanned from the late 1960s to 1999. Some of his top horses include Grade I–winner Lets Don't Fight and Grade II–winners Highland Park and Fortnightly. Basile won the 1967 Arlington-Washington Futurity with T.V. Commercial. (Courtesy of Midwest Outdoors.)

Three

Million Dollar Legacy

1980–August 1985

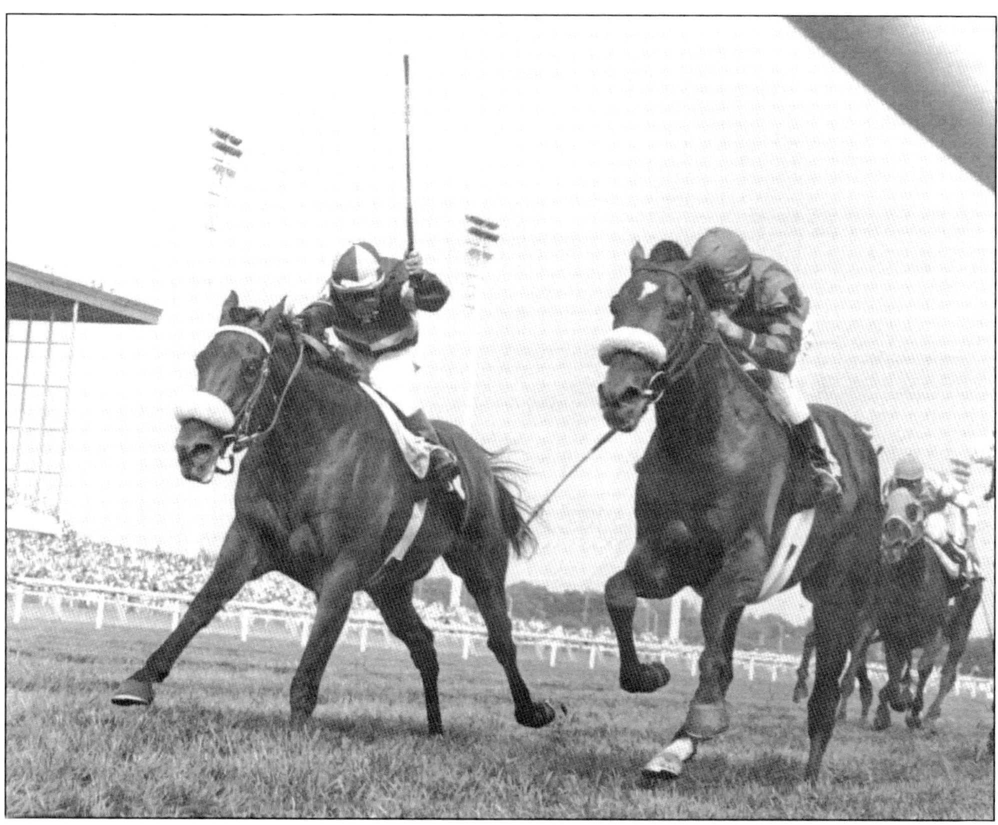

John Henry's spectacular nose victory over 40-1 longshot The Bart in the first running of the Arlington Million on August 30, 1981, saw a crowd of 30,637 watch as he and jockey Bill Shoemaker covered the one-and-one-quarter-mile turf test in 2:07.36. The Bart led most of the way, but the Ron McAnally-trained John Henry unleashed a tremendous late brush to beat him by a whisker at the wire. (Author's collection.)

The "Million" was the brainchild of Arlington president Joe Joyce, who joined the track in 1976. Sonny Werblin, Joyce's boss at Arlington's parent company, Madison Square Garden, loved the idea when Joyce proposed it to him in 1980. Joyce enticed international horses to come to Arlington—with horses coming from England, Ireland, and France—and was looking to instill prestige the track had enjoyed during the 1930s, 1940s, and 1950s. Beginning with John Henry, California-based horses dominated the Million—especially those conditioned by Ron McAnally and Charlie Whittingham—who each won the race three times. The 1981 Million is commemorated with the sculpture *Against All Odds*, which sits above Arlington's paddock area. Joyce left Arlington in 1982, and owned Wyoming Downs from 1990 to 1998. A decorated veteran, Joyce passed away on November 27, 2006, at age 77. (Courtesy of Midwest Outdoors.)

Spectacular Bid was a 1976 Bold Bidder colt, sold to the Maryland-based Hawksworth Farm for $37,000 as a yearling. Trained by Grover "Bud" Delp, he won the 1979 Kentucky Derby and Preakness and the 1980 Washington Park Handicap (Gr. III) by 10 lengths carrying 130 pounds, stopping the clock in a new track record of 1:46.2. He retired with $2.7 million in earnings from 26 wins in 30 starts. (Author's collection.)

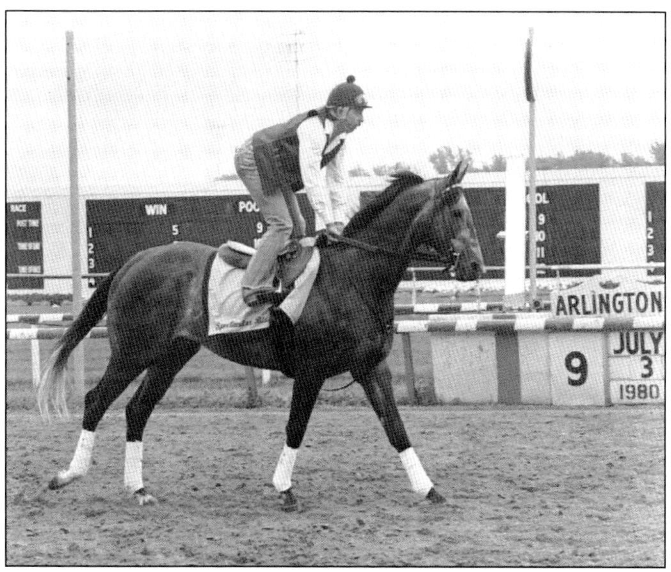

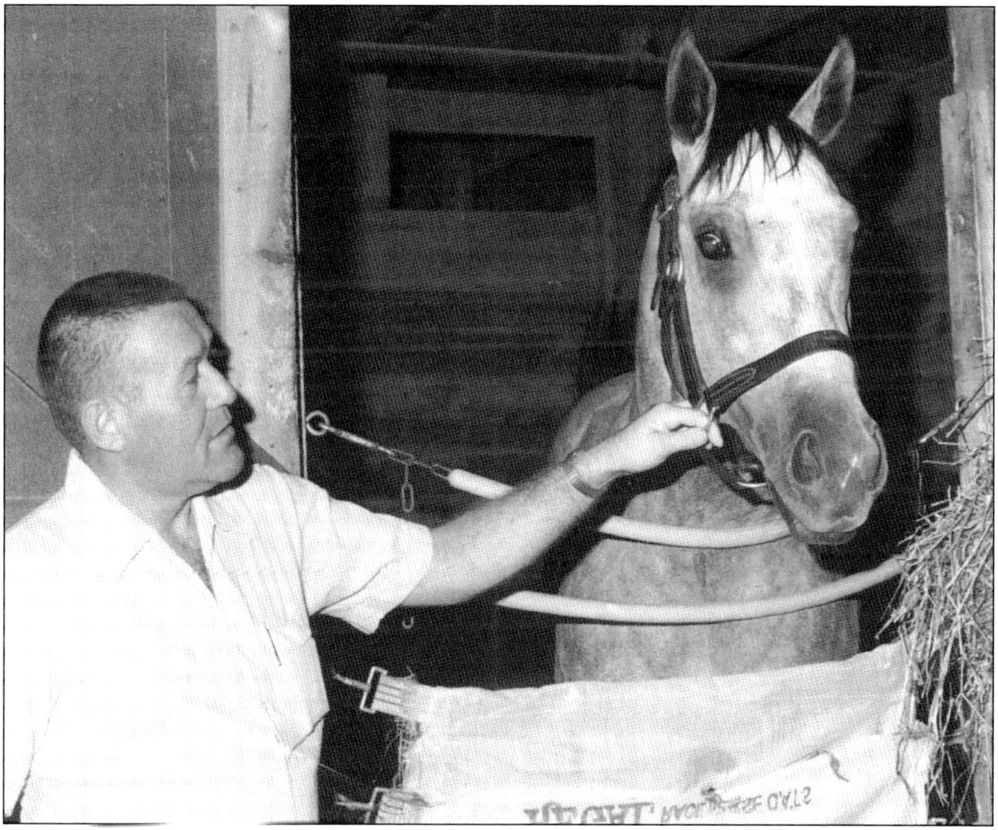

Golden Derby, shown here with trainer William "Smiley" Adams, was a 1978 roan son by Master Derby who rarely missed a check in graded stakes. Golden Derby earned $244,729 from six wins, five seconds, and seven thirds in 28 starts for breeder/owner Gaines and Lehmann. He won the 1981 Olympia Handicap and was second in the 1981 Arlington Handicap. He later sold for $500,000 as a stallion. (Courtesy of Midwest Outdoors.)

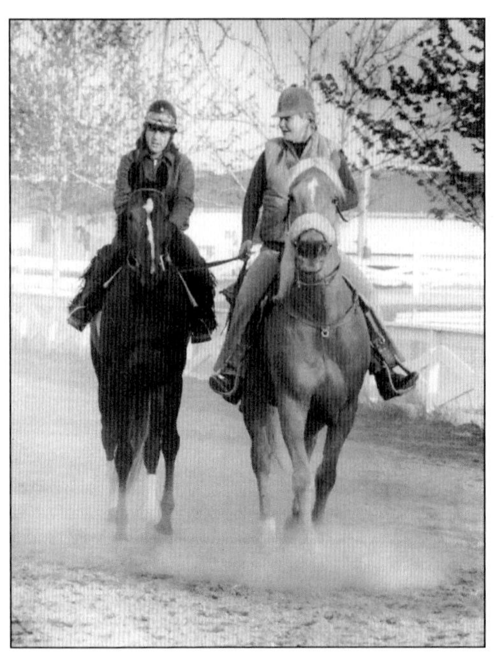

Producer, trotting to the track for a morning workout, was a 1976 daughter of Nashua who won an Allowance test and the Susan's Girl Handicap in 1980 at Arlington. The multiple graded stakes–placed mare began her career in England and France before coming to America, where she earned $423,678 from 10 wins in 24 starts. She sold for $5,250,000 in foal to Northern Dancer to a British nursery. (Courtesy of Midwest Outdoors.)

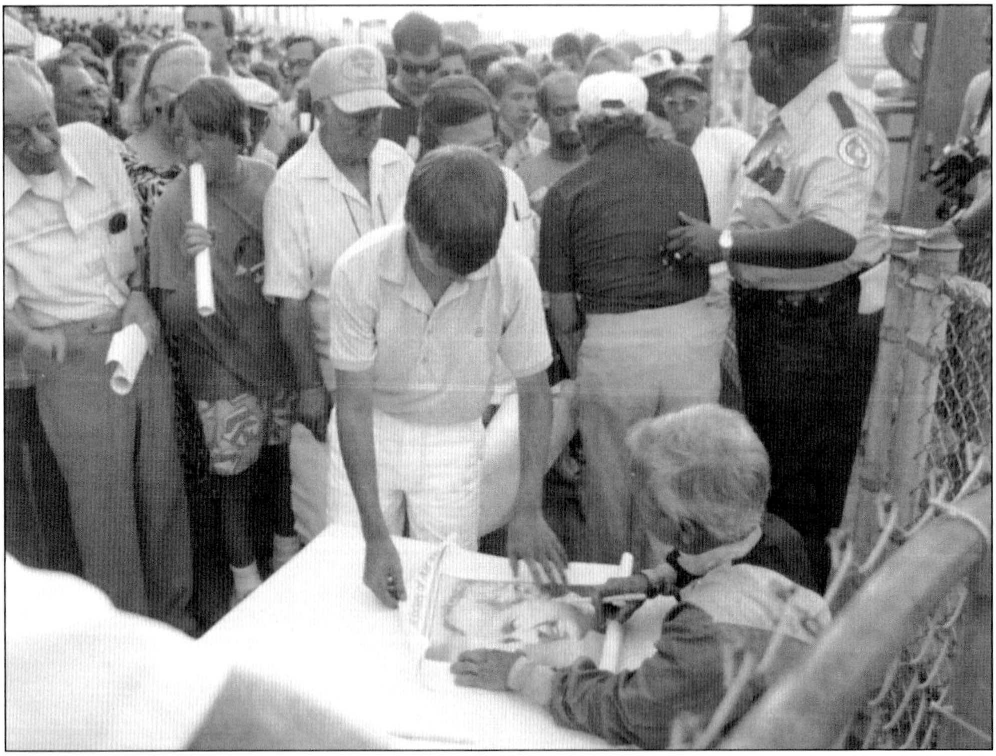

Bill Shoemaker Day was September 23, 1984, at Arlington. Born August 19, 1931, in Fabens, Texas, "The Shoe" tied for the Arlington riding title in 1958 with jockey Luis Cook with 52 wins. Shoemaker won the Arlington Handicap four times, twice with Round Table (1958 and 1959) and with Chieftain (1965) and Palikariki (1983). He rode 41 years, amassing 8,833 victories with $123,375,524. Shoemaker died on October 12, 2003. (Courtesy of Midwest Outdoors.)

Jinxed was a 1978-foaled, Illinois-bred daughter by Recaptured, and she was trained by Harvey Vanier for breeder Mary Lou Cashman. The multiple-stakes winner raced at Arlington in all nine of her career starts, before being sold for $62,000 in foal to Crafty Prospector. She won the 1981 editions of the Colfax Maid and Anita Peabody Stakes as well as four allowance races at Arlington with $89,495 from six wins. (Courtesy of Midwest Outdoors.)

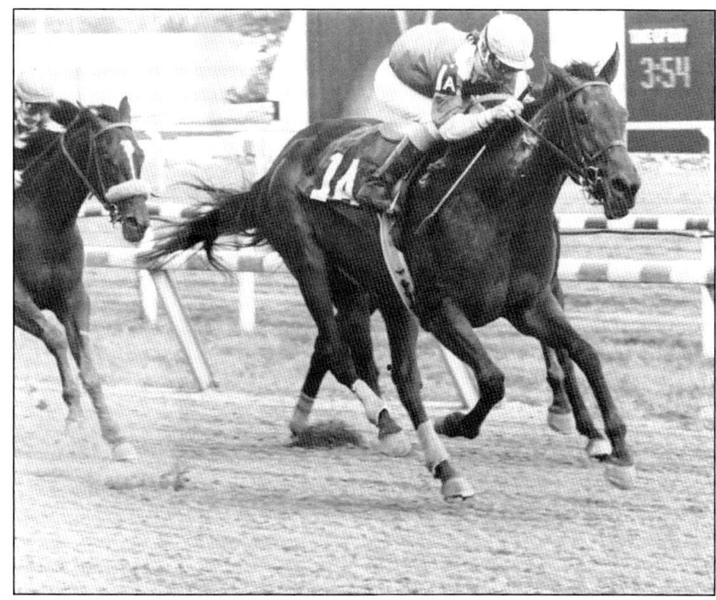

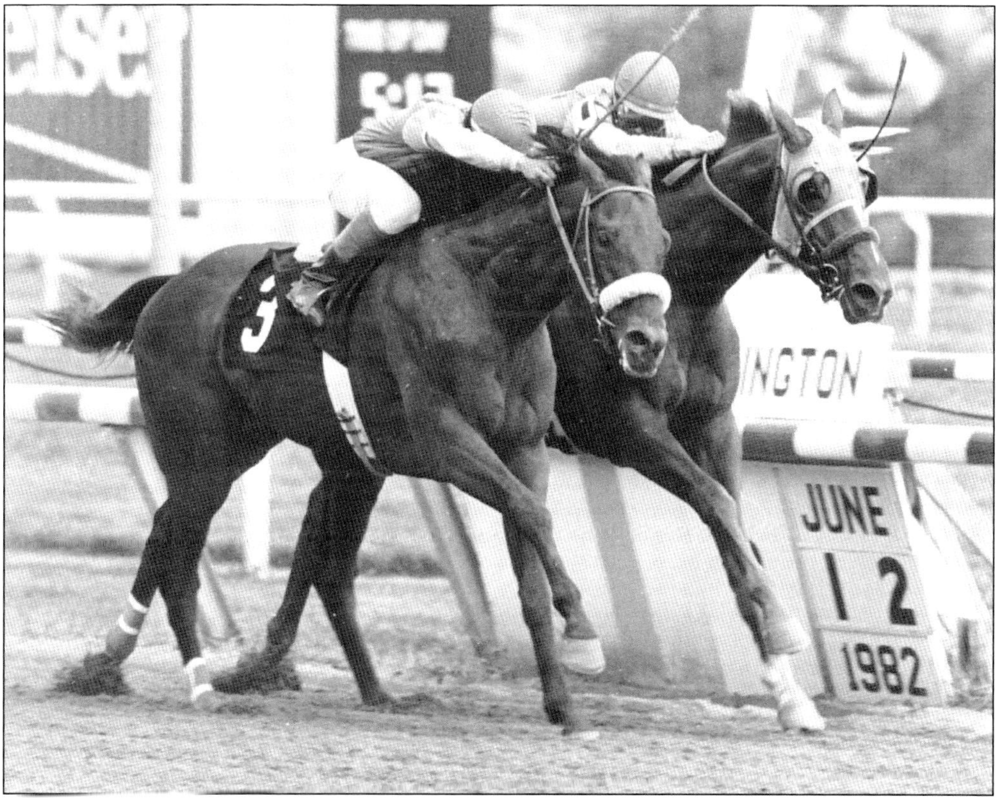

Wolfie's Rascal was a 1975 son of London Company trained by Howard Tesher. He is shown here winning the 1982 Arlington Classic (Gr. I) for rider Angel Cordero Jr. (No. 3), besting Drop Your Drawers (No. 10) by a nose. He also won the July 10, 1982, Arlington Derby (Gr. I) for owners Sy Cohen and Sid Port. Wolfie's Rascal earned $321,061 from 26 starts, with 9 wins, 1 second, and 3 thirds. (Courtesy of Midwest Outdoors.)

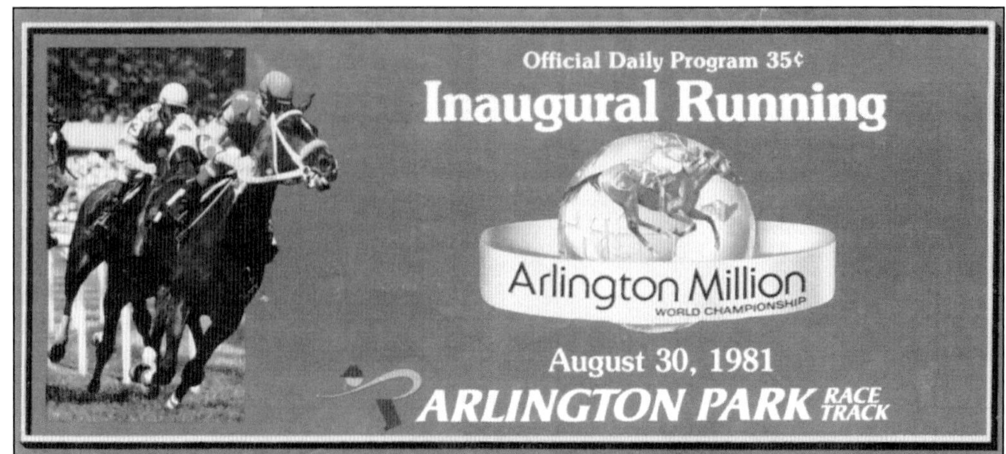

The first Arlington Million program featured an international field of Thoroughbreds, while the jockeys read like a who's who of the best riders ever, including Lestor Piggot, Bill Shoemaker, Pat Day, Angel Cordero Jr., Steve Cauthen, Eddie Delahoussaye, Laffit Pincay Jr., Don Brumfield, and Sandy Hawley, among others. Four European runners were part of that field, including Madam Gay, who would finish third for Lester Piggott, and another filly, Mrs. Penny, along with France's Argument and Fingal's Cave, and Irish five-year-old The Bart. Still the closest finish in Million history, that 1981 edition boosted John Henry to a new plateau. The six-year-old son by Ole Bob Bowers upped his career earnings to $2,464,510 with that victory. John Henry's owner, Sam Rubin, who was a New York–based bicycle importer, had purchased the gelding as a three-year-old for a mere $25,000 sight unseen. (Author's collection.)

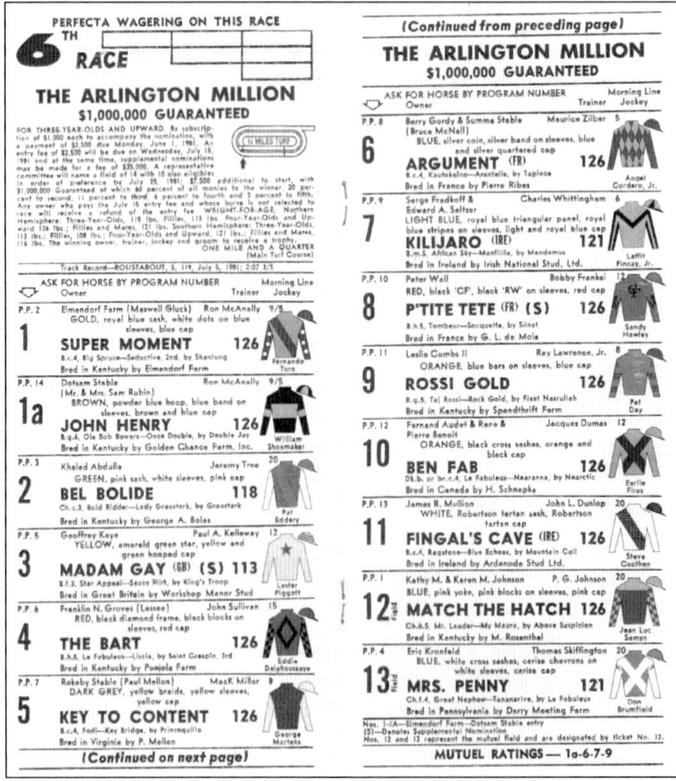

PERFECTA WAGERING ON THIS RACE

6TH RACE

THE ARLINGTON MILLION

$1,000,000 GUARANTEED

FOR THREE-YEAR-OLDS AND UPWARD. By subscription of $1,000 each to accompany the nomination, with a payment of $2,500 due Monday, June 1, 1981. An entry fee of $2,500 will be due on Wednesday, July 15, 1981 and at the same time, supplemental nominations may be made for a fee of $35,000. A representative committee will name a field of 14 with 10 also eligibles in order of preference by July 25, 1981; $7,500 additional to start, with $1,000,000 Guaranteed of which 60 percent of all monies to the winner, 20 percent to second, 11 percent to third, 6 percent to fourth and 3 percent to fifth. Any owner who pays the July 15 entry fee and whose horse is not selected to race will receive a refund of the entry fee. WEIGHT-FOR-AGE. Northern Hemisphere: Three-Year-Olds, 118 lbs. Fillies, 113 lbs. Four-Year-Olds and Upward 126 lbs.; Fillies and Mares, 121 lbs. Southern Hemisphere: Three-Year-Olds, 113 lbs.; Fillies, 108 lbs.; Four-Year-Olds and Upward, 121 lbs.; Fillies and Mares, 116 lbs. The winning owner, trainer, jockey and groom to receive a trophy.

ONE MILE AND A QUARTER (Main Turf Course)

1¼ MILES TURF

Track Record—ROUSTABOUT, 5, 119, July 5, 1981; 2:07 3/5

ASK FOR HORSE BY PROGRAM NUMBER — Owner / Trainer / Morning Line / Jockey

P.P. 2 — **1** — Elmendorf Farm (Maxwell Gluck) — Ron McAnally — 9/5
GOLD, royal blue sash, white dots on blue sleeves, blue cap
SUPER MOMENT 126
B.c.4, Big Spruce—Seductive, 2nd, by Shantung
Bred in Kentucky by Elmendorf Farm — Fernando Toro

P.P. 14 — **1a** — Dotsam Stable (Mr. & Mrs. Sam Rubin) — Ron McAnally — 9/5
BROWN, powder blue hoop, blue band on sleeves, brown and blue cap
JOHN HENRY 126
B.g.6, Ole Bob Bowers—Once Double, by Double Jay
Bred in Kentucky by Golden Chance Farm, Inc. — William Shoemaker

P.P. 3 — **2** — Khaled Abdulla — Jeremy Tree — 20
GREEN, pink sash, white sleeves, pink cap
BEL BOLIDE 118
Ch.c.3, Bold Bidder—Lady Graustark, by Graustark
Bred in Kentucky by George A. Bolas — Pat Eddery

P.P. 5 — **3** — Geoffrey Kaye — Paul A. Kelleway — 12
YELLOW, emerald green star, yellow and green hooped cap
MADAM GAY (GB) (S) 113
B.f.3, Star Appeal—Saucy Flirt, by King's Troop
Bred in Great Britain by Workshop Manor Stud — Lester Piggott

P.P. 6 — **4** — Franklin N. Groves (Lessee) — John Sullivan — 15
RED, black diamond frame, black blocks on sleeves, red cap
THE BART 126
B.h.5, Le Fabuleux—Lisela, by Saint Crespin, 3rd
Bred in Kentucky by Pomjola Farm — Eddie Delahoussaye

P.P. 7 — **5** — Rokeby Stable (Paul Mellon) — MacK Miller — 8
DARK GREY, yellow braids, yellow sleeves, yellow cap
KEY TO CONTENT 126
B.c.4, Forli—Key Bridge, by Princequillo
Bred in Virginia by P. Mellon — George Martens

(Continued on next page)

(Continued from preceding page)

THE ARLINGTON MILLION

$1,000,000 GUARANTEED

ASK FOR HORSE BY PROGRAM NUMBER — Owner / Trainer / Morning Line / Jockey

P.P. 8 — **6** — Berry Gordy & Summa Stable (Bruce McNall) — Maurice Zilber — 5
BLUE, silver coin, silver band on sleeves, blue and silver quartered cap
ARGUMENT (FR) 126
B.c.4, Kautokeino—Arantelle, by Tapioca
Bred in France by Pierre Ribes — Angel Cordero, Jr.

P.P. 9 — **7** — Serge Fradkoff & Edward A. Seltzer — Charles Whittingham — 6
LIGHT BLUE, royal blue triangular panel, royal blue stripes on sleeves, light and royal blue cap
KILIJARO (IRE) 121
B.m.5, African Sky—Manfilia, by Mandamus
Bred in Ireland by Irish National Stud, Ltd. — Laffit Pincay, Jr.

P.P. 10 — **8** — Peter Wall — Bobby Frankel — 12
RED, black 'CF', black 'RW' on sleeves, red cap
P'TITE TETE (FR) (S) 126
B.h.5, Tombeur—Socquette, by Silnet
Bred in France by G. L. de Mola — Sandy Hawley

P.P. 11 — **9** — Leslie Combs II — Ray Lawrence, Jr. — 8
ORANGE, blue bars on sleeves, blue cap
ROSSI GOLD 126
B.g.5, Taj Rossi—Rock Gold, by Fleet Nasrullah
Bred in Kentucky by Spendthrift Farm — Pat Day

P.P. 12 — **10** — Fernand Audet & Rene & Pierre Benoit — Jacques Dumas — 12
ORANGE, black cross sashes, orange and black cap
BEN FAB 126
Dk.b. or br.c.4, Le Fabuleux—Nearanna, by Nearctic
Bred in Canada by H. Schnepka — Earlie Fires

P.P. 13 — **11** — James R. Mullion — John L. Dunlop — 20
WHITE, Robertson tartan sash, Robertson tartan cap
FINGAL'S CAVE (IRE) 126
B.c.4, Ragstone—Blue Echoes, by Mountain Call
Bred in Ireland by Ardenode Stud Ltd. — Steve Cauthen

P.P. 1 — **12 Field** — Kathy M. & Karen M. Johnson — P. G. Johnson — 20
BLUE, pink yoke, pink blocks on sleeves, pink cap
MATCH THE HATCH 126
Ch.h.5, Mr. Leader—My Maura, by Above Suspicion
Bred in Kentucky by M. Rosenthal — Jean Luc Samyn

P.P. 4 — **13 Field** — Eric Kronfeld — Thomas Skiffington — 20
BLUE, white cross sashes, cerise chevrons on white sleeves, cerise cap
MRS. PENNY 121
Ch.f.4, Great Nephew—Tananarive, by Le Fabuleux
Bred in Pennsylvania by Derry Meeting Farm — Don Brumfield

Nos. 1-1A—Elmendorf Farm—Dotsam Stable entry
(S)—Denotes Supplemental Nomination
Nos. 12 and 13 represent the mutuel field and are designated by ticket No. 12.

MUTUEL RATINGS — 1a-6-7-9

Trainer Frank Gomez is with his three-year-old ace Smile after a morning workout at Arlington. The Florida-bred Smile was a dark bay horse foaled March 26, 1982, a son of In Reality–Sunny Smile, by Boldnesian. He was bred and owned by Frances Genter, earning $1,664,027 for her with 14 wins, 4 seconds, and 3 thirds in 27 career starts. He raced from 1984 through 1987 throughout the South and Midwest. (Courtesy of Midwest Outdoors.)

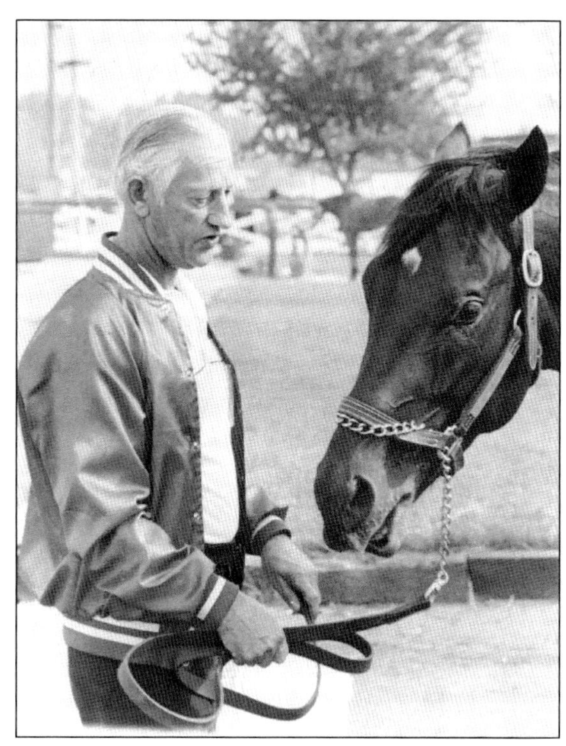

Smile goes postward for the 1985 edition of the $100,000 Arlington Classic (Gr. I), which he won easily for jockey Jacinto Vasquez, before finishing a solid third 15 days later in the American Derby (Gr. I) on July 6. Smile returned to Chicago the following summer, capturing the Equipoise Mile Handicap (Gr. III) on August 30, 1986—again with Vasquez in the irons. (Courtesy of Midwest Outdoors.)

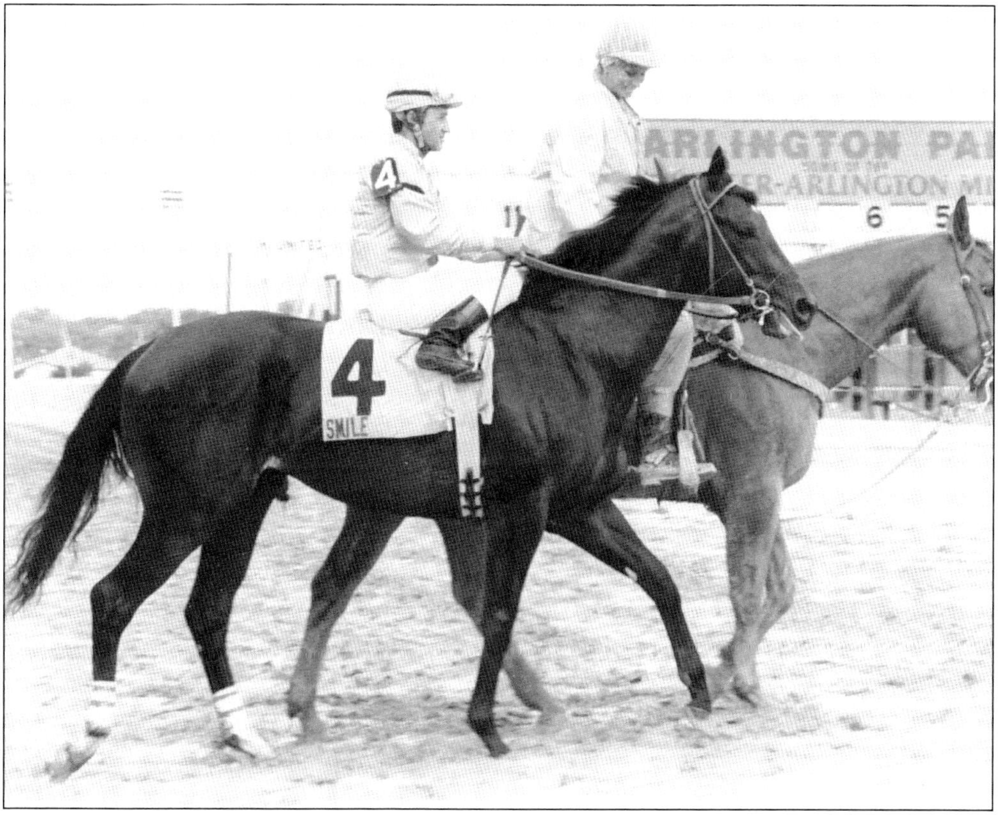

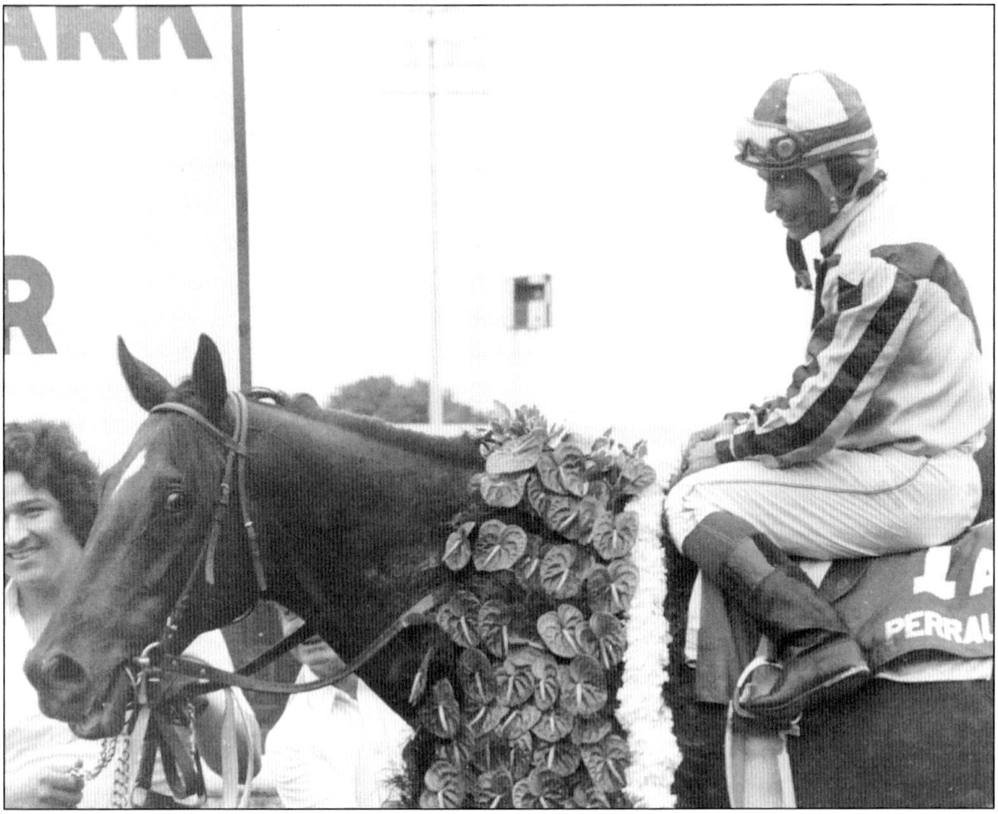

Perrault captured the 1982 Arlington Million in a stakes record 1:58.4 for Laffit Pincay Jr. A member of the National Museum of Racing and Hall of Fame, the Panama native began riding in 1966, before becoming a seven-time leading jockey and four-time Eclipse winner in America. Pincay won the 1984 Kentucky Derby with Swale and three consecutive Belmonts (1982–1984), retiring in 2002 with 9,530 winners. (Author's collection.)

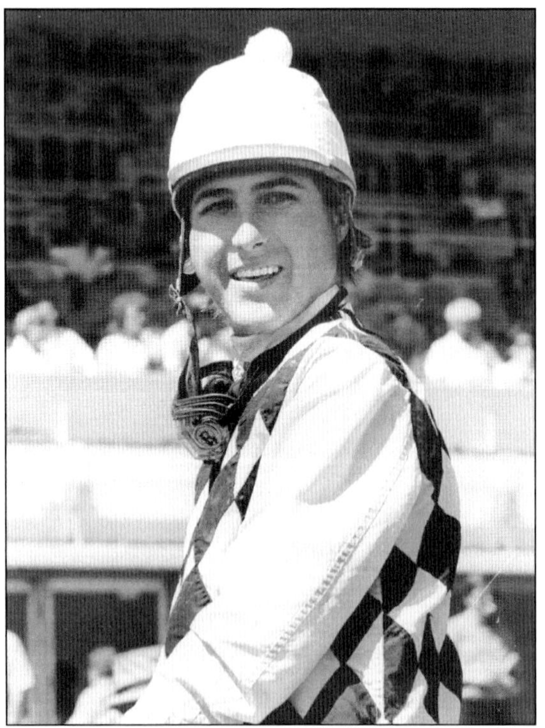

Randy Romero, born December 22, 1957, at Erath, Louisiana, was known as the "Ragin' Cajun" and set an Arlington Park record of 181 wins for the season in 1982. Despite a Hall of Fame career beginning in 1975, Romero was plagued throughout with race-related injuries, which ultimately caused his retirement in July 1999 after having ridden 4,285 winners. He was elected into the Thoroughbred Racing Hall of Fame May 27, 2010. (Author's collection.)

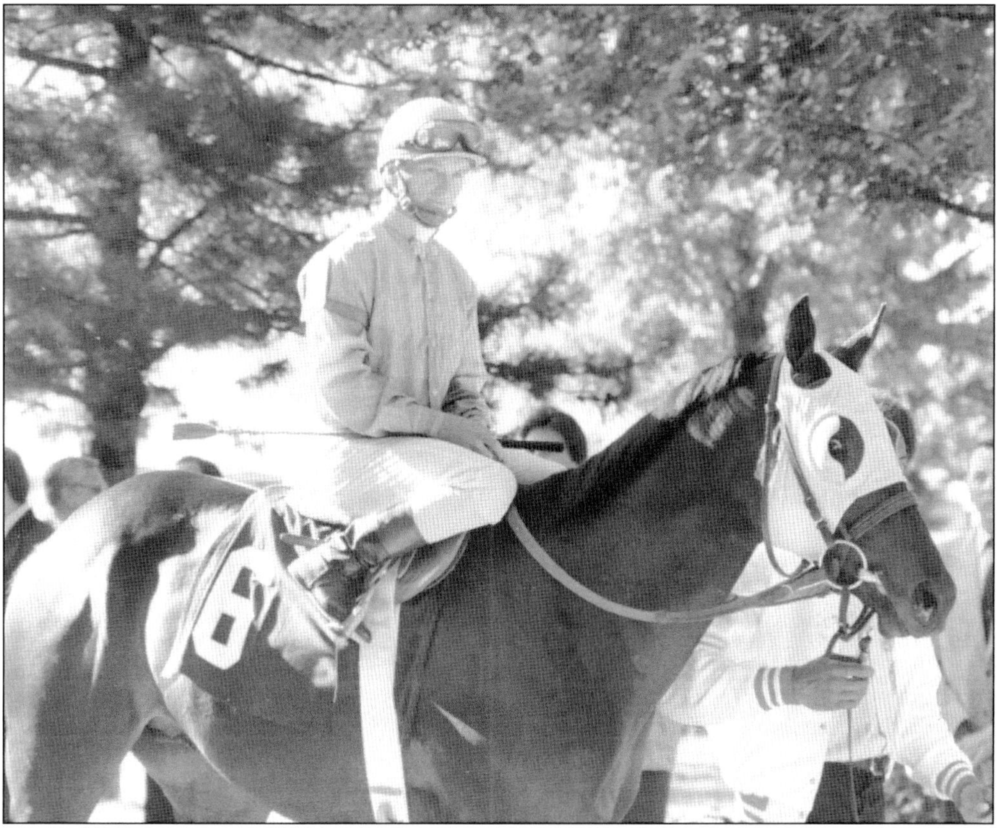

Pat Day, born October 13, 1953, in Brush, Colorado, is a 1991 Hall of Fame inductee and four-time Eclipse Award–winning jockey, as well as a George Woolf Memorial Jockey Award (1985) winner and 1995 Mike Venezia Memorial recipient. At Arlington, Day set a North American record when he won eight of nine races in 1989. He retired on Aug. 3, 2005, after 32 years and 8,804 wins. (Courtesy of Midwest Outdoors.)

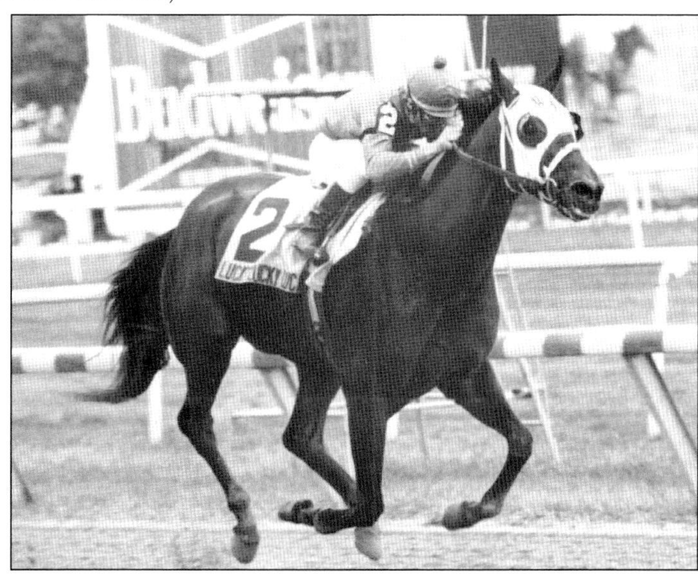

Lucky Lucky won the one-and-one-eighth-mile $75,000 Arlington Oaks (Gr. III) in 1984 for jockey Robbie Davis in 1:49.4. The 1981-foaled daughter of Chieftain was owned by Leslie Combs II and Equiets Stable and trained by D. Wayne Lukas. She earned $847,126 from 6 wins, 5 seconds, and 5 thirds in 22 starts and later was sold in foal to Northern Dancer for $3 million. (Courtesy of Midwest Outdoors.)

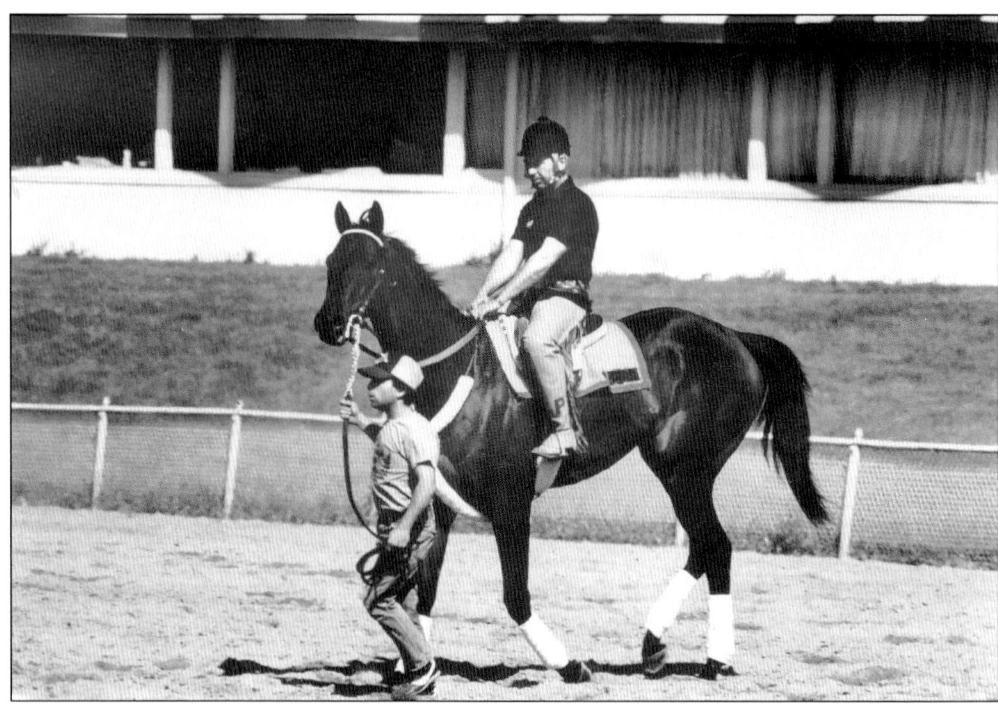

Rossi Gold was a Kentucky-bred foal of 1976 popular with Chicago fans. The son of Taj Rossi was trained by Ray Lawrence, bred by Spendthrift Farm, and owned by Leslie Combs III, and became a multiple graded stakes winner of $794,718 with stats of 16-8-5 from 43 starts, with the vast majority of his victories coming at Arlington. He won his debut there on November 18, 1978, and later scored triumphs in the 1979 Round Table Handicap (Gr. III); 1980 Sea O Erin Handicap; 1981 Washington Park Stakes; 1980 and 1981 Swoon's Son Handicap; and 1981 and 1982 Laurence Armour Handicap. Rossi Gold won the Stars & Stripes Handicap (Gr. II) at Arlington three consecutive years—1981, 1982, and 1983. Above, Rossi Gold prepares for a workout; below, he takes a carrot from trainer Lawrence. (Courtesy of Midwest Outdoors.)

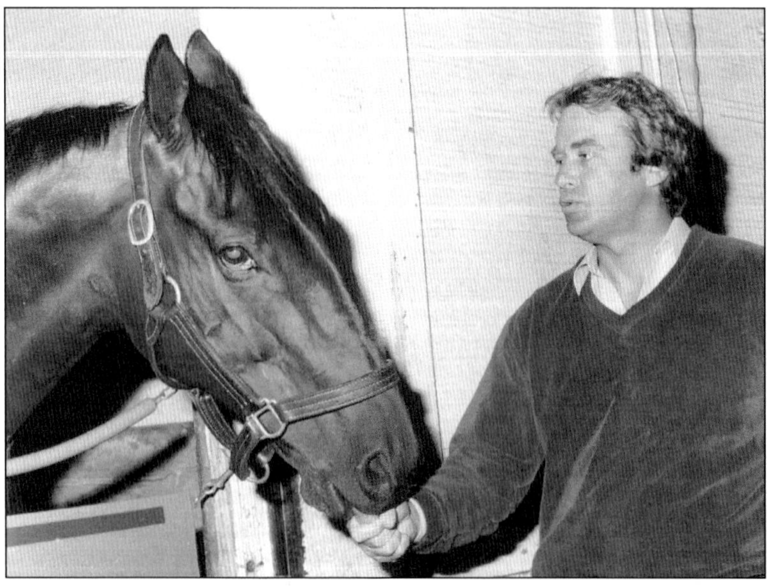

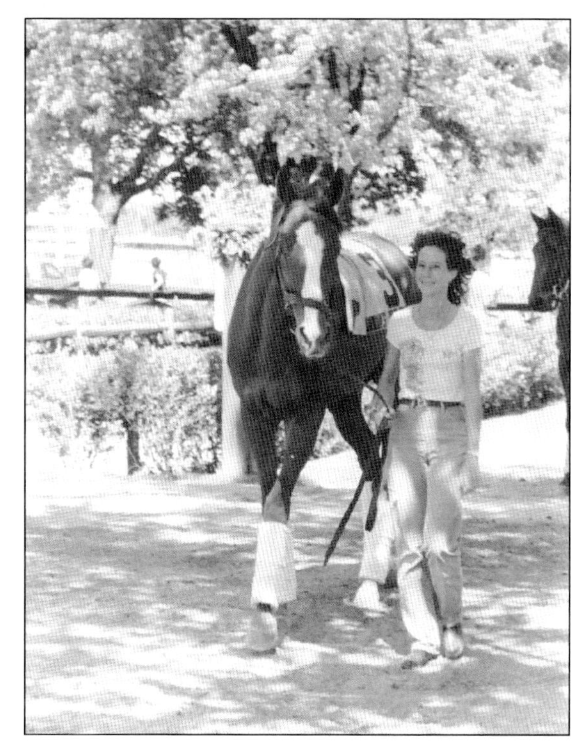

Harham's Sizzler and his groom go for a stroll in the Arlington Park saddling area. The 1979 foal by Good Behaving was trained by Lou Goldfine for breeder/owner Harold Florsheim. A multiple graded stakes winner that raced from 1981 to 1987, Harham's Sizzler was hometown favorite who amassed $843,406 from 24 wins, 11 seconds, and 13 thirds in 73 starts. (Courtesy of Midwest Outdoors.)

Harham's Sizzler captures the $100,000 Washington Park Stakes (Gr. II) on July 9, 1983, with Juvenal Diaz in the irons. The precocious Illinois-bred won stakes at all five of the Prairie State's Thoroughbred venues—Arlington, Sportsman's Park, Hawthorne, Balmoral, Fairmount Park—and at historic Keeneland. He was known to have a special liking for a muddy track. (Courtesy of Midwest Outdoors.)

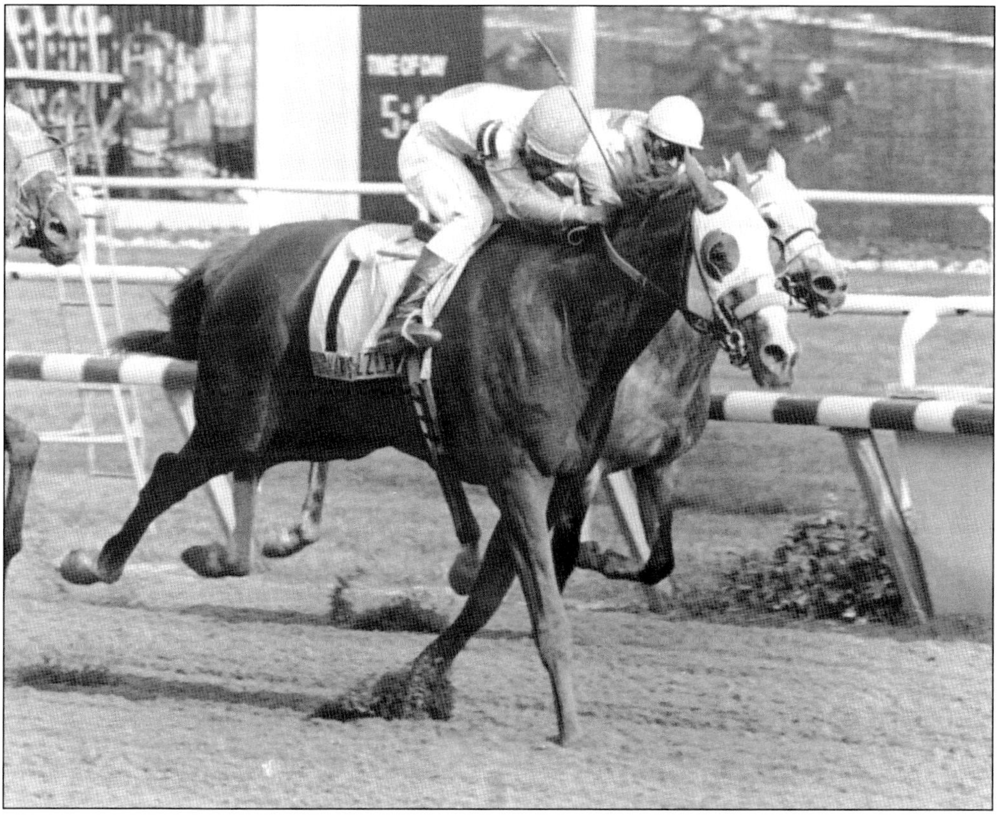

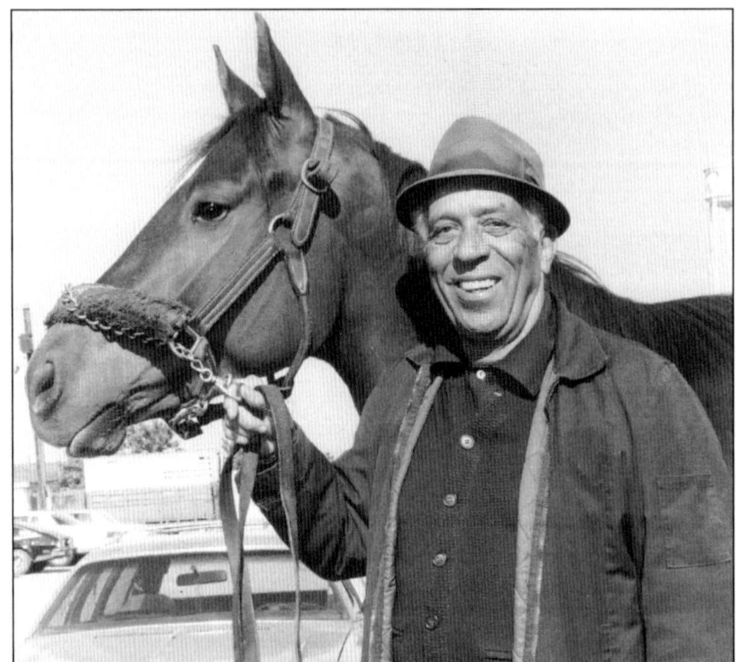

Trainer Clifford Scott poses here with his top charge, Cream, a 1977 Kentucky-bred son by Prove Out, who was co-owned by Scott. Ridden by Carlos Silva, Cream won the 1980 Olympia Stakes at Arlington. From 26 starts, he won 4 races and earned $73,899. Scott was a multiple graded stakes winning trainer who conditioned 579 winners of $45.9 million from 1960 until 1992, including Balotra and Jeremy Jet. (Courtesy of Midwest Outdoors.)

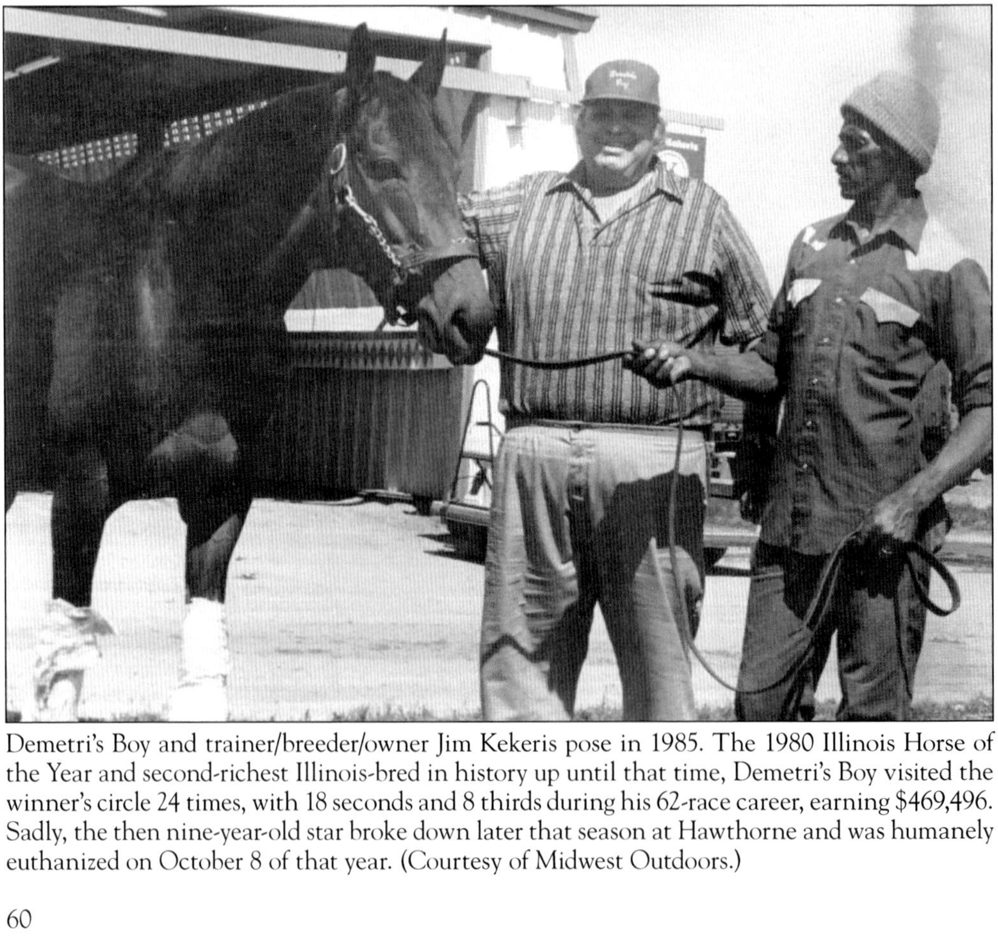

Demetri's Boy and trainer/breeder/owner Jim Kekeris pose in 1985. The 1980 Illinois Horse of the Year and second-richest Illinois-bred in history up until that time, Demetri's Boy visited the winner's circle 24 times, with 18 seconds and 8 thirds during his 62-race career, earning $469,496. Sadly, the then nine-year-old star broke down later that season at Hawthorne and was humanely euthanized on October 8 of that year. (Courtesy of Midwest Outdoors.)

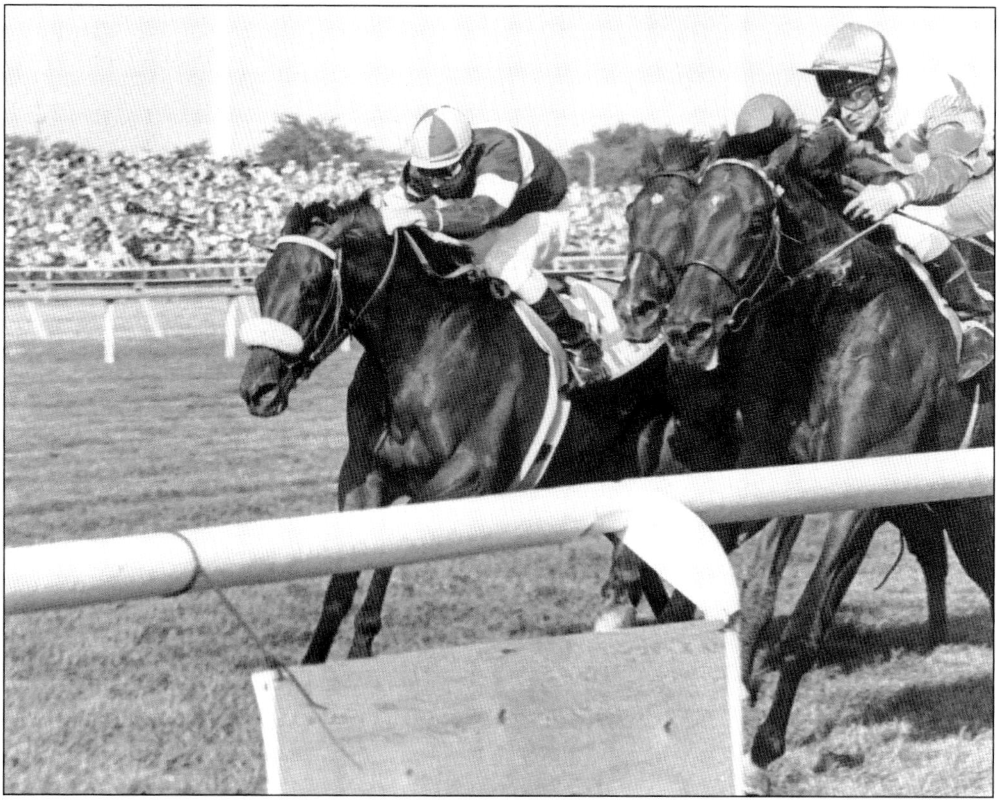

In 1983, Tolomeo (on the inside rail, right) upset John Henry (on the outside, left) in becoming the first European winner of the Arlington Million. The Irish-bred son of Lypheor was foaled January 1, 1980, and was a graded stakes winner who bested the eight-year-old John Henry at 38-1 odds. Tolomeo snuck through on the rail in mid-stretch and held off John Henry by a neck, with Nijinsky's Secret (center) third. (Courtesy of Midwest Outdoors.)

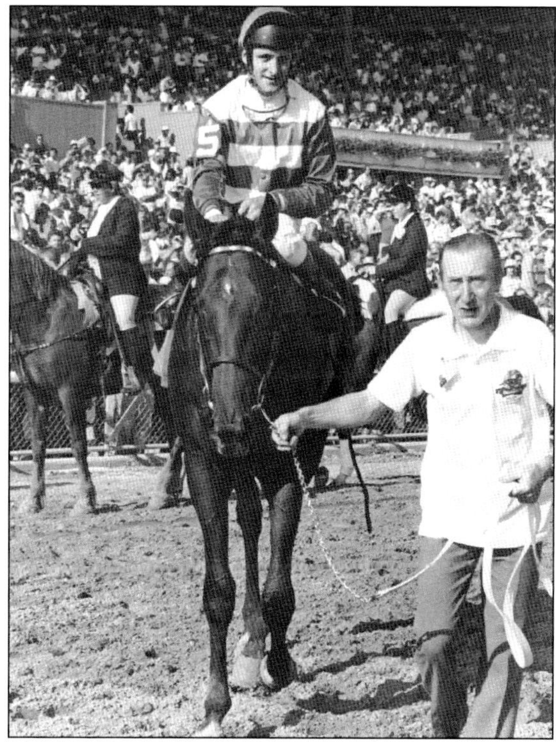

Tolomeo, only three when he won the Million, paid $78.40 for $2 to win and covered the one-and-a-quarter-mile turf contest in 2:04.2. Tolomeo and Irish jockey Pat Eddery carried 118 pounds, 8 fewer than John Henry, who, with Chris McCarron up, was a neck back and half a length in front of Nijinsky's Secret. Tolomeo was trained by Luca Cumani for Carlo d'Alessio, a 78-year-old retired Italian attorney. (Courtesy of Midwest Outdoors.)

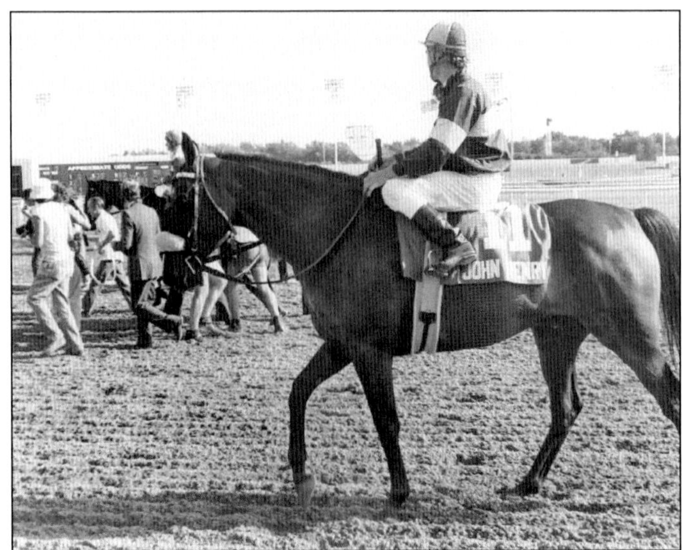

John Henry and rider Chris McCarron watch as Tolomeo is surrounded by his connections after winning the 1983 Arlington Million. John Henry had looked like an almost sure winner in the stretch before the longshot Tolomeo brushed up the rail to prevail over the Chicago favorite. (Courtesy of Midwest Outdoors.)

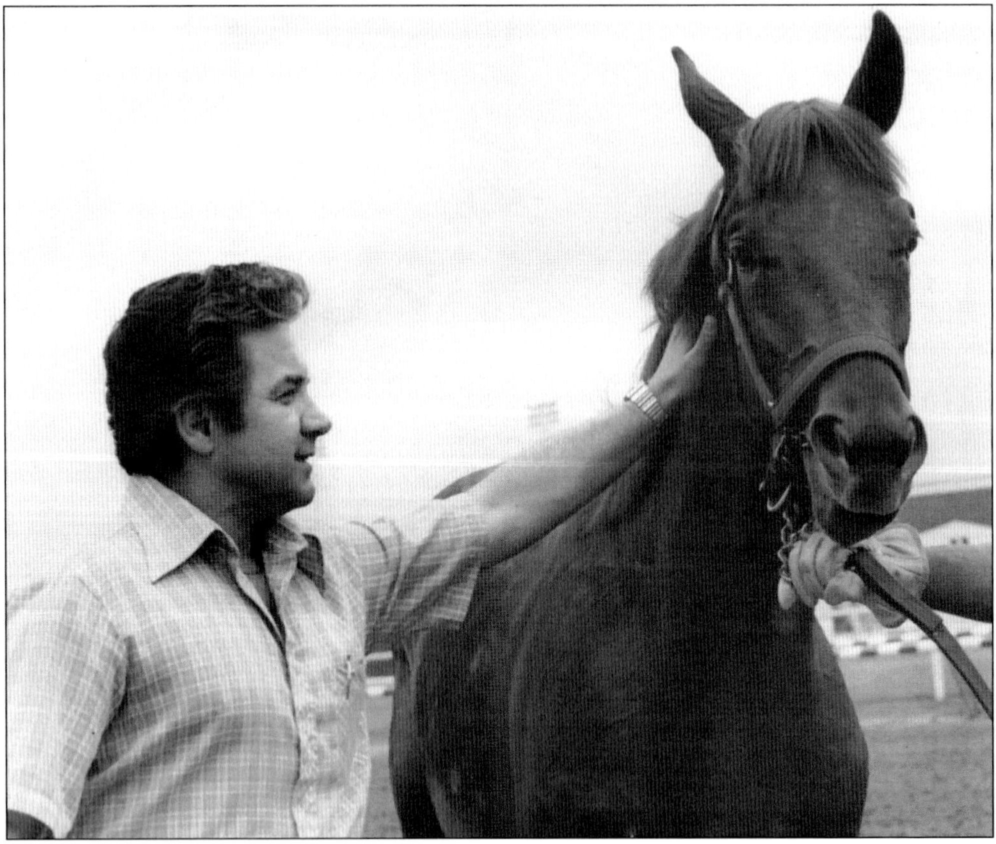

Track announcer Phil Georgeff stands alongside his namesake, the Illinois-bred Georgeff, a 1978 son by Raise a Native. Georgeff the horse won 4 of 51 starts and $78,112. Georgeff the human was known as the "Voice of Arlington" and called over 95,000 Chicagoland races in his 32-year career. His catchphrase, "Here they come spinning out of the turn," is one of the most famous in all of horse racing. (Courtesy of Midwest Outdoors.)

The California-bred Pole Position was a 1976 Draft Card colt who raced throughout America from 1978 through 1980. Trained by George Goodwin, he was unraced at two but went on to win numerous graded stakes for the Eldorado Stable in Chicago, earning $507,402 from 16 wins in 35 career starts. He had a modest stud career, siring 18 crops of runners who earned $5.4 million. (Courtesy of Midwest Outdoors.)

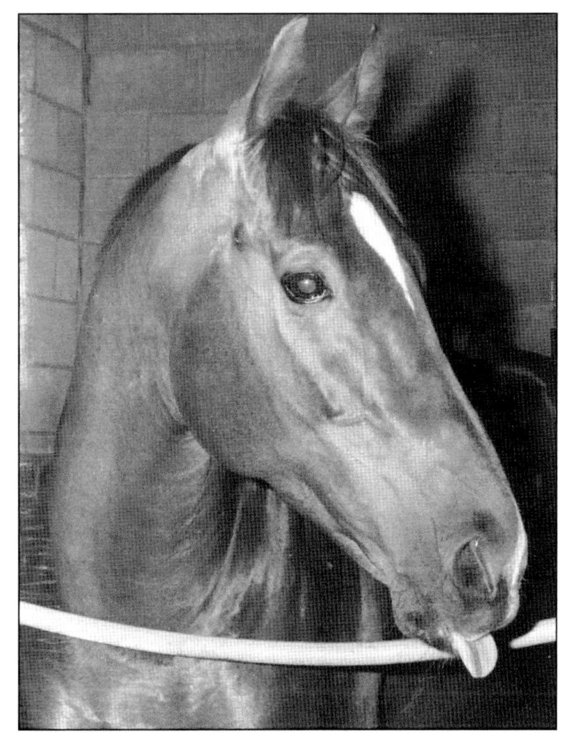

Aspro was a Maryland-bred roan son of Double Edge Sword conditioned by Grover "Bud" Delp. Foaled April 5, 1978, Aspro earned $416,587 for owner/breeder Mrs. James Bayard from 15 wins, 7 seconds, and 10 thirds in 43 starts. Here, the multiple graded stakes winner captures the $38,000 Shecky Greene Handicap at Arlington on May 13, 1984. (Courtesy of Midwest Outdoors.)

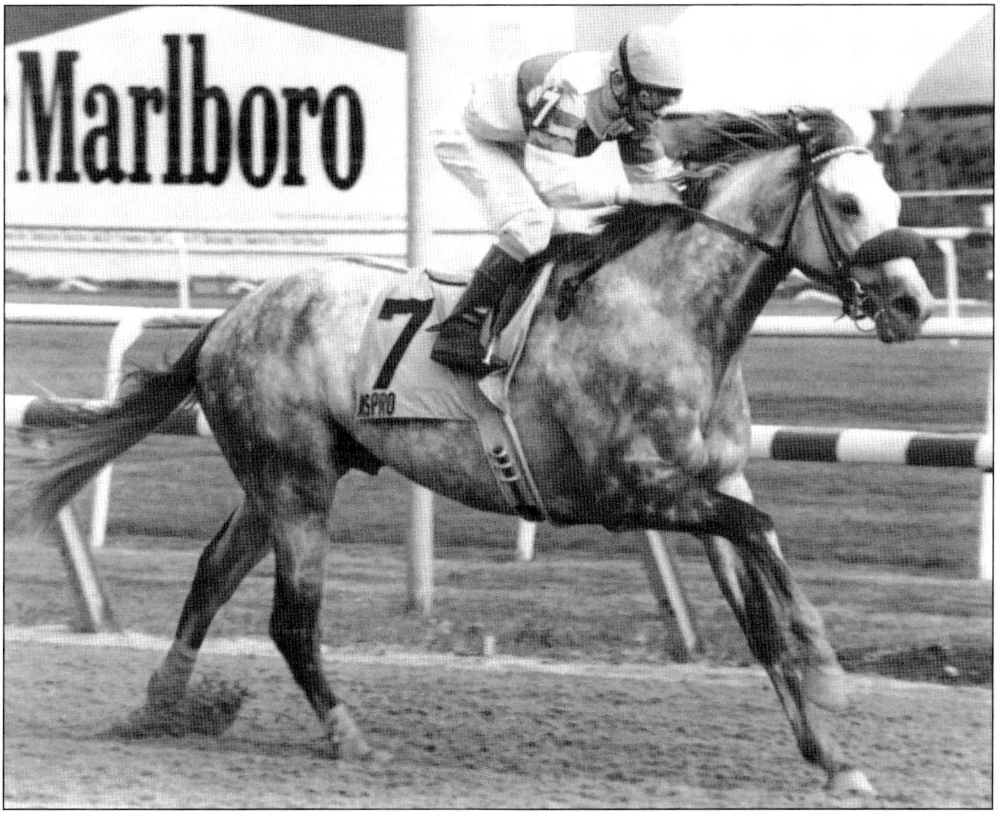

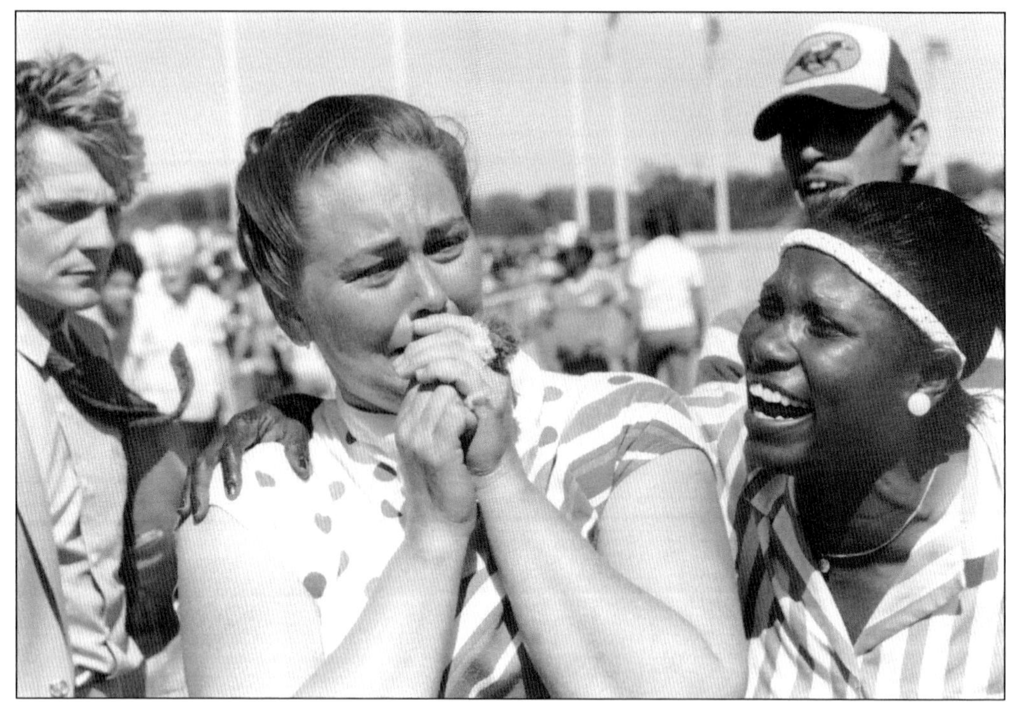

Kindance was an Illinois-bred mare, foaled April 19, 1982, a daughter of Kinsman Hope, bred and owned by the Amcan Stables and trained by Wilton Predium. Here, her caretaker and hotwalker celebrate after she won the first division of the Colfax Maid Stakes on June 10, 1984, at Arlington Park. Caretakers spend more time with their horses than almost anyone else and form a deep attachment to them. (Courtesy of Midwest Outdoors.)

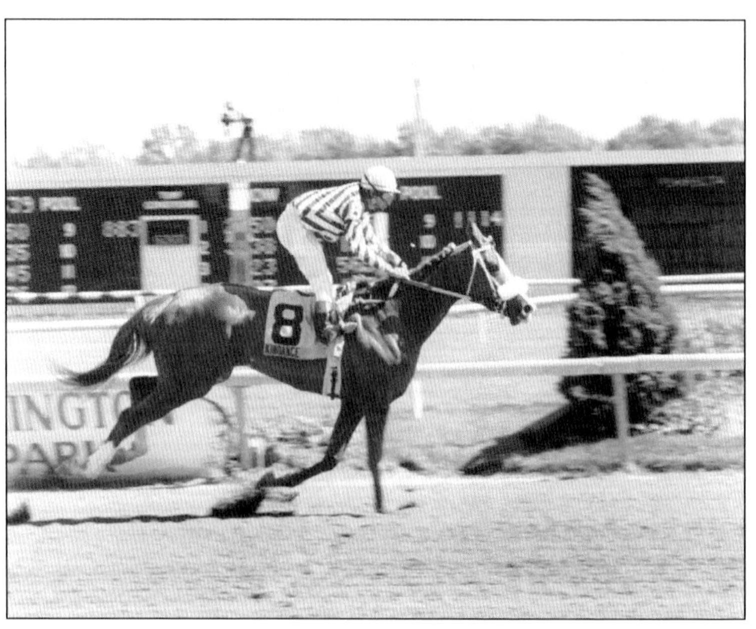

Clocked in 1:24.20 for the seven-furlong contest, Kindance is all alone at the wire in the first division of the 1984 Colfax Maid Stakes at Arlington Park. Racing from 1983 through 1985, the striking chestnut mare with the big white blaze earned $150,341 from 9 wins, 10 seconds, and 5 thirds in 38 starts. (Courtesy of Midwest Outdoors.)

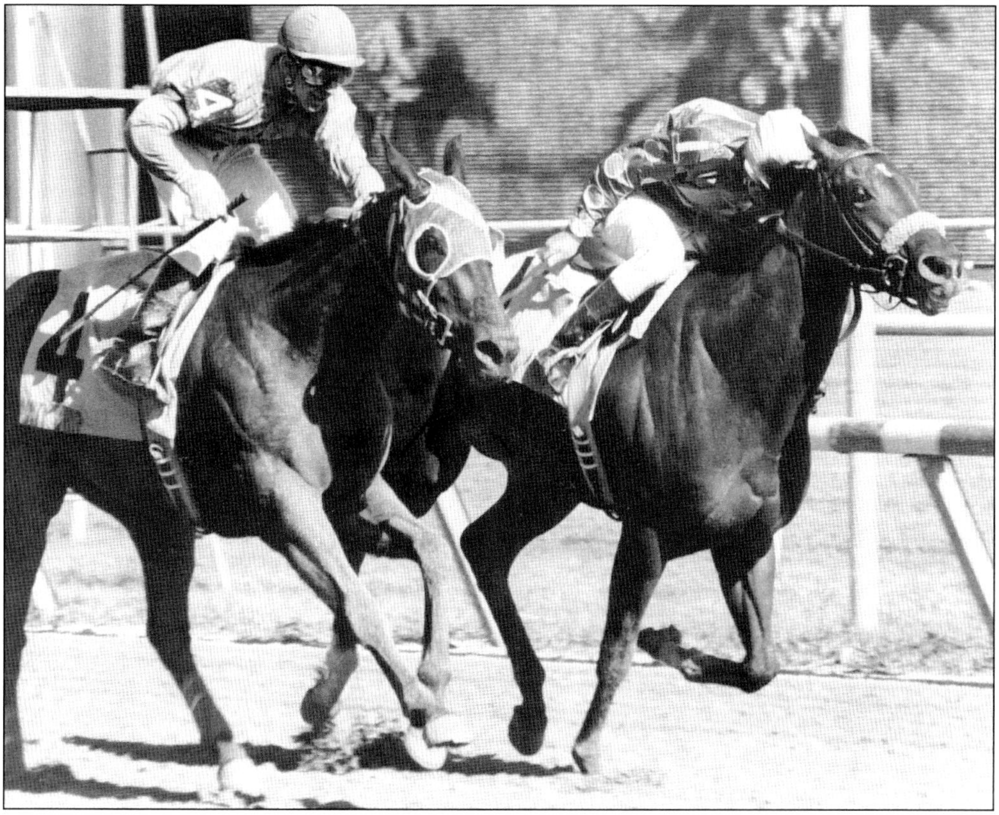

Le Bag Lady (right) was a 1981-foaled, Illinois-bred filly bred by Hill 'n' Dale Farm and owned by Arlington proprietor Richard Duchossois. Trained by Mickey Goldfine, she won several Illinois stakes, earning $103,903. She won her career debut at Arlington on July 15, 1983, and captured three consecutive races there in 1984, including the seven-furlong Colfax Maid (2nd division) with Juvenal Diaz up in 1:25.2, besting Party Whip (left). (Courtesy of Midwest Outdoors.)

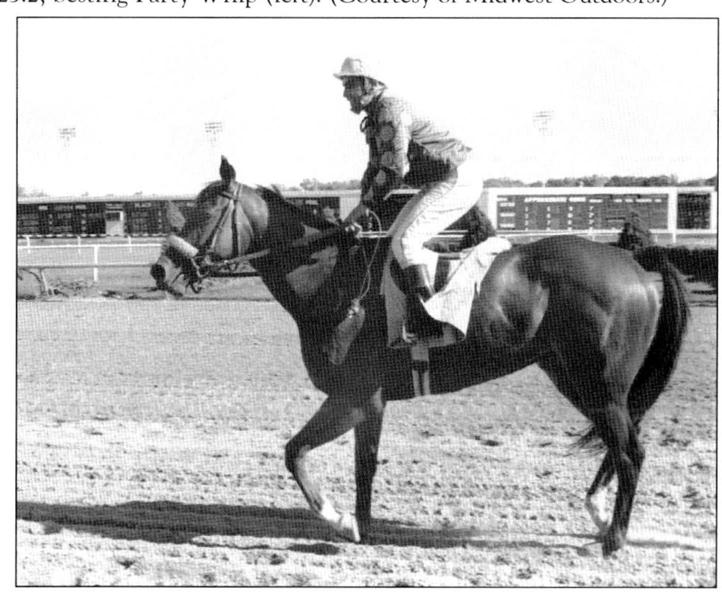

Le Bag Lady trots back to the winner's circle for jockey Juvenal Diaz. The daughter by Sauce Boat-Hunting Pink, by Jacinto won several allowance races at Arlington, as well as finishing a solid third in the 1984 Anita Peabody Handicap. As a two-year-old, she had won the Miss Collinsville Stakes at Fairmount Park. (Courtesy of Midwest Outdoors.)

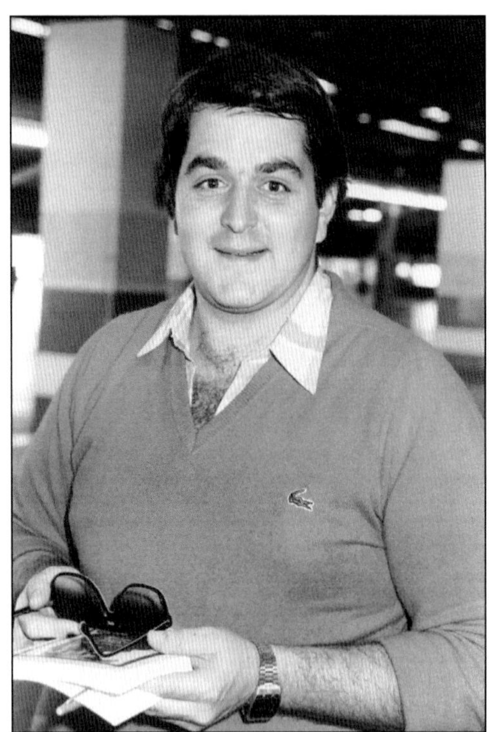

Mickey Goldfine is trainer Lou Goldfine's son, born in 1952 in Chicago. His father's assistant until going out on his own in the late 1970s, Mickey is a graded stakes winning trainer who continues to ply his wares at Arlington. He has trained 255 winners to more than $5.6 million in earnings, including the $321,994-earning Galic Boy, as well as top mares Souper Miss ($220,149) and Atlantic Frost ($186,840). (Courtesy of Midwest Outdoors.)

Don Brumfield steers Mr. Japan (No. 8) to victory in Arlington's fifth race on June 24, 1982, becoming the 17th rider in racing history to score his 4,000th career win at age 46. Mr. Japan nosed out Take the Flack (center) and Rich Butterfly (right) in the one-and-one-sixth-mile turf test, timed in 1:45.1. A 1996 Hall of Fame inductee, Brumfield scored 4,573 wins with $43,567,861 in earnings. (Courtesy of Midwest Outdoors.)

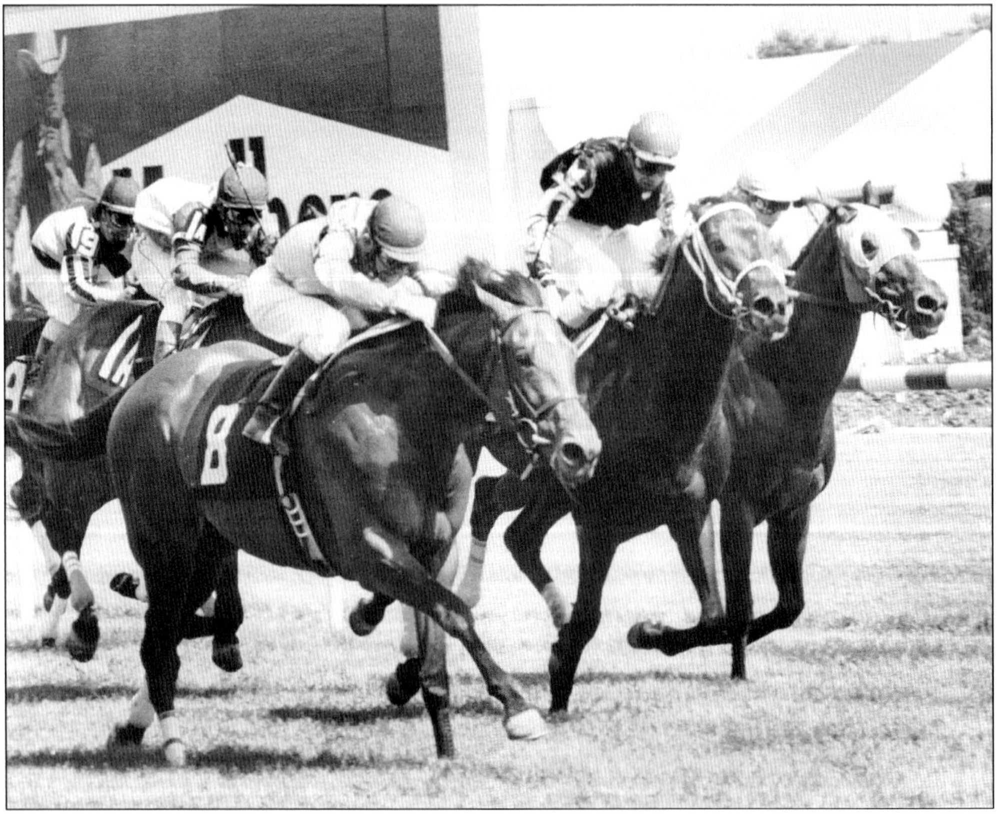

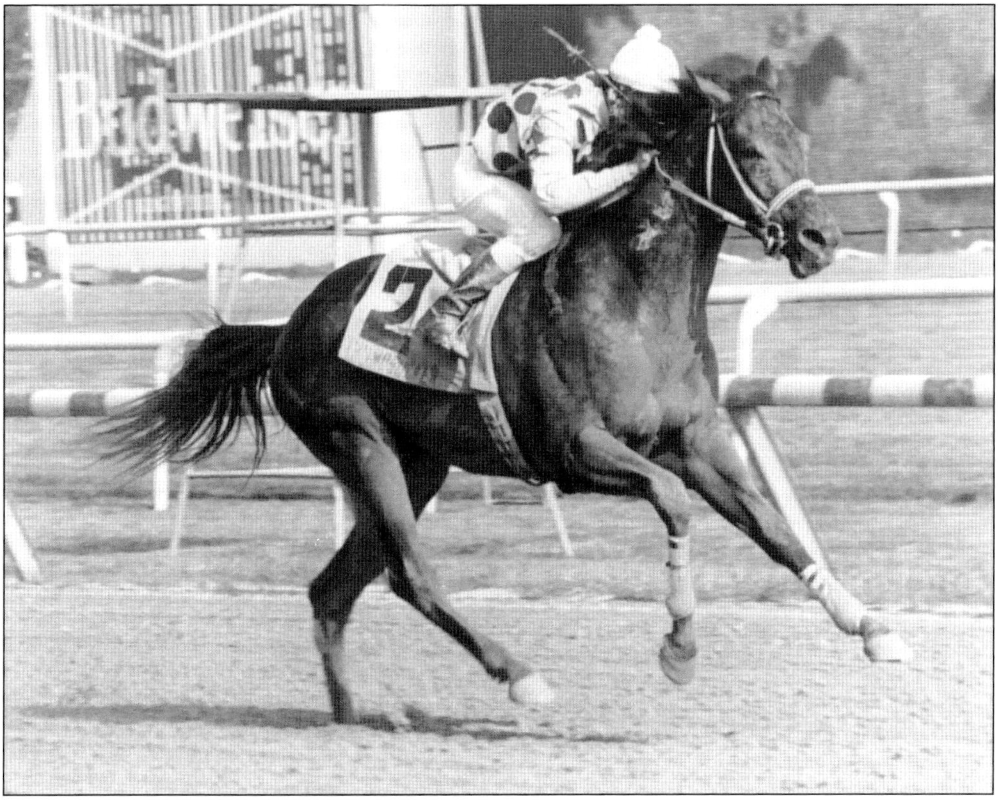

Thumbsucker was a 1979 Great Sun colt, trained by John Drumwright for breeders/owners GAT Stable. Considered the best Michigan-bred ever, this multiple graded stakes winner earned $525,553 from 16 wins in 31 starts, racing from 1981 through 1984. Here, he captures the 57th running of the $137,400 Washington Park Handicap (Gr. II) on June 23, 1984, for Sam Maple in 1:48.60, besting Timeless Native by two lengths, with Le Cou third. (Courtesy of Midwest Outdoors.)

In Full View (right) was a 1983 Kentucky-bred Full Out filly, trained by George Arnold for Glencrest Farm. The winner of $143,337 from 4 wins in 19 starts, In Full View won her debut at Arlington on July 15, 1985, following that up with a Mademoiselle Stakes triumph on July 28, before capturing the Bassinet Stakes on August 25 at River Downs. She was later sold to Japanese interests for $100,000. (Courtesy of Midwest Outdoors.)

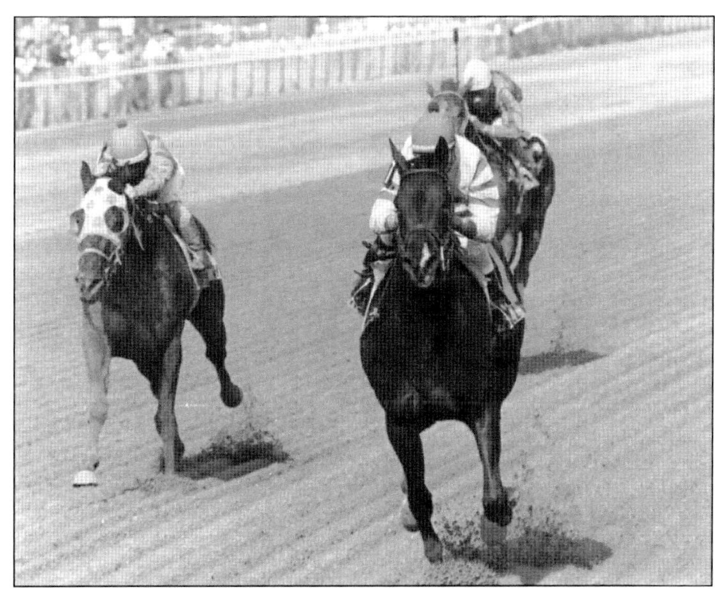

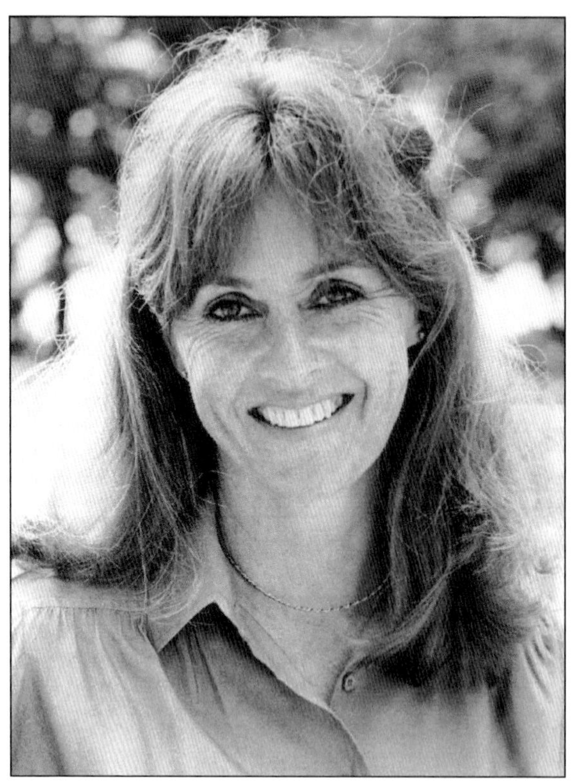

Christine Janks became one of the most successful women trainers of all time on the Chicagoland Thoroughbred circuit. She also was elected as president of the Chicago chapter of the Horsemen's Benevolent & Protective Association (HBPA) in the 1990s. From 12,851 starters, she has amassed 1,723 wins, 1,742 seconds, and 1,626 third-place finishes, with $29,731,708 in career earnings. Her top charges include High Expectations ($679,248) and Pretty Jenny ($534,262). (Courtesy of Midwest Outdoors.)

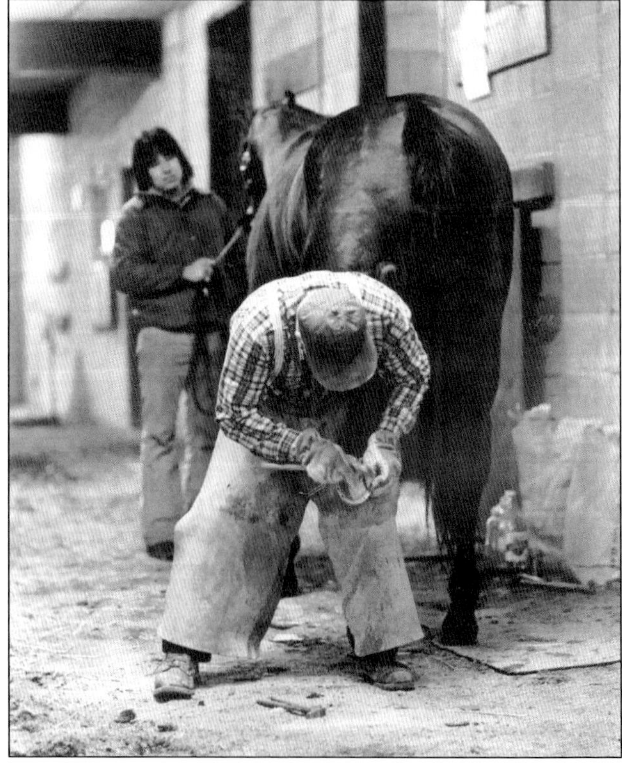

In this photograph, a blacksmith taps on a left hind shoe while a caretaker stands at the horse's head. Blacksmiths or farriers are an intricate and essential part of life on the backstretch of Arlington Park, as trainers rely on these skilled tradesmen to fit the shoe to the hoof, not the other way around. The old adage "no foot, no horse" certainly applies to the Thoroughbred racing industry. (Courtesy of Midwest Outdoors.)

Juvenal Diaz was a multiple graded stakes winning jockey who rode from the early 1970s until 2000, scoring 3,164 wins, 2,797 seconds, and 2,570 thirds from 20,808 career starts, and steering the winners of $41,589,019. His major Arlington victories include the Washington Park Stakes (Gr. II) with Harham's Sizzler; the American Derby (Gr. II) with Jaunatxo; the Arlington-Washington Futurity (Gr. I) with Meadowlake; and the Arlington Handicap (Gr. I) with Pass the Line. (Courtesy of Midwest Outdoors.)

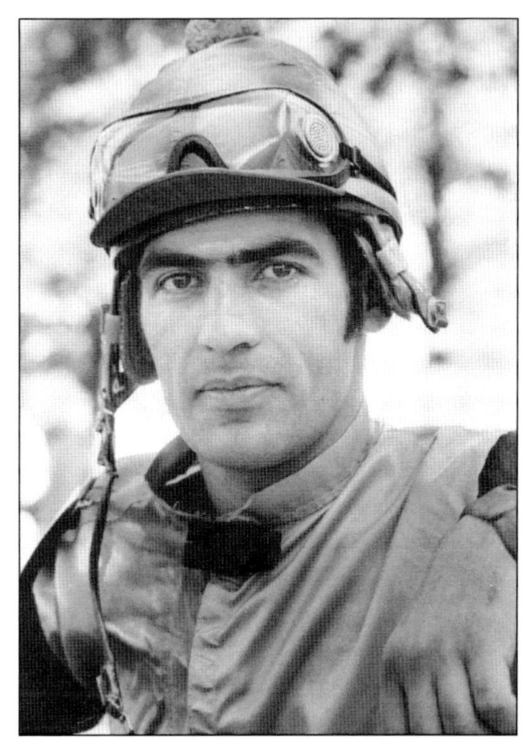

In this photograph, Juvenal Diaz rides Dictina to victory in the Pucker Up Stakes (Gr. III) at Arlington on August 5, 1984. Foaled April 15, 1981, Dictina was a French-bred mare by Dictus. Trained by Harry Trotsek for E.A. Seltzer, Dictina was a graded stakes winner of $243,571 from 4 wins, 3 seconds, and 4 thirds in 24 starts. She was later sold for $350,000 in foal to Zilzal. (Courtesy of Midwest Outdoors.)

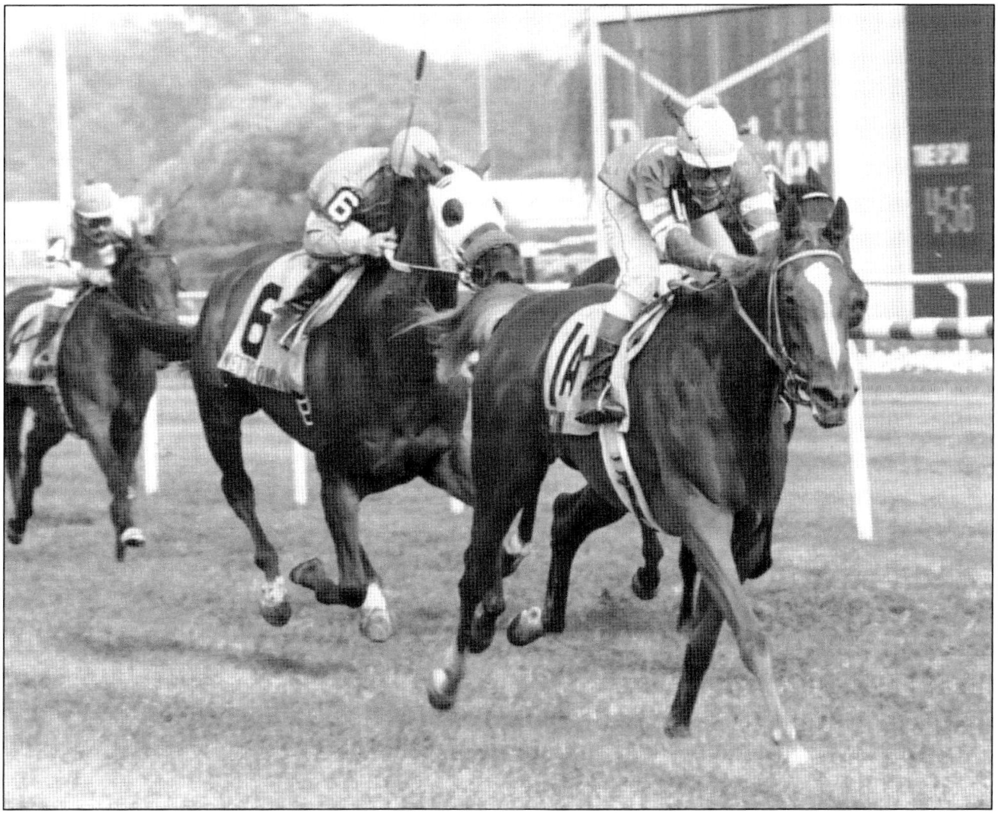

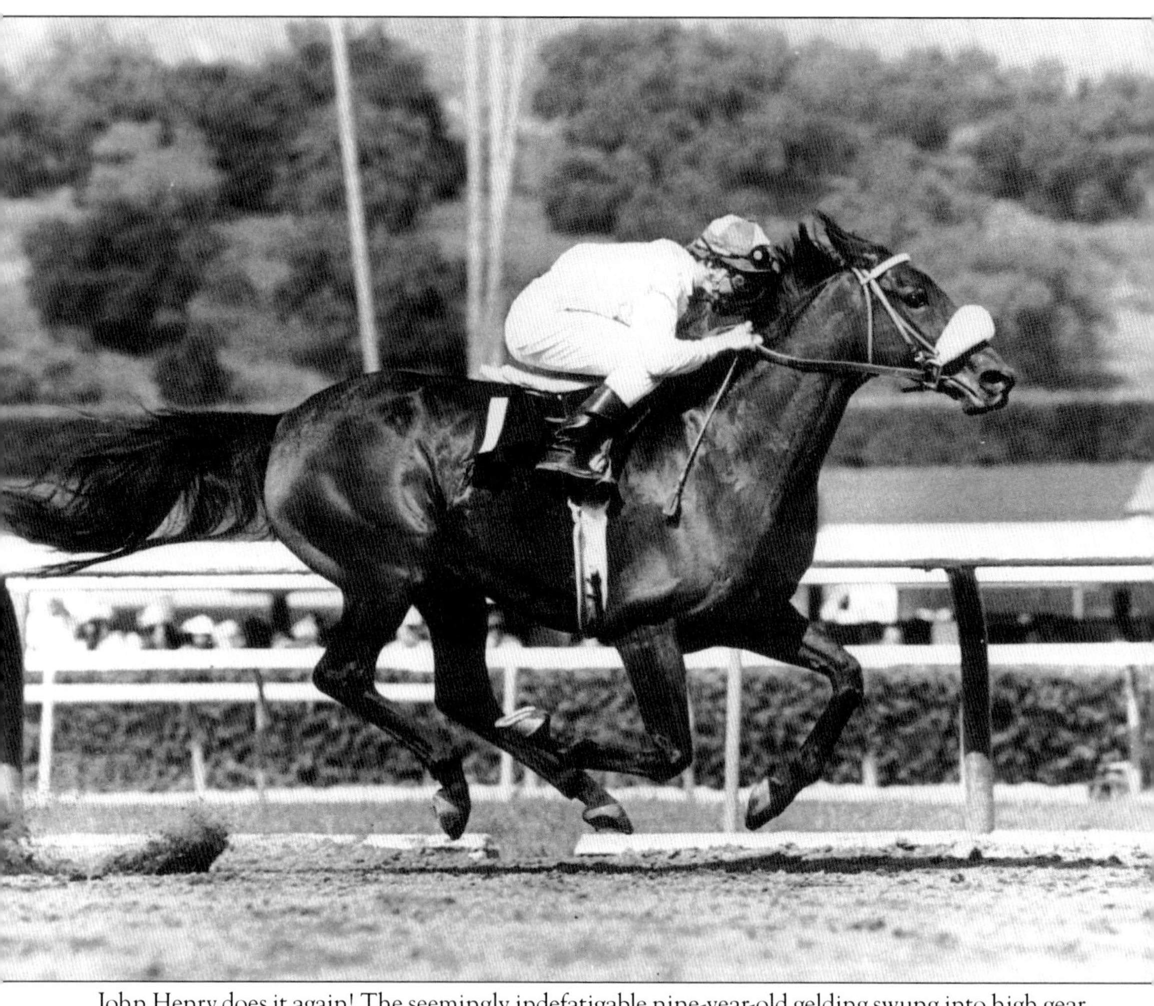

John Henry does it again! The seemingly indefatigable nine-year-old gelding swung into high gear to notch his second Arlington Million in his third try, drawing away by one and three-quarters lengths to best the top grass filly Royal Heroine, with 1982 Kentucky Derby winner Gato del Sol another three lengths back in third, besting three others in a four-horse photo finish. Nijinsky's Secret was fourth, followed by Hot Touch and Majesty's Prince. Slightly more than 39,000 fans came out to watch as favorite John Henry, who paid $4.20 on a $2 ticket, was clocked in 2:01.2 for jockey Chris McCarron. The win upped John Henry's earnings to $5,482,797. After winning the inaugural Million in 1981, he sat out the 1982 Million due to a pulled muscle, and was second by a neck to Tolomeo in 1983. John Henry raced from 1977 to 1989 and had 39 wins from 83 starts and was twice Horse of the Year, winning 17 Grade I stakes over 19 different racetracks. (Author's collection.)

John Henry readies to leave Arlington on Monday morning following his 1984 Arlington Million triumph. He was preparing to fly to Belmont Park to prepare for his next start in the Man O' War Stakes on September 22, 1984. Standing at John Henry's head is his longtime caretaker, Jose Mercado, who referred to the gelding as "El Viejo," or "The Old One." (Author's collection.)

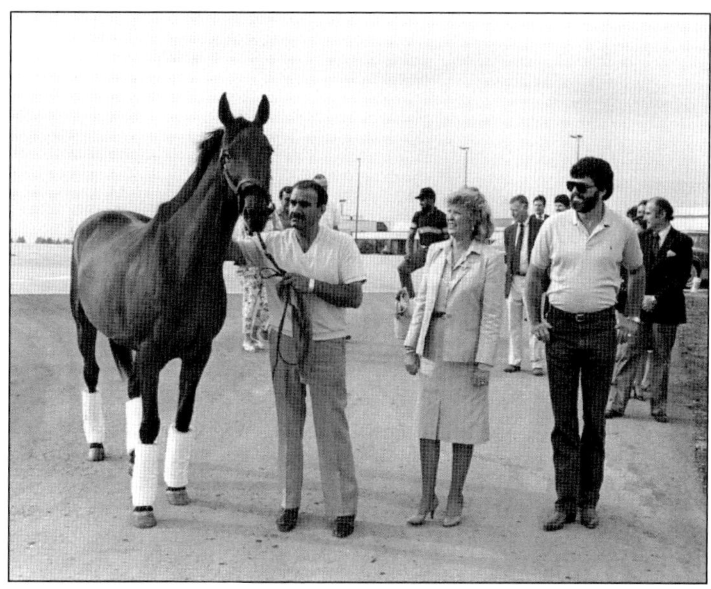

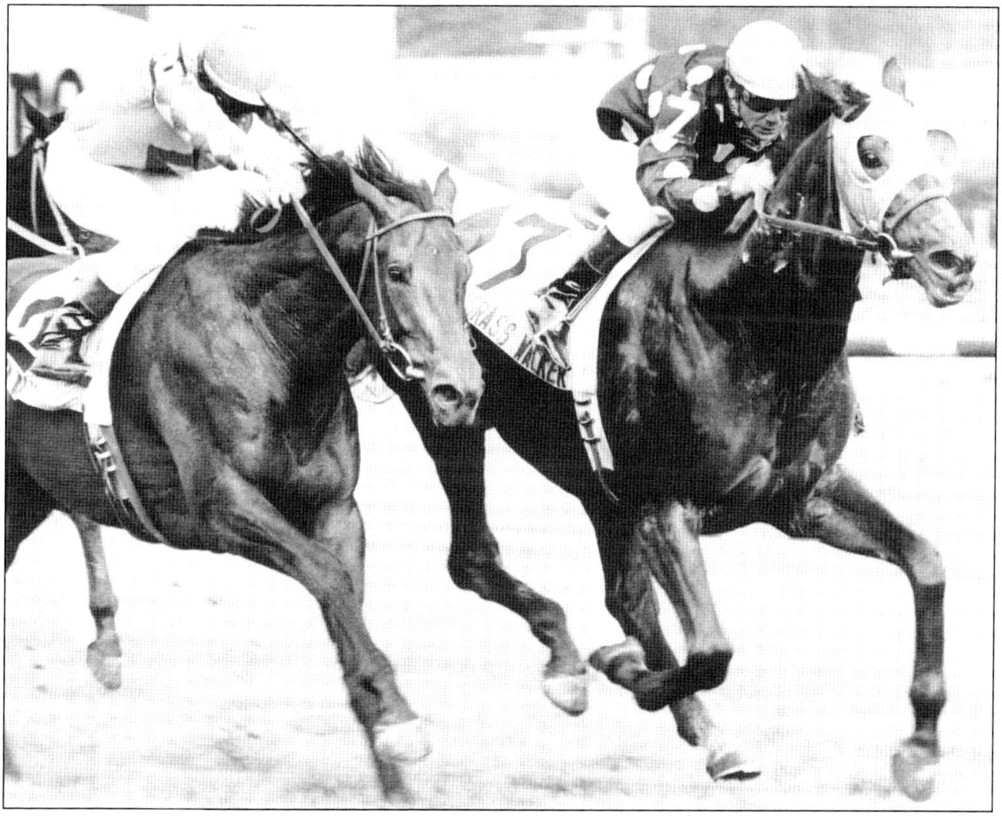

Tall Grass Walker was a 1981 Kentucky-bred son of Navaj and owned by K.C. Plattner. Trained by Henry M. "Pete" Wylie, Tall Grass Walker amassed stats of 11-6-0 from 34 starts and $171,670. He captured the 1984 edition of the $50,000 Round Table Handicap at Arlington in 1:53.2 for jockey Earlie Fires. Raja Native was second and Onyxly third in the one-and-one-eighth-mile turf contest. (Courtesy of Midwest Outdoors.)

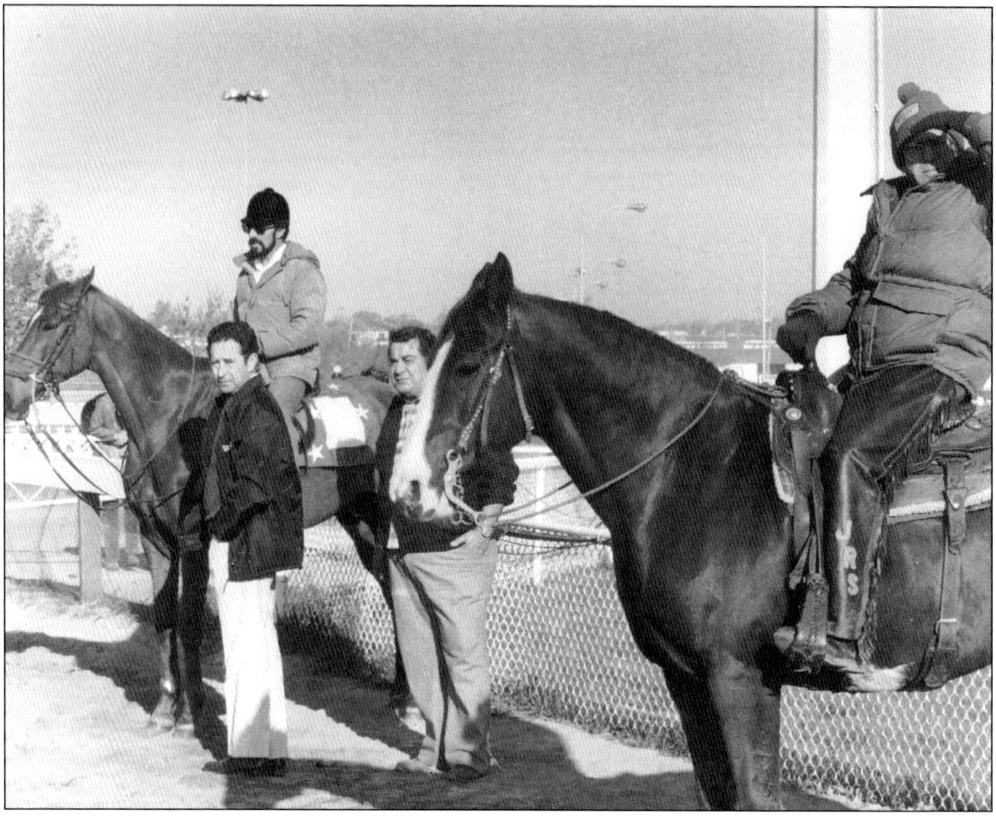

On August 18, 1983, the quartet of Joseph Joyce, Sheldon Robbins, Ralph Ross, and Richard L. Duchossois purchased Arlington Park for $18 million from Madison Square Garden, a subsidiary of Gulf and Western. In this photograph, Arlington Park president Joe Joyce and chief outrider Vince Dimeo watch the Thoroughbreds work out on a chilly morning. (Courtesy of Midwest Outdoors.)

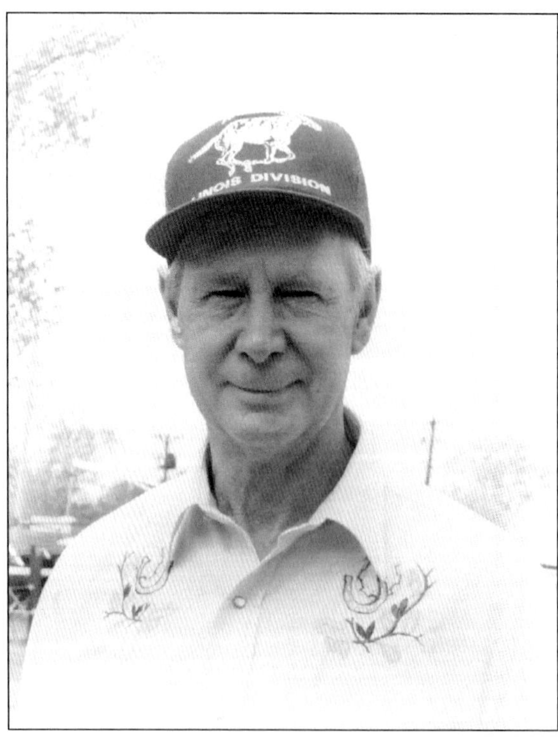

Trainer Elmer Miller was a fixture on the Chicago scene. He was best known as the conditioner of Toy Tiger, an Illinois-bred son of Zen, the top Prairie State stallion of the day, who was owned by Richard L. Duchossois's Hill 'n' Dale Farm. Toy Tiger won $106,791 for owner John Bauman, winning numerous allowance and claiming races at Arlington and the other Chicago racetracks. (Courtesy of Midwest Outdoors.)

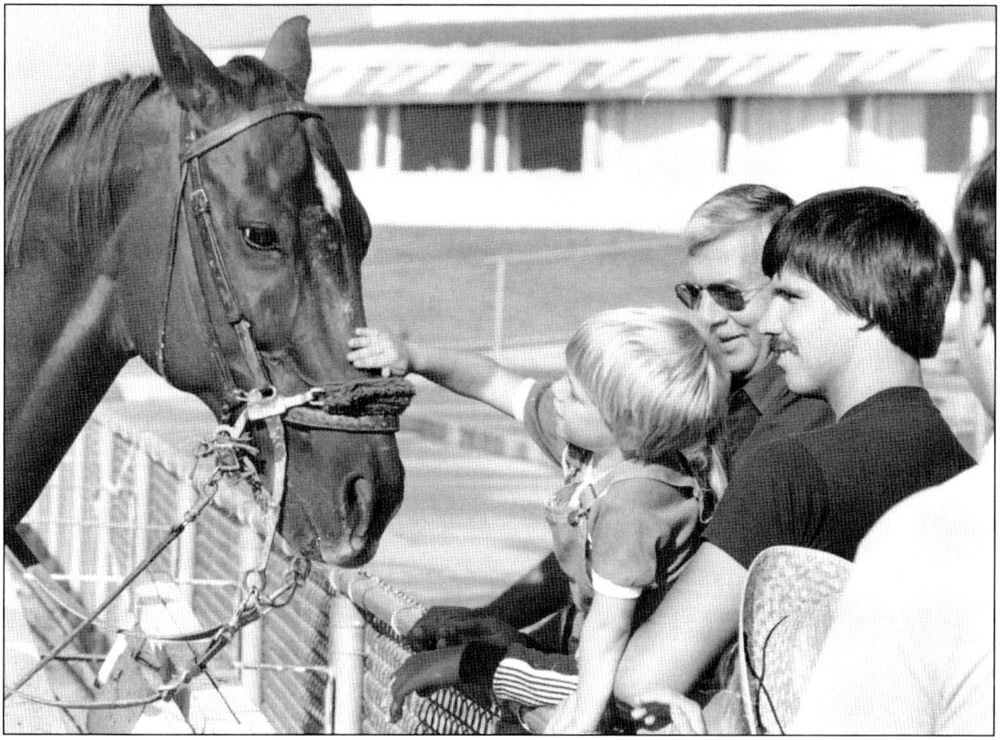

Racing fans love horses, and none are too young or too old to visit Arlington Park. Here, a youngster reaches out to pet one of the outriders' horses who work during the races. These horses, commonly referred to as "pony" horses, are often retired racers themselves. Many do not have the desire or speed to be a successful racehorse but often make good companions to high-strung runners. (Courtesy of Midwest Outdoors.)

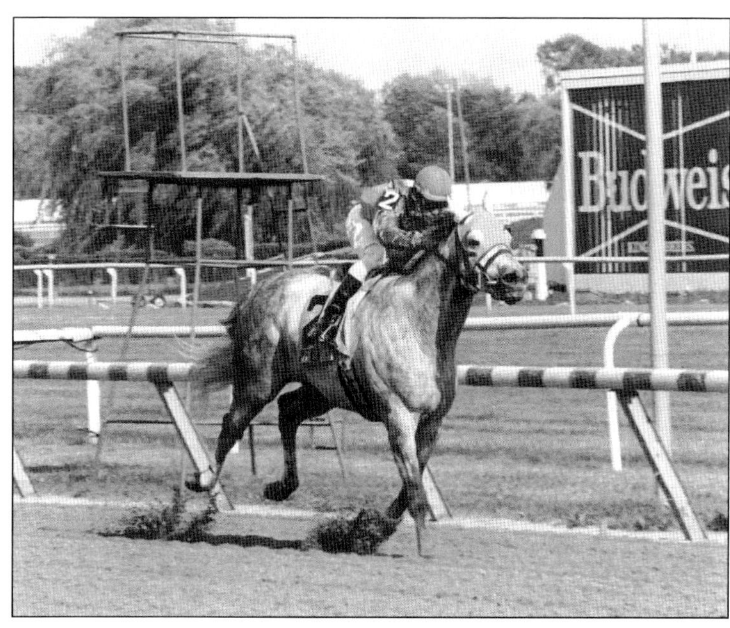

Par Flight strides out to win the Shecky Greene Handicap at Arlington on May 25, 1985. The grey Kentucky-bred by Reality was a 1981 foal trained by Carl Nafzger and owned by Tadahiro Hotehama. Par Flight broke her maiden on July 4, 1983, at Arlington with Earlie Fires up and won the Washington Park Stakes (Gr. II) in 1985. She earned $209,357, winning 6 of 14 starts. (Courtesy of Midwest Outdoors.)

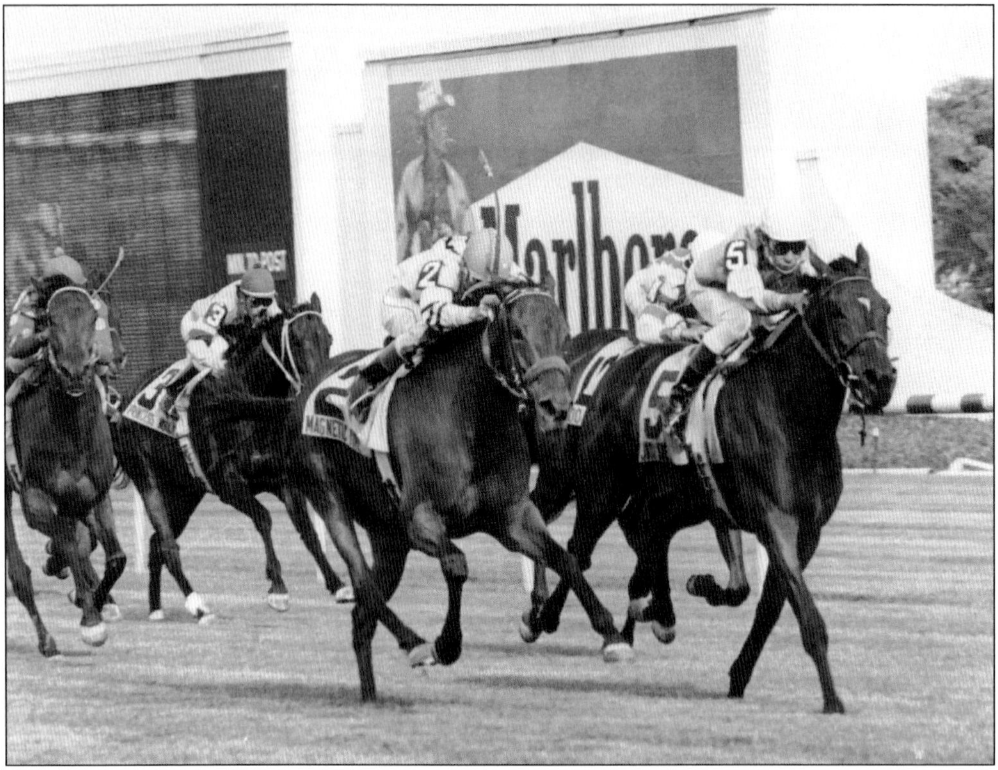

Jay's Sue (No. 5, right) captures the Pattee Canyon Handicap at Arlington Park on July 1, 1984, for jockey Earlie Fires, owner C. P. Blake, and trainer Jerry Calvin. La Erudite and Pretty Perfect (No. 7) finished in a dead heat for second in the one-and-one-eighth-mile turf race, timed in 1:49.2. Jay's Sue went on to earn $282,560 from 18 wins in 51 starts. (Courtesy of Midwest Outdoors.)

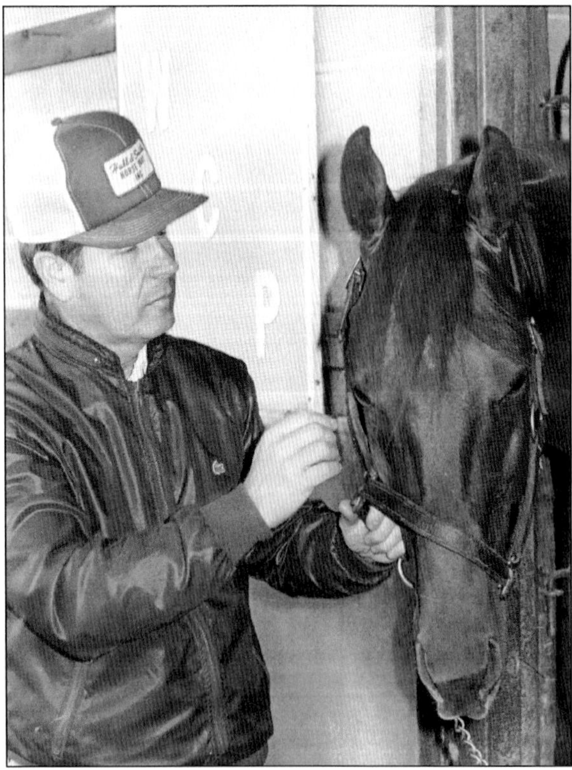

Trainer Lynn Whiting adjusts the halter on Big Pistol, a Kentucky-bred, multiple graded stakes winner who finished second in the Washington Park Handicap (Gr. II) on June 29, 1985. Big Pistol had won the Haskell (Gr. I) prior to coming to Arlington and went on to earn $558,521 lifetime. Whiting trained the winners of $23,960,058, including Kentucky Derby winner Lil E. Tee ($1,425,026) and Arlington Classic winner At the Threshold ($668,495). (Courtesy of Midwest Outdoors.)

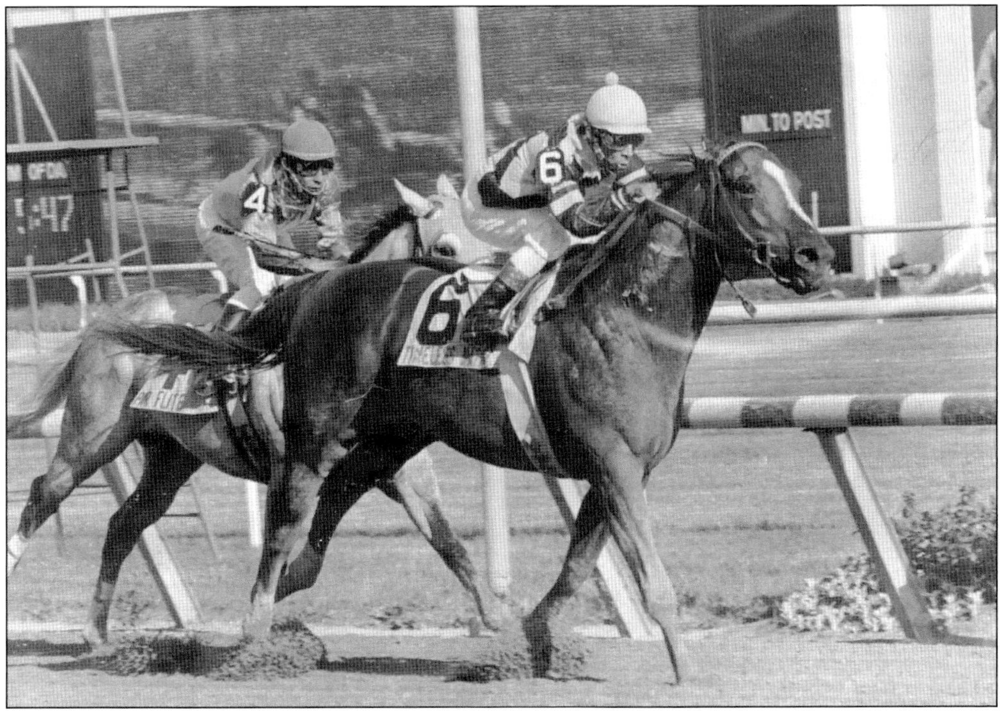

A chestnut son of Timeless Moment, Timeless Native was foaled May 23, 1980, and trained by Grover "Bud" Delp—who also trained Spectacular Bid. Timeless Native won Arlington's Equipoise Mile (Gr. III) on June 8, 1985, and was second in the Washington Park Stakes (Gr. II) and Shecky Greene Handicap that same year. He also finished second in the 1984 Washington Park Handicap (Gr. II) and fifth in the 1984 Sea O'Erin Handicap. (Courtesy of Midwest Outdoors.)

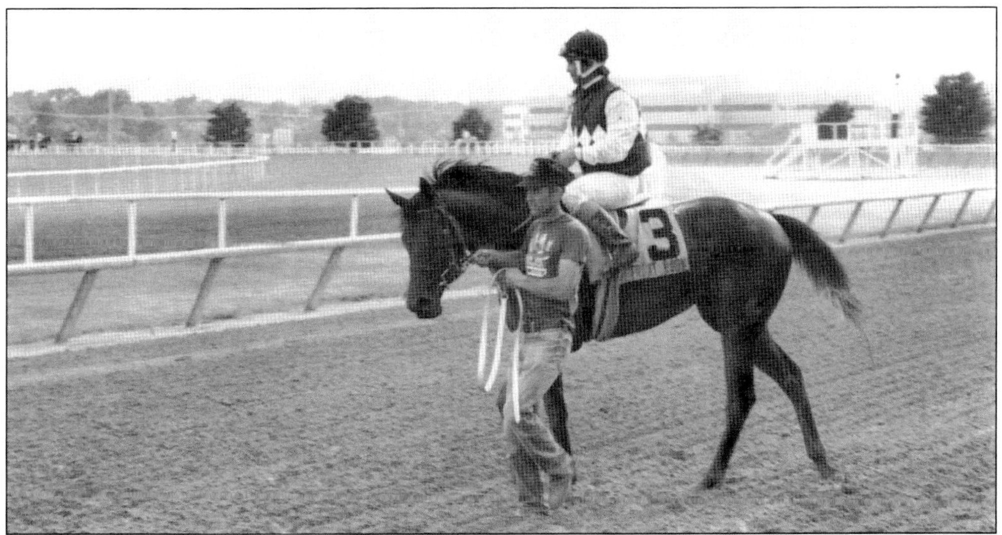

Front Room and her caretaker are seen after winning the $50,000 Colfax Maid Stakes on July 14, 1985, for jockey Gerry Gallitano in 1:22.4. It was the filly's third consecutive triumph, as she had won her previous two allowances races at Arlington. The daughter of Mr. Leader was trained, owned, and bred by Harvey and Nancy Vanier and earned $138,142 for this husband-wife team. (Courtesy of Midwest Outdoors.)

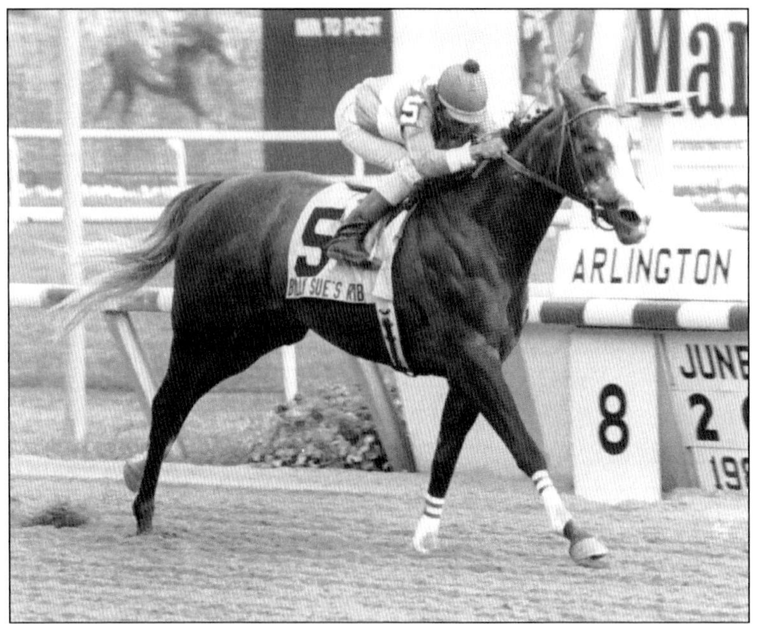

An Illinois-bred daughter by Al Hattab, Billy Sue's Rib was a grey mare foaled March 7, 1980, who won the June 26, 1983, edition of the Colfax Maid for jockey Richard Strauss and was second in the Anita Peabody Stakes that same year. A $60,000 yearling who earned $289,645 from 13 wins in 22 starts, she later sold for $175,000 in foal to the ill-fated Ferdinand. (Courtesy of Midwest Outdoors.)

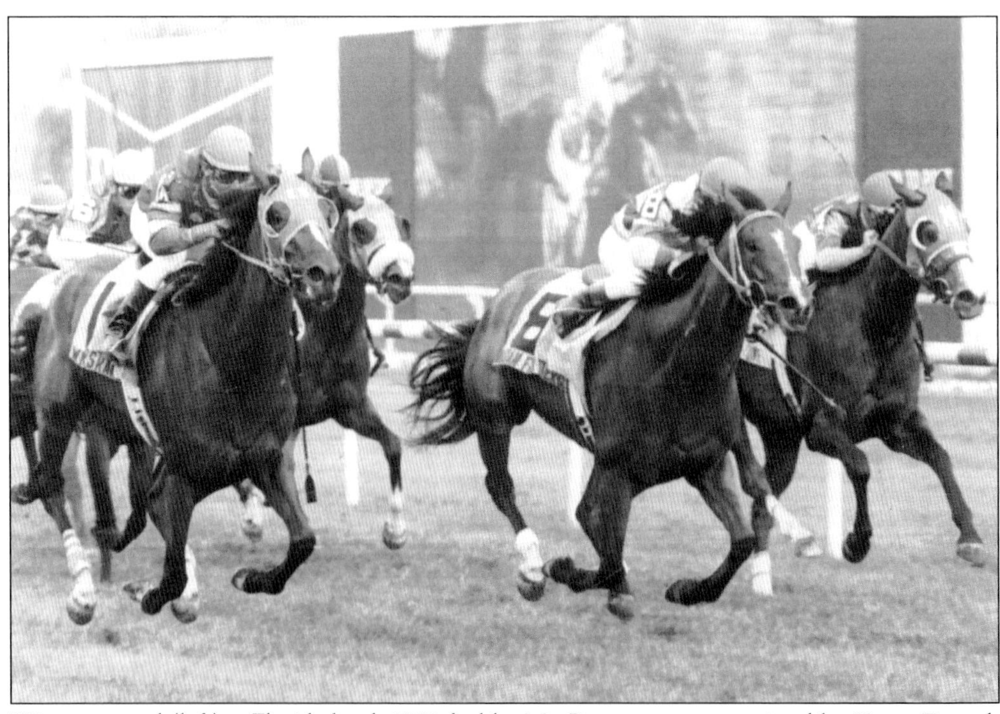

Witwatersrand (left), a Florida-bred, 1981 foal by Mr. Prospector, was trained by Harry Trotsek for Ed Seltzer. She won the Grade III Pucker Up Stakes at Arlington on August 5, 1984, for rider Earlie Fires. Though she earned just $66,006 from 2 wins and 3 thirds in 12 starts, Witwatersrand sold for $775,000 in foal to Manila at the Keeneland Sale. (Courtesy of Midwest Outdoors.)

Carl Nafzger, born August 29, 1941, in Plainview, Texas is a Hall of Fame trainer best known for conditioning 1990 Kentucky Derby and Breeders' Cup Classic winner Unbridled and 2007 Derby winner Street Sense. He won numerous Arlington stakes, including the 1981 Arlington Classic, the 1985 Washington Park Handicap, and the 1990 Secretariat Stakes, among others. To date, he has saddled more than 1,150 winners to $51.9 million in earnings. (Courtesy of Midwest Outdoors.)

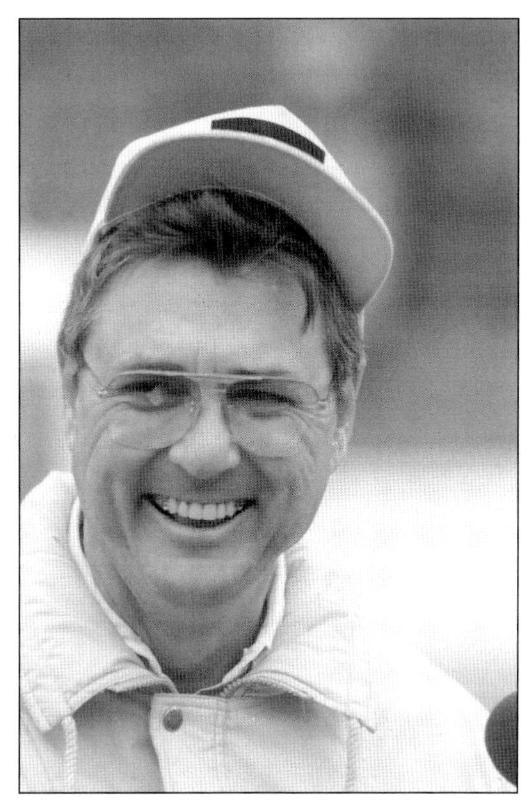

Mr. T's Tune was a grey mare foaled May 12, 1981 by Al Hattab, trained by Carl Nafzger for owner Terry T. She won $255,560 and 10 of 41 starts, including the Cleopatra Handicap on June 9, 1985, and was a strong second to Queen Alexander in the Arlington Matron Handicap (Gr. II) on August 30, 1986. She sold at the 1998 Keeneland Sale for $105,000 in foal to Dehere. (Courtesy of Midwest Outdoors.)

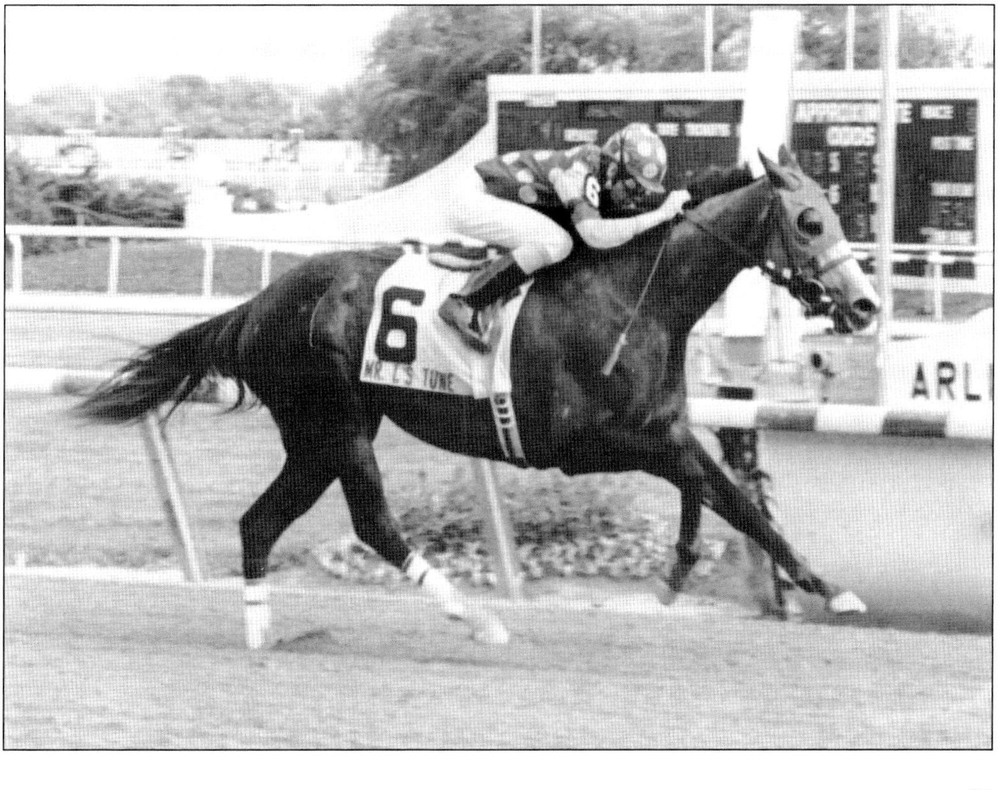

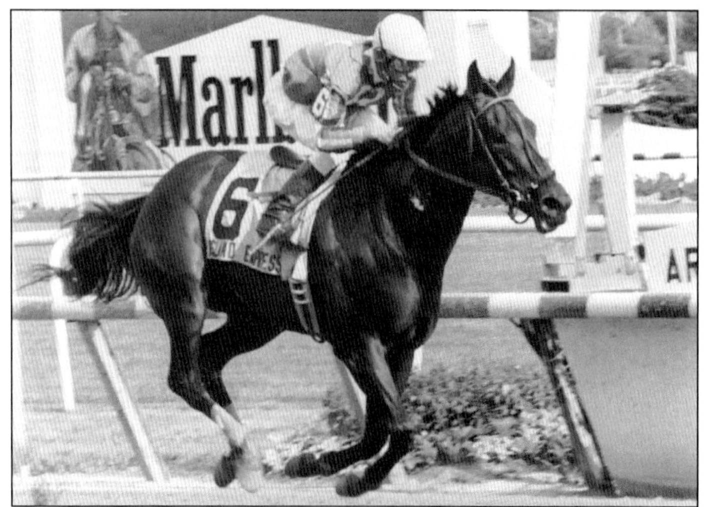

Island Empress, a Kentucky filly by King Pellinore and foaled May 11, 1982, won three consecutive Arlington races in 1985, including an allowance test on May 30, the Ta Wee Handicap on June 15, and the June 23 Princess Doreen Stakes. Trained by Philip Gleaves for the Reineman Stable, Island Empress won 7 of 30 starts and $113,914, racing from 1984 through 1986. (Courtesy of Midwest Outdoors.)

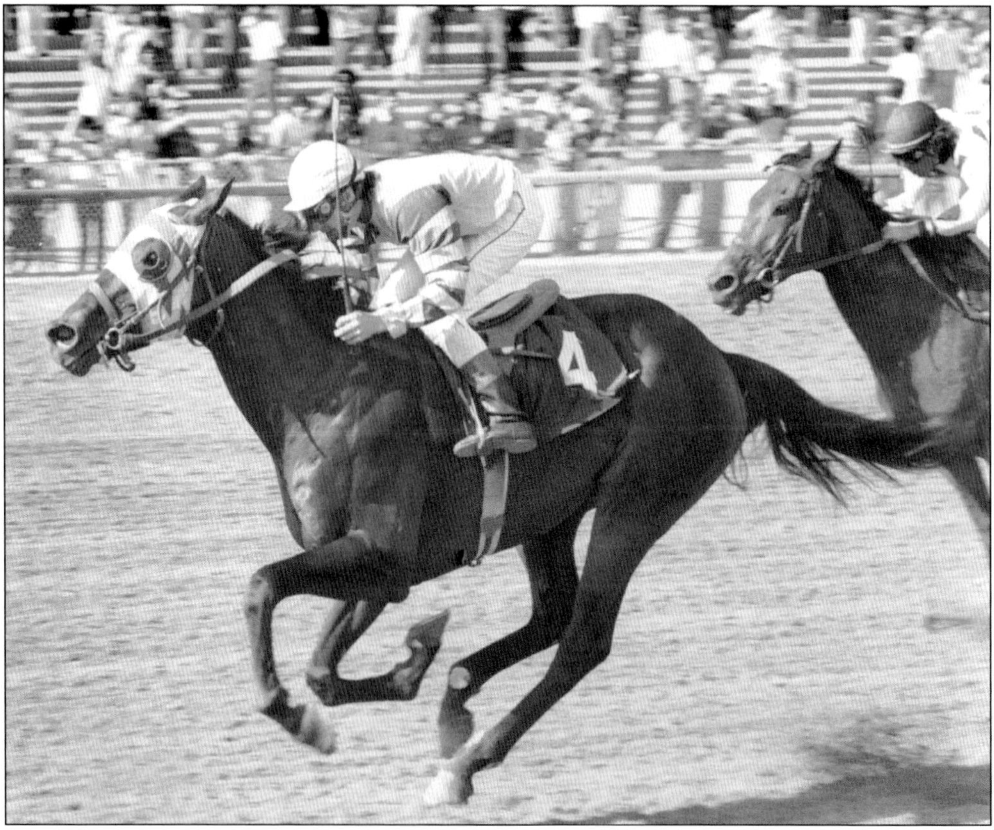

Jockey Ray Sibille rode for 35 years before retiring on July 24, 2004, at age 51. A recipient of the 2005 George Woolf Award, he won the 1988 Breeders' Cup Turf with Great Communicator. Sibille began competing in Chicago in 1973, winning multiple titles at Arlington, Hawthorne, and Sportsman's Park and now works as an officer of the MacBeth Memorial Jockey Fund and the Andre Agassi Charitable Foundation. (Courtesy of Midwest Outdoors.)

Four

The Miracle
August 25, 1985–1989

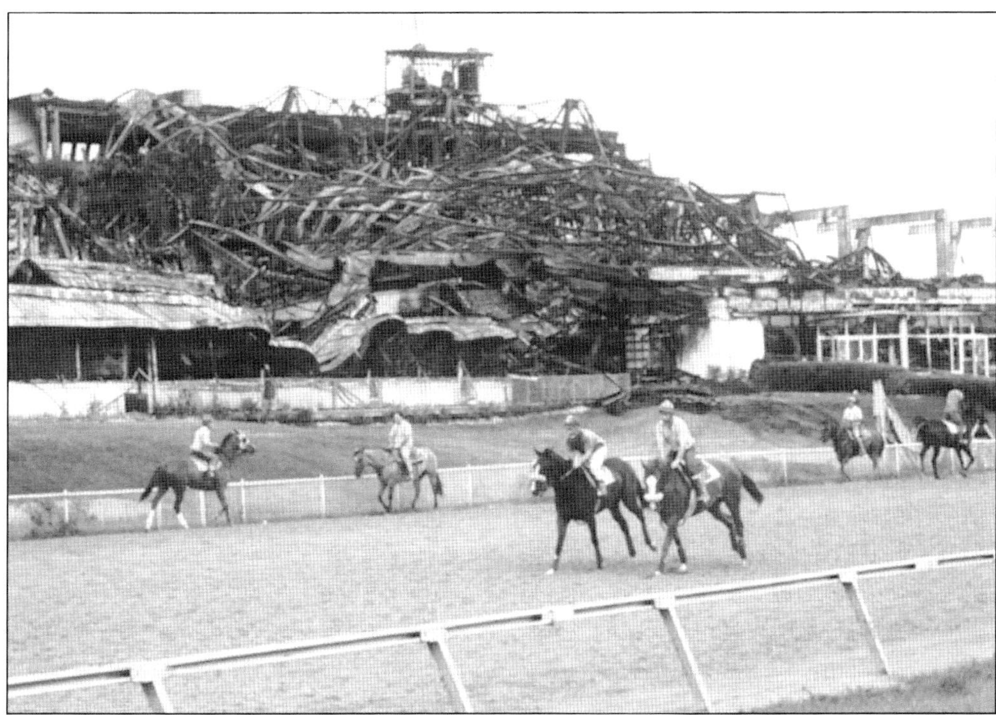

On July 31, 1985, Arlington Park's horseman's lounge caught fire due to an electrical malfunction. Soon, the small blaze morphed into a five-alarm fire, ravaging the grandstand into a charred, twisted pile of metal. More than 150 firemen were required to keep the blaze contained. Despite the devastation, the Arlington Million—just 26 days away—was contested in elegant fashion. Here, horses work out in front the charred grandstand. (Courtesy of Arlington Park.)

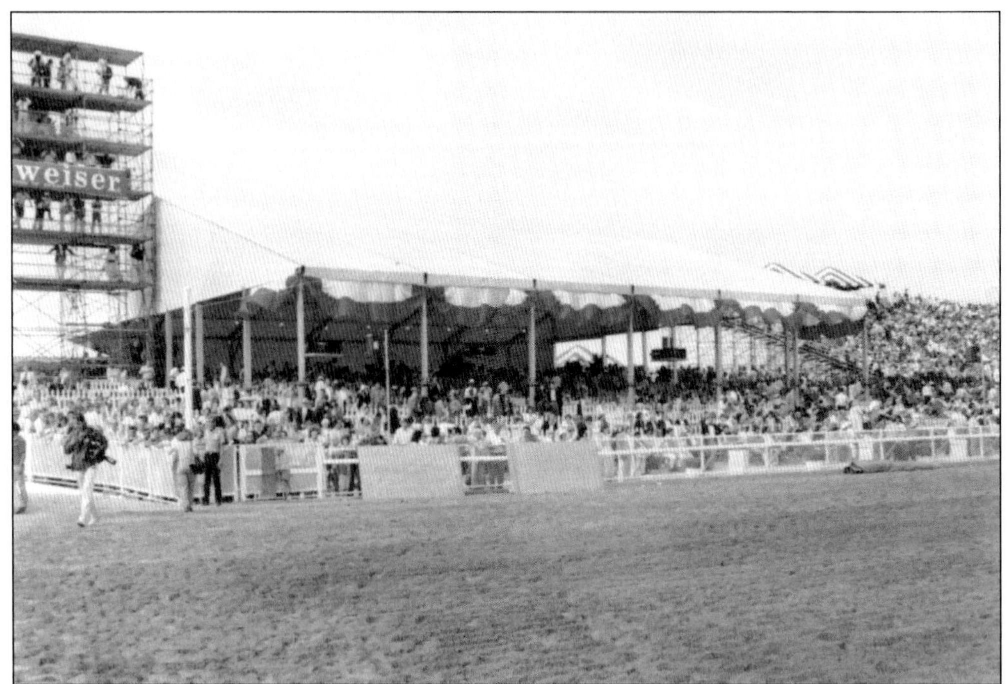

After the fire, Arlington built tents and temporary stands to accommodate thousands of racing fans, with working facilities for the stewards, track announcer, and NBC-TV crew. Betting windows were also installed, with crews working in 24-hour shifts to haul off the remains of the burnt clubhouse and grandstand. The 121-day Arlington meeting scheduled to run through September 30 resumed the Monday after the fire at Hawthorne under a lease arrangement. (Courtesy of Midwest Outdoors.)

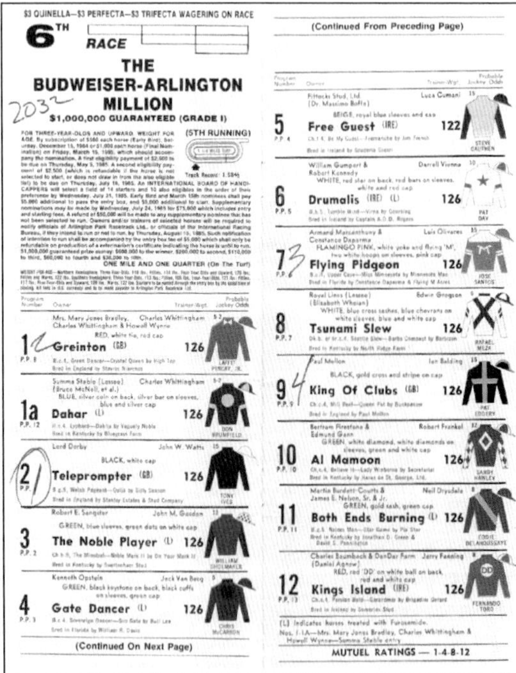

$3 QUINELLA—$3 PERFECTA—$3 TRIFECTA WAGERING ON RACE

6TH RACE

THE BUDWEISER-ARLINGTON MILLION

$1,000,000 GUARANTEED (GRADE I)

(5TH RUNNING)

Track Record: 1.58⅘

ONE MILE AND ONE QUARTER (On The Turf)

Program Number	Owner	Trainer	Wgt.	Probable Odds	Jockey
1 P.P. 8	Mrs. Mary Jones Bradley, Charles Whittingham & Howell Wynne — RED, white tie, red cap — **Greinton** (GB)	Charles Whittingham	126	5-2	LAFFIT PINCAY, JR.
1a P.P. 12	Summa Stable (Lessee) (Bruce McNell, et al.) — BLUE, silver coin on back, silver bar on sleeves, blue and silver cap — **Dahar** (L)	Charles Whittingham	126	5-2	DON BRUMFIELD
2 P.P.	Lord Derby — BLACK, white cap — **Teleprompter** (GB)	John W. Watts	126	15	TONY IVES
3 P.P. 2	Robert E. Sangster — GREEN, blue sleeves, green dots on white cap — **The Noble Player** (L)	John M. Gosden	126	12	WILLIAM SHOEMAKER
4 P.P. 3	Kenneth Opstein — GREEN, black keystone on back, black cuffs on sleeves, green cap — **Gate Dancer** (L)	Jack Van Berg	126	5	CHRIS McCARRON

(Continued On Next Page)

(Continued From Preceding Page)

Program Number	Owner	Trainer	Wgt.	Probable Odds	Jockey
5 P.P. 4	Fittocks Stud, Ltd. (Dr. Massimo Boffa) — BEIGE, royal blue sleeves and cap — **Free Guest** (IRE)	Luca Cumani	122	15	STEVE CAUTHEN
6 P.P. 5	William Gumpert & Robert Kennedy — WHITE, red star on back, red bars on sleeves, white and red cap — **Drumalis** (IRE) (L)	Darrell Vienna	126	10	PAT DAY
7 P.P. 6	Armand Marcanthony & Constance Daparma — FLAMINGO PINK, white yoke and flying 'M', two white hoops on sleeves, pink cap — **Flying Pidgeon**	Luis Olivares	126	15	JOSE SANTOS
8 P.P. 7	Royal Lines (Lessee) (Elisabeth Whelan) — WHITE, blue cross sashes, blue chevrons on white sleeves, blue and white cap — **Tsunami Slew**	Edwin Gregson	126	5	RAFAEL MEZA
9 P.P. 9	Paul Mellon — BLACK, gold cross and stripe on cap — **King Of Clubs** (GB)	Ian Balding	126	15	PAT EDDERY
10 P.P. 10	Bertram Firestone & Edmund Gann — GREEN, white diamond, white diamonds on sleeves, green and white cap — **Al Mamoon**	Robert Frankel	126	12	SANDY HAWLEY
11 P.P. 11	Martin Burdett-Coutts & James E. Nelson, Sr. & Jr. — GREEN, gold sash, green cap — **Both Ends Burning** (L)	Neil Drysdale	126	8	EDDIE DELAHOUSSAYE
12 P.P. 13	Charles Baumbach & DanDar Farm (Daniel Agnew) — RED, red 'DD' on white ball on back, red and white cap — **Kings Island** (IRE)	Jerry Fanning	126	8	FERNANDO TORO

(L) Indicates horses treated with Furosemide.
Nos. 1-1A—Mrs. Mary Jones Bradley, Charles Whittingham & Howell Wynne—Summa Stable entry

MUTUEL RATINGS — 1-4-8-12

The program pages from the 1985 "Miracle Million." The grandstand and clubhouse's skeletal remains had been removed, and the world's richest race went off without a hitch. Teleprompter (Tony Ives) edged Greinton (Laffit Pincay Jr.) with Flying Pidgeon third by three and a half lengths. King of Clubs was fourth, with The Noble Player fifth, followed by Al Mamoon, Tsunami Slew, Both Ends Burning, Dehar, Gate Dancer, Drumalis, Free Guest, and Kings Island. (Author's collection.)

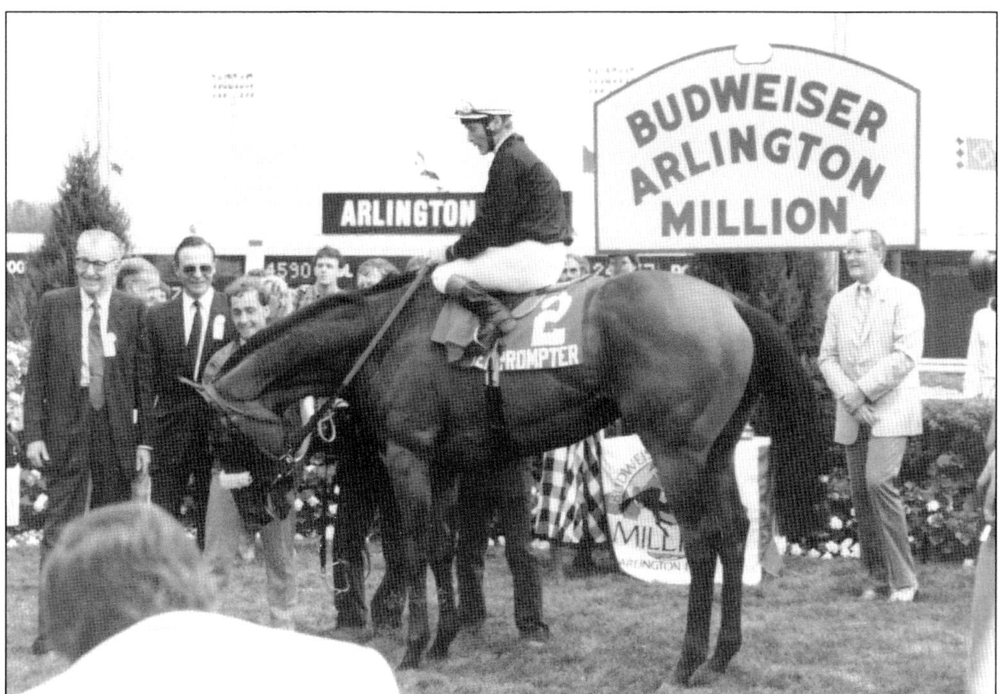

Teleprompter stands in the winner's circle after winning the 1985, "Miracle Million" with jockey Tony Ives in the saddle, clocked in 2:03.2. Trained by John Watts, Teleprompter, a five-year-old gelding at the time, was known as the "John Henry" of Great Britain. He had won 9 of 21 races prior to his Million victory. (Courtesy of Midwest Outdoors.)

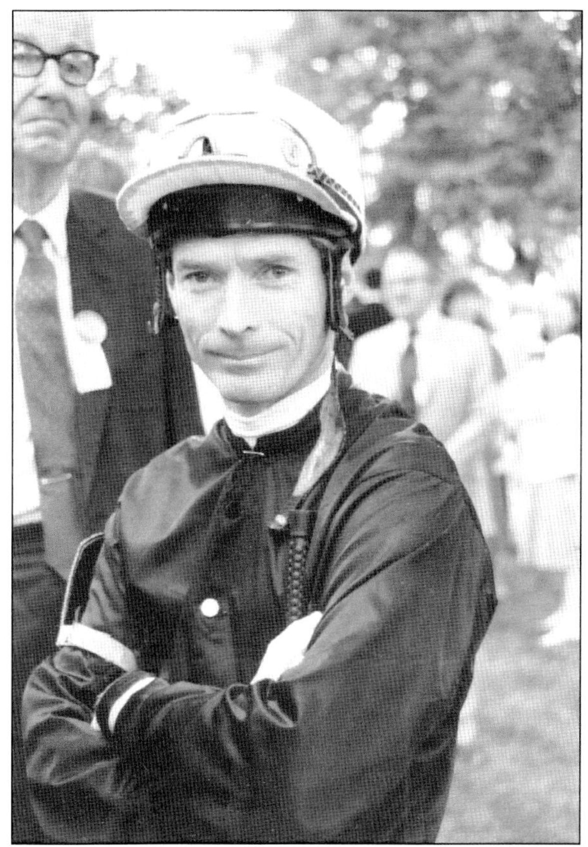

Tony Ives, the jockey aboard 14-1 Teleprompter, was kicked in the head by a horse in Britain the Monday prior to the 1985 Arlington Million. When Ives was first examined, English racing officials did not clear him to race. But the rider persisted, took another physical two days after the accident, passed, and soon after was on a plane to Chicago to ride Teleprompter in the world's only million-dollar race. (Courtesy of Midwest Outdoors.)

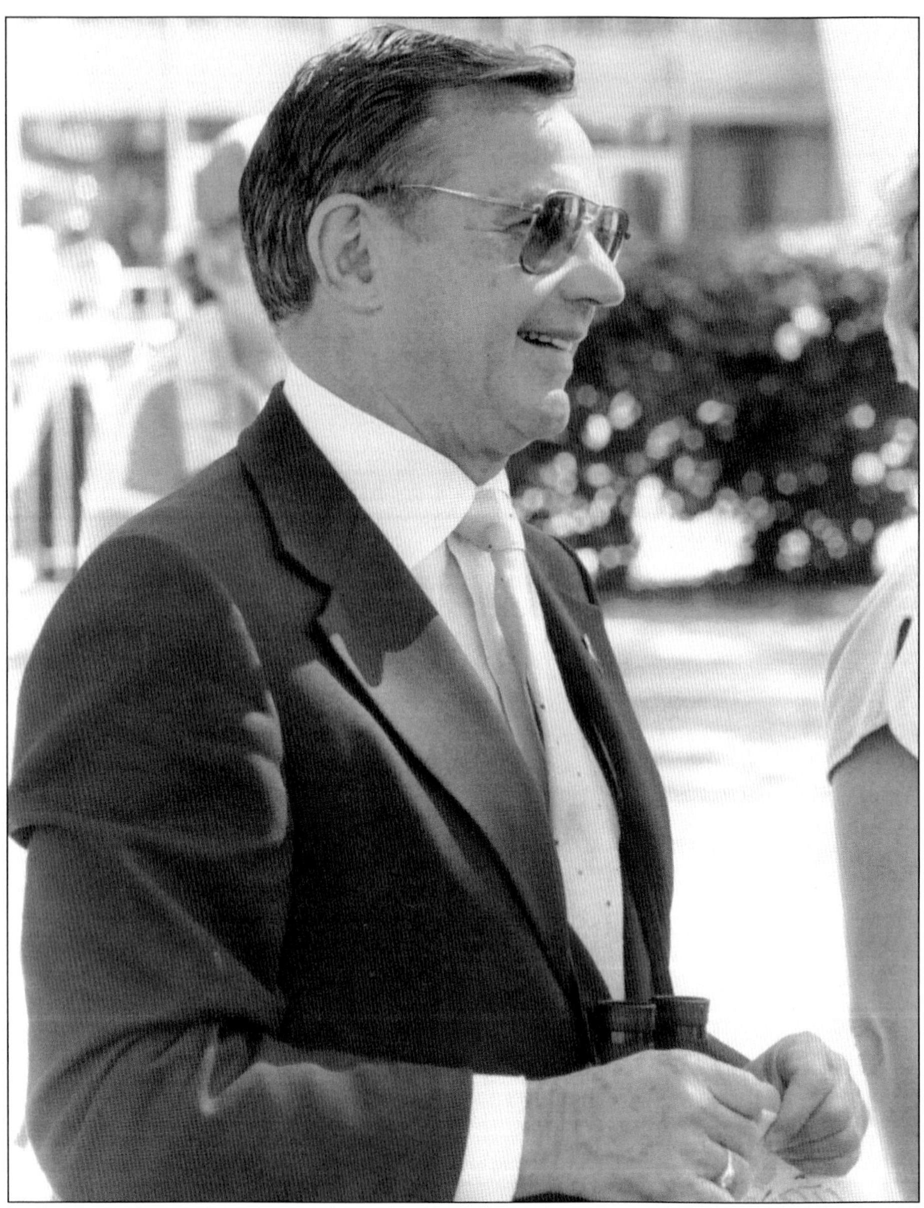

Richard L. "Dick" Duchossois was born on October 7, 1921, and raised on Chicago's southwest side, graduating from the Morgan Park Military Academy. He enrolled at Washington and Lee University in Lexington, Virginia, but left in 1942 and was commissioned lieutenant at age 20, assigned as commander of the 610th Tank Destroyer Battalion. He saw military action in Normandy, serving under Gen. George Patton in combat at the Falaise Gap, the Moselle River, and the Battle of the Bulge. Duchossois returned to Chicago, married childhood sweetheart Beverly Thrall, and in 1952 became CEO of the Thrall Car Manufacturing Company, the second-largest freight car builder in the world. The Duchossoises had four children, and in the 1960s established the 600-acre Hill 'n' Dale Farm, a Thoroughbred breeding facility. Duchossois helped form the ITBOA and became one of the leading breeders and owners in Illinois. After his wife passed away from cancer in 1980, he purchased the majority share of Arlington for $17.8 million, with the $19 million price making him the major investor. (Courtesy of Midwest Outdoors.)

After the daylong firestorm that ravaged Arlington Park in its 58th year, a $100 million rebuilding of the 323-acre site was proposed. The 350 employees who worked on the management side of Arlington were now without an office or duties, while for the more than 2,000 backstretch workers, life continued, as the barns and stable area were unscathed from the incident. (Courtesy of Midwest Outdoors.)

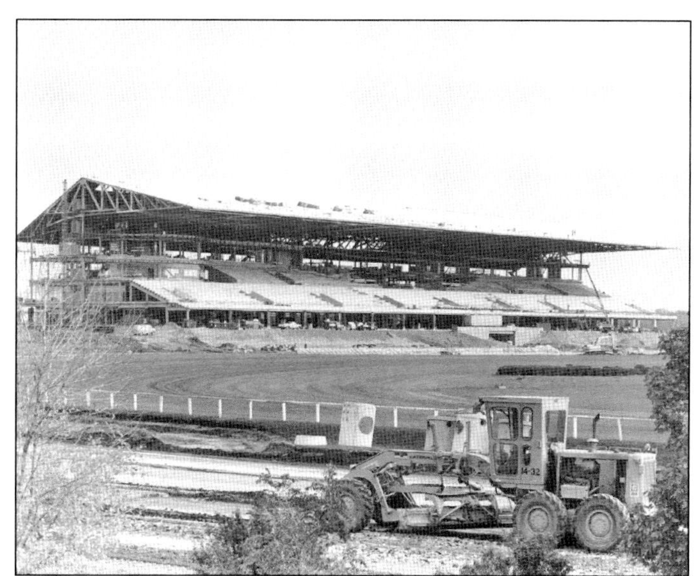

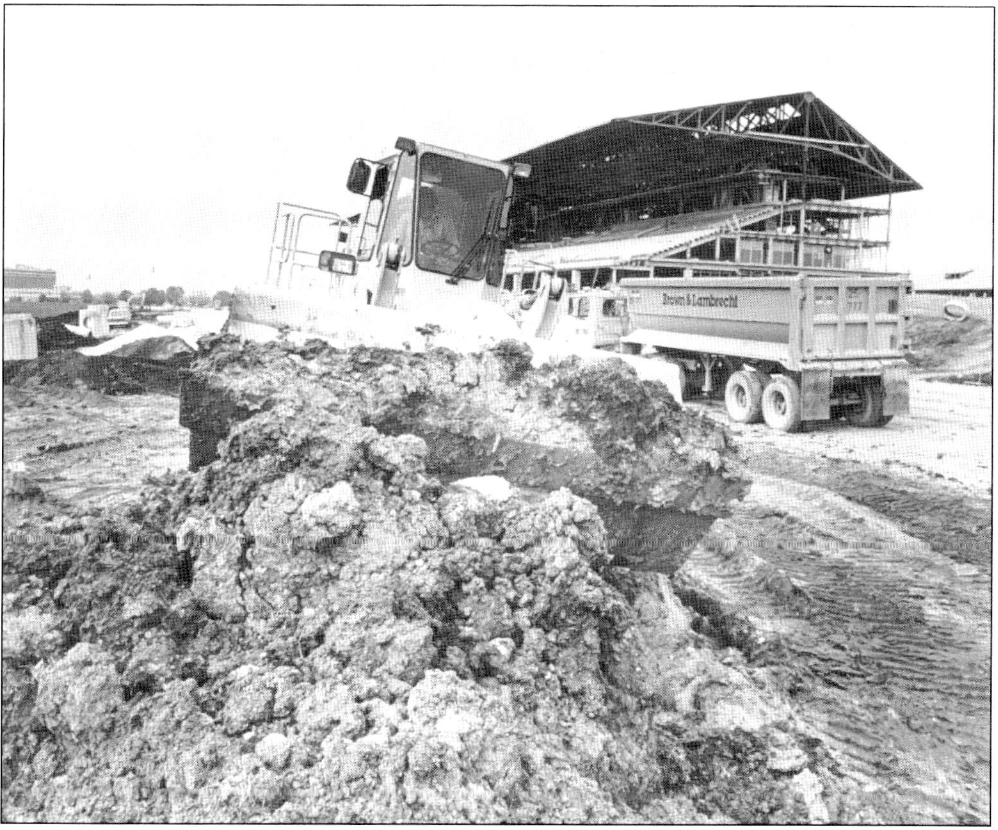

The reconstruction took 19 months and cost $175 million. Richard Duchossois, then 68, went from being a silent partner to being the sole owner of Arlington. It was estimated that the Arlington Park fire caused the State of Illinois to lose $8.6 million in tax revenue, and that had Arlington not been rebuilt, the Village of Arlington Heights would have lost as much as $15 million a year. (Courtesy of Midwest Outdoors.)

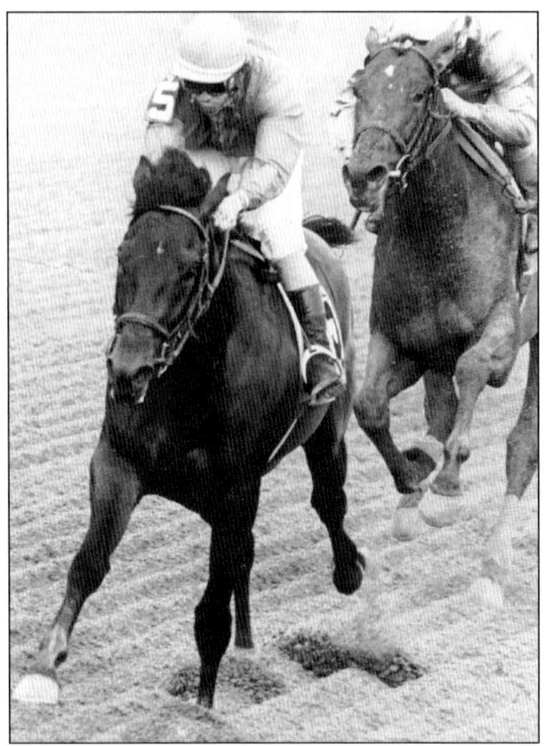

Holme on Top was a Florida-bred, 1981 foal, conditioned by James Levitch Sr. for breeder-owner Mary Zimmerman. The son of Noholme II won several Arlington allowance races and the 1983 edition of the Primer Stakes. Ridden in many of his starts by Jean Cruguet—who rode Seattle Slew to Triple Crown status—the graded stakes–placed Holme on Top earned $225,772 from 7 wins in 32 starts. (Courtesy of Midwest Outdoors.)

The new Arlington Park opened June 28, 1989, with a six-story, 700,000-square-foot clubhouse and grandstand and seating for more than 35,000. In 1986, Arlington had introduced its International Festival of Racing, a 13-day extravaganza that included three Grade I turf races—the Arlington Million, the Beverly D., and the Secretariat Stakes. In 1988, the Million was moved to Woodbine Race Course in Toronto while the new Arlington was being built. (Courtesy of Midwest Outdoors.)

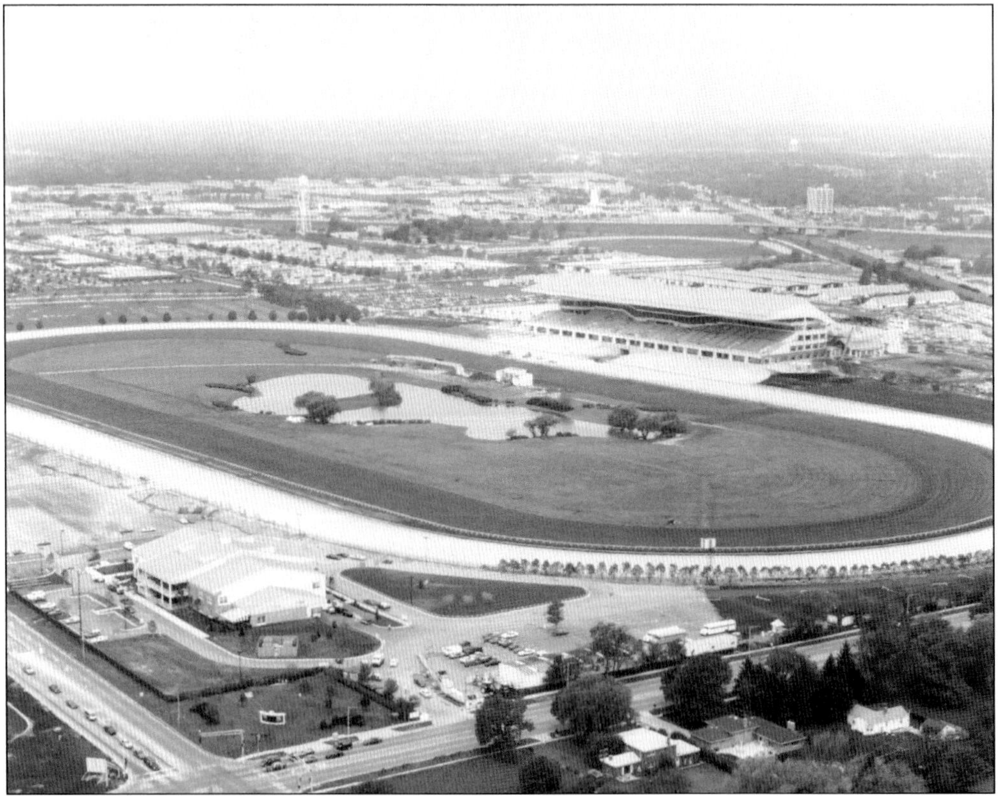

Gerry Gallitano was a Chicago riding fixture who later became a local television personality. Raised in Jacksonville, Florida, Gallitano became a jockey at age 19 and enjoyed a successful career—winning nearly 2,000 races from more than 10,000 mounts and earning $12 million-plus in purses. He was best known for his partnership with Gallant Bob, with whom he won 14 of 18 stakes in 1975 and who was a champion sprinter that year. (Courtesy of Midwest Outdoors.)

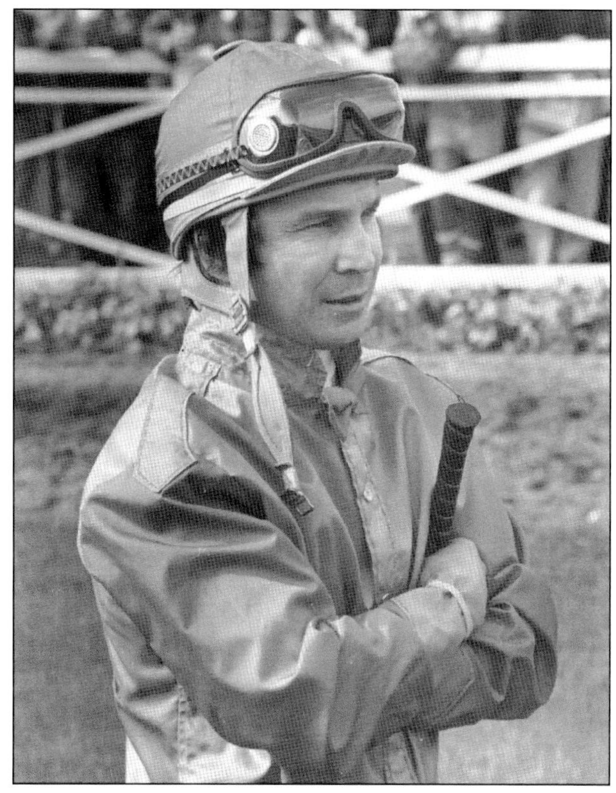

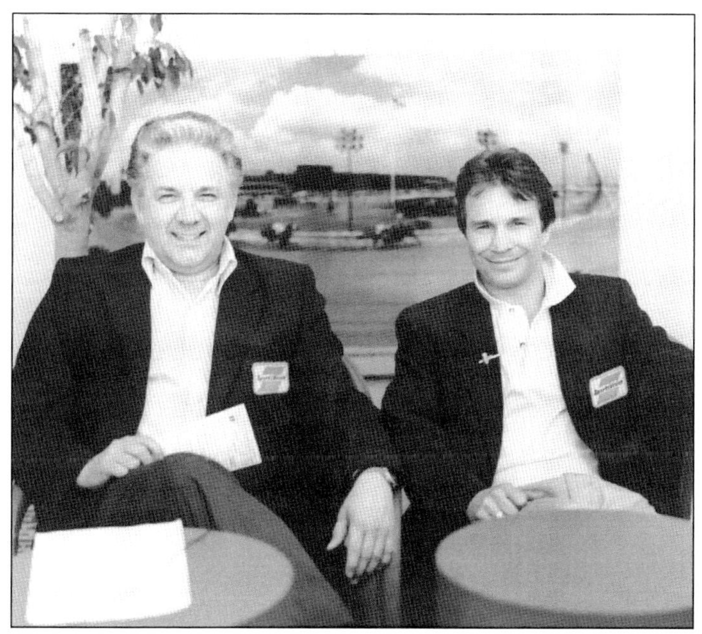

Gerry Gallitano (right) and Arlington's "Voice of Chicago Racing," Phil Georgeff, were in front of the cameras every afternoon for their *Chicago Racing Report*, which appeared on SportsChannel, a local cable line catering to some two million Chicagoland households. Providing fans with the latest racing news and updates, the half-hour racing information and results show was produced via Gallitano's production company ThoroughVision. (Courtesy of Midwest Outdoors.)

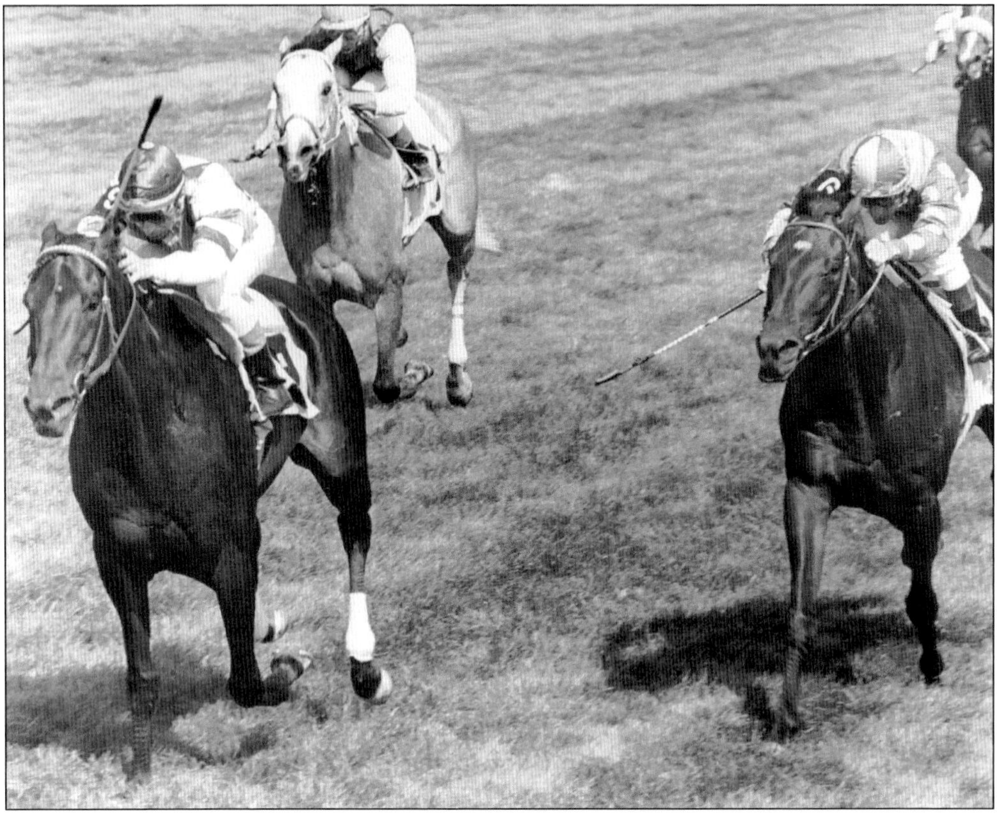

Mourjane captured the Arlington Park Handicap on August 31, 1986, in rein to Jose Santos, who was riding for trainer Tom Skiffington Jr., and the Fernwood Stable. The Irish-bred horse had finished seventh in the 1984 Arlington Million in his first start stateside after racing in Ireland and France. He went on to earn $747,747 from 10 wins, 7 seconds, and 6 thirds in 36 starts. (Courtesy of Midwest Outdoors.)

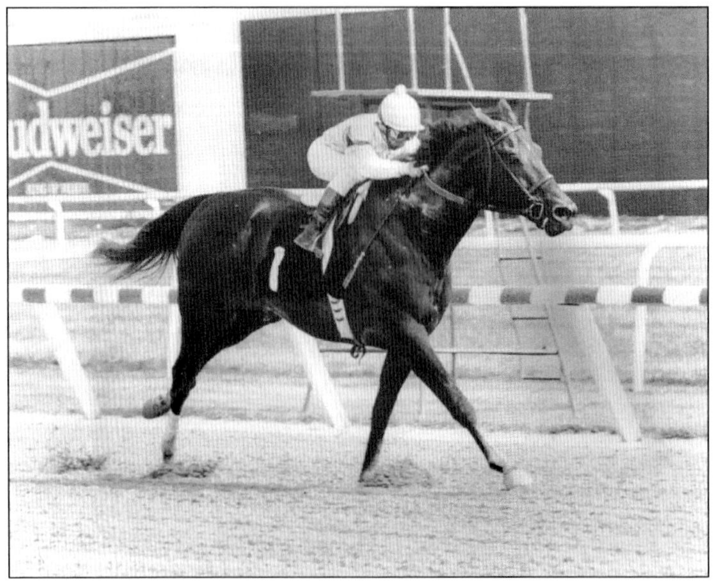

Taylor's Special was a 1981 Kentucky-bred son of Hawkin's Special and was trained by Bill Mott for W.F. Lucas. This multiple graded stakes winner was a tough sprinter who earned $1,065,805 from 21 wins, 7 seconds, and 2 thirds in 41 starts, racing from 1983 through 1987. He won the 1986 and 1987 editions of the Isaac Murphy Handicap and the 1987 Washington Park Handicap (Gr. II), among others. (Courtesy of Midwest Outdoors.)

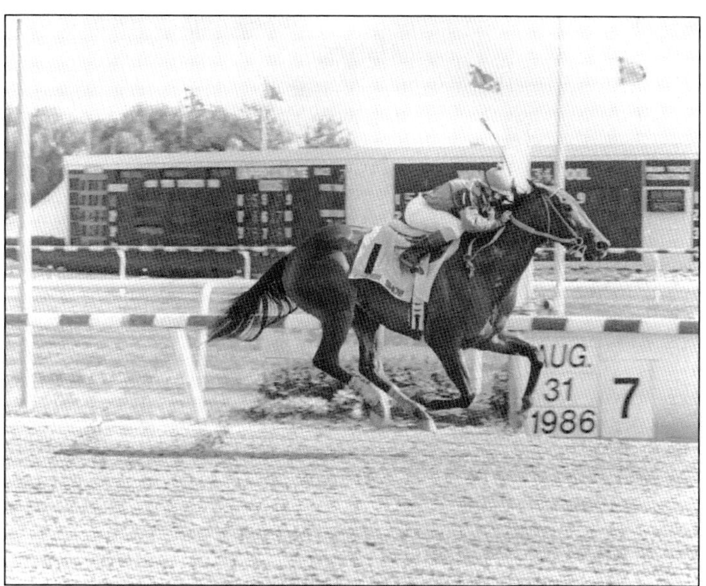

Lazer Show, with Pat Day up, won the Arlington-Chicago Budweiser Breeders' Cup Handicap two years in a row—in 1986 and 1987. The 1983 Kentucky-bred Apalachee daughter was trained by Don Winfree for owner James Devaney. A winner of $948,446 from 14 wins, 5 seconds, and 1 third in 14 starts, Lazer Show was later sold in foal to Seeking the Gold for $550,000. (Courtesy of Midwest Outdoors.)

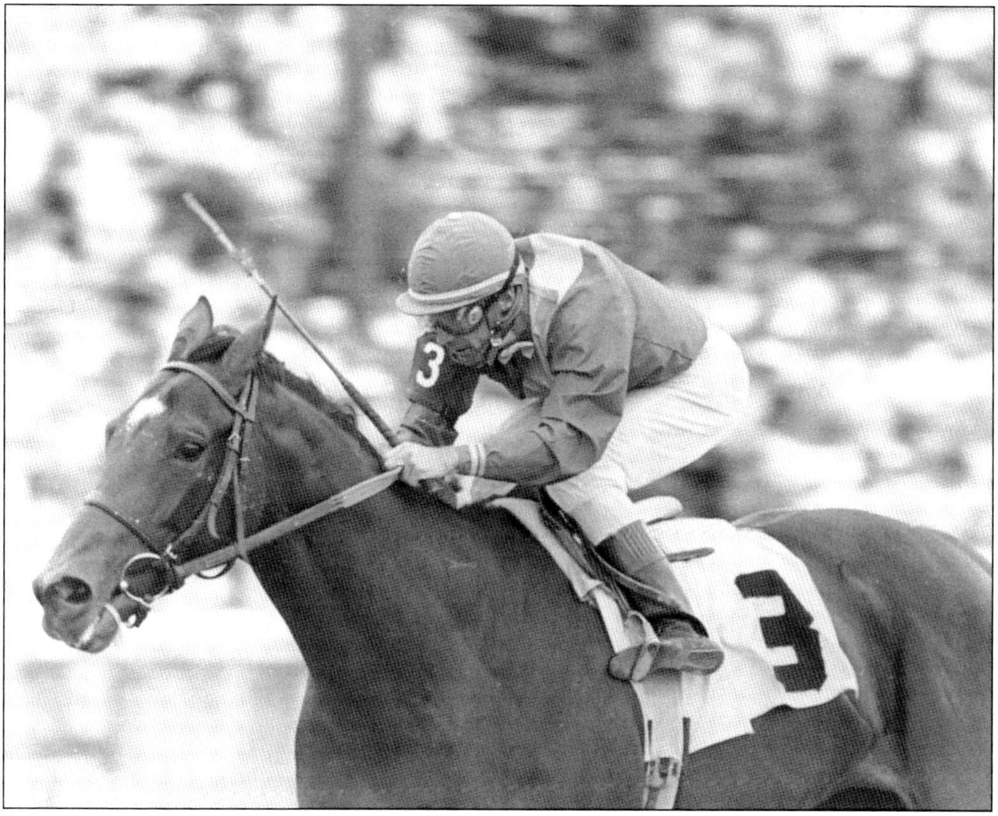

Orono and jockey Sandy Hawley are shown here winning the Arch Ward Stakes on August 24, 1986. The 1984 Illinois-bred son by Codex was trained by Carl Nafzger for the Bayview Stable and was a sprinter of modest success, earning $141,121 from 3 wins in 10 career starts. The stake was named in honor of the former sports editor of the *Chicago Tribune* newspaper. (Courtesy of Midwest Outdoors.)

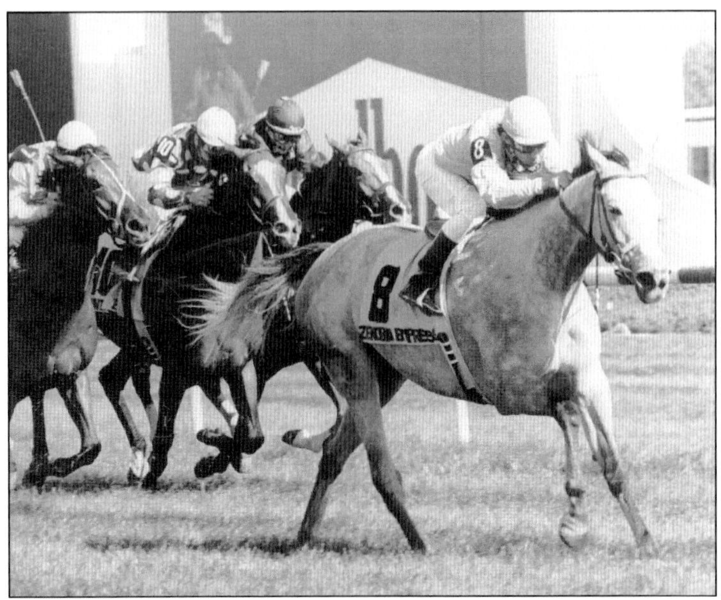

Zenobia Empress, with Earlie Fires in the saddle, outran 10 other fillies and mares to win the Grade II $92,000 Modesty Handicap on the turf in August 1986, when trainer Joe Bollero was 75. Earlie Fires was in the saddle before a crowd of 12,216 on the third day of Arlington's International Festival of Racing. Zenobia Empress retired a 15-time winner from 32 starts and $368,134. (Courtesy of Midwest Outdoors.)

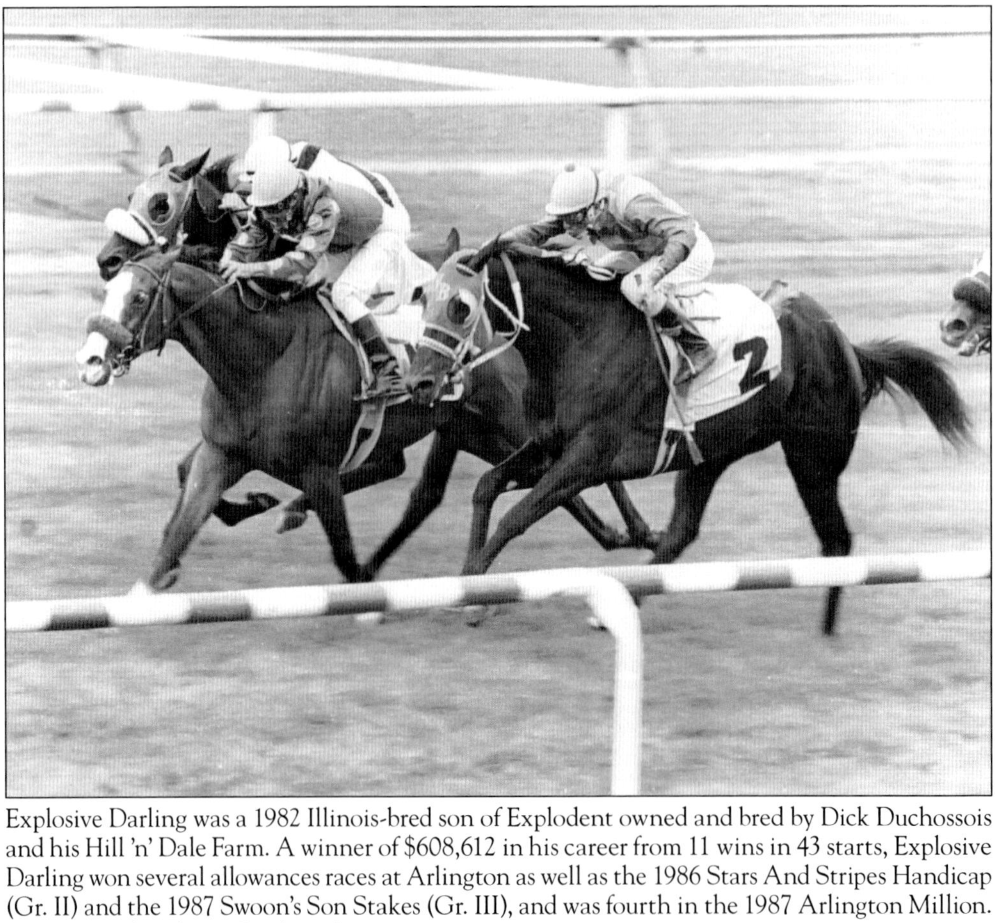

Explosive Darling was a 1982 Illinois-bred son of Explodent owned and bred by Dick Duchossois and his Hill 'n' Dale Farm. A winner of $608,612 in his career from 11 wins in 43 starts, Explosive Darling won several allowances races at Arlington as well as the 1986 Stars And Stripes Handicap (Gr. II) and the 1987 Swoon's Son Stakes (Gr. III), and was fourth in the 1987 Arlington Million. (Courtesy of Midwest Outdoors.)

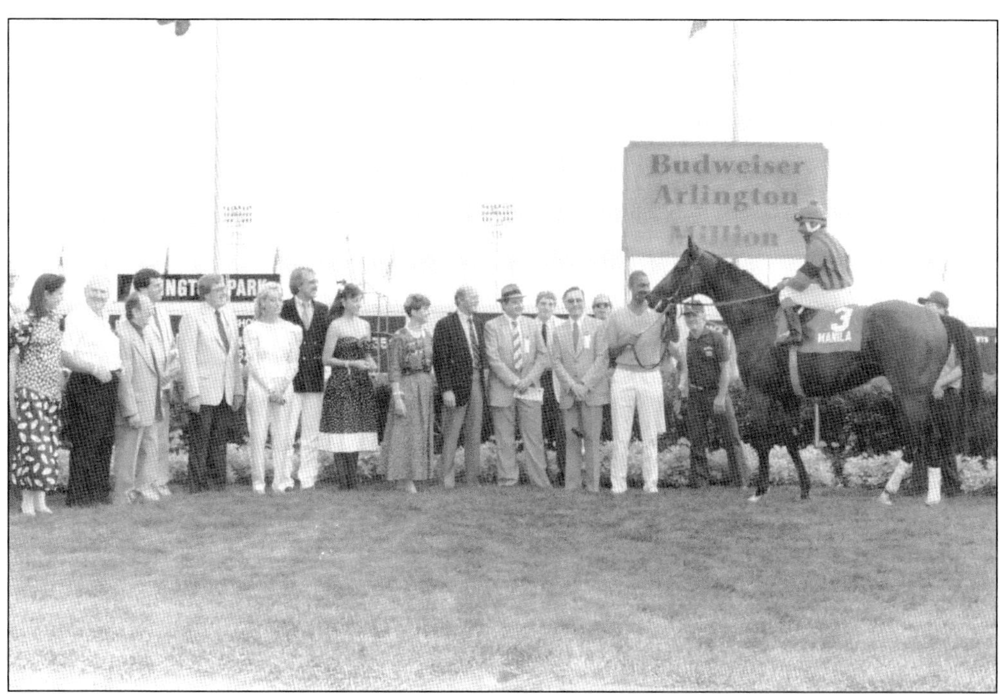

Manila, the 1986 Grass Champion, captured the 1987 Arlington Million with ease for rider Angel Cordero Jr. Sharrood was second, three and a quarter lengths ahead of 2-1 second choice Theatrical in the seventh running of the stake. Sadly, the Million was to be his last race as Manila broke a cannon bone two weeks later and was retired. He had earned $2,692,799 from 12 wins and 5 seconds in 18 starts. (Courtesy of Midwest Outdoors.)

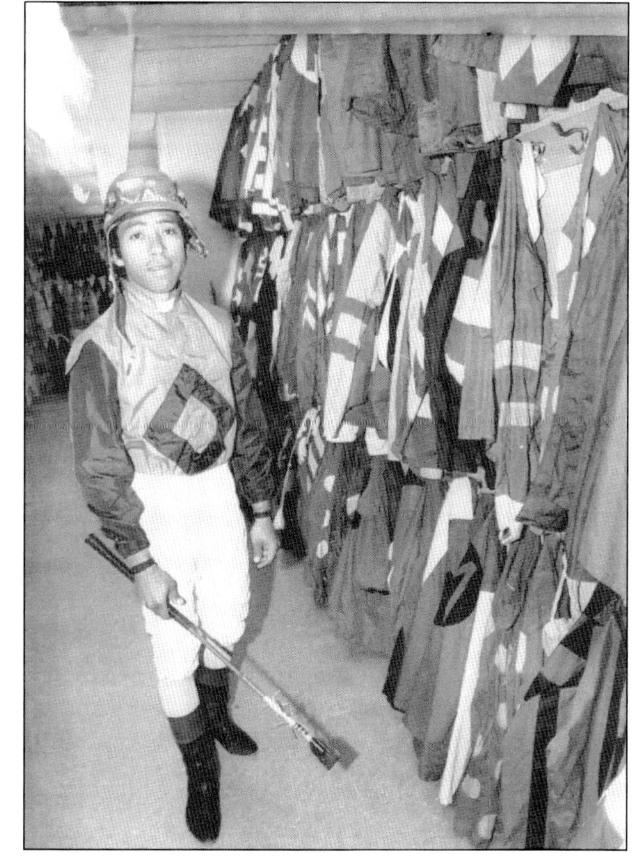

Angel Cordero Jr., the Eclipse award–winning jockey of 1982 and 1983 and a 1988 Hall of Fame inductee, rode a plethora of Grade I winners, including 1987 Arlington Million winner Manila. Known for his aggressive riding style, Cordero retired with more than $164 million in career earnings, with 7,057 wins, 6,136 seconds, and 5,359 thirds from 38,658 lifetime mounts. (Courtesy of Midwest Outdoors.)

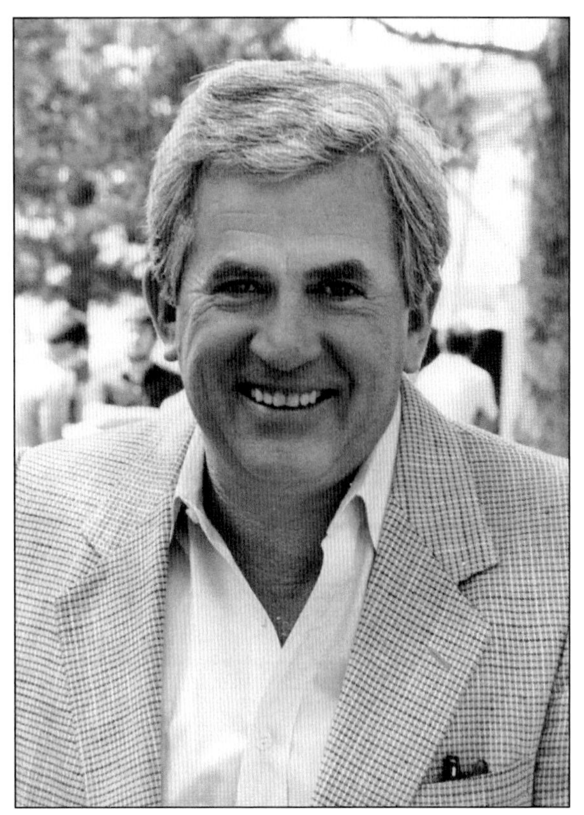

James Bert Sonnier, born October 1, 1938, in Church Point, Louisiana, was Arlington's leading trainer in 1983 and 1985. This Cajun-raised conditioner began galloping horses at age eight and went on to have a successful training career. In 1979, he became the first trainer to bridle up the winners of both the Arlington-Washington Futurity Stakes (with Execution's Reason) and the Arlington-Washington Lassie stakes (with Sissy's Time) in the same season. (Courtesy of Midwest Outdoors.)

Western Playboy, a chestnut son of Illinois sire Play Fellow, was foaled March 20, 1986, and became a multiple graded stakes winner of $1,128,449. Bred, trained, and owned by Harvey Vanier and the Script R Farm, Western Playboy won the 1989 Hertz Stakes at Arlington as well as the Jim Beam (Gr. II) and Bluegrass Stakes (Gr. I) and the Pennsylvania Derby (Gr. I). (Courtesy of Midwest Outdoors.)

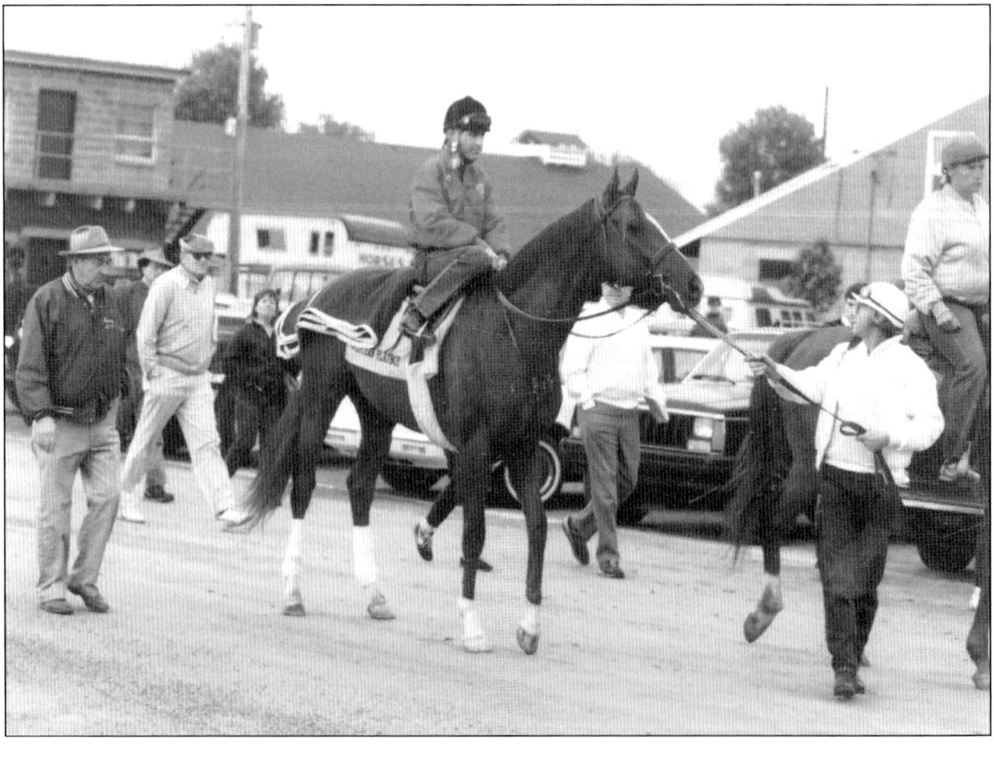

Five

Rebirth 1990–1999

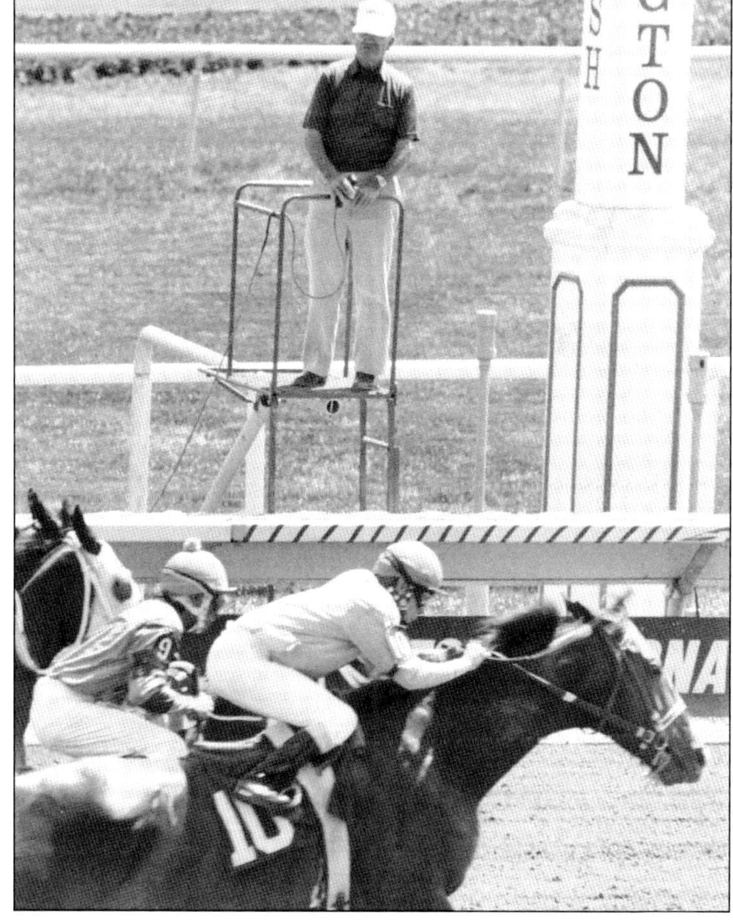

Arlington Park starter Jimmy Canard watches after giving a field of nine Thoroughbreds their freedom from the starting gate. After the horses are loaded into the starting gate and stand quietly, Canard will press a button, sounding a bell that simultaneously opens the gate doors, releasing the horses. Talented starters such as Canard get to know the quirks and nuances of all the horses he starts at a racing meet. (Courtesy of Midwest Outdoors.)

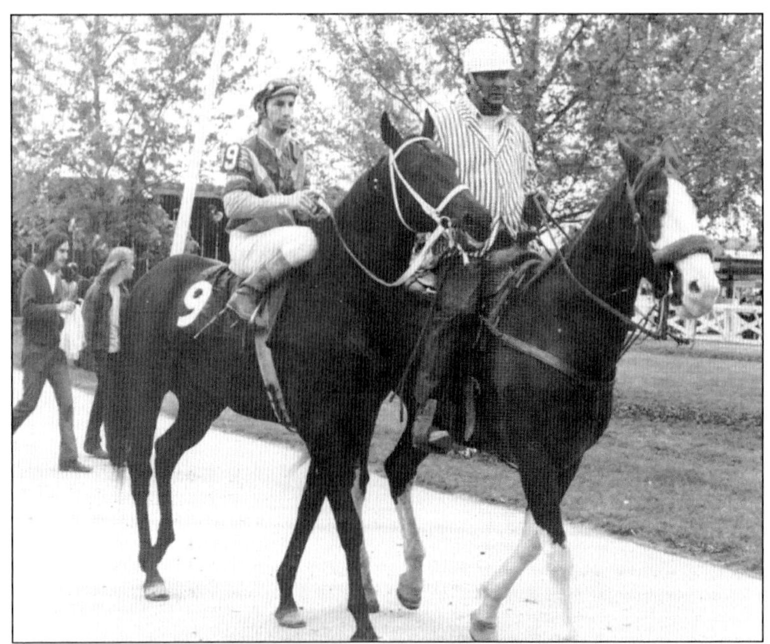

Jockey Ray Sibille is led to the post by an Arlington Park outrider and his piebald pony horse (right). The pony horses are necessary to the welfare of both the horse and rider, helping to calm the often-fractious Thoroughbreds who become excited and keyed up on race day. (Courtesy of Midwest Outdoors.)

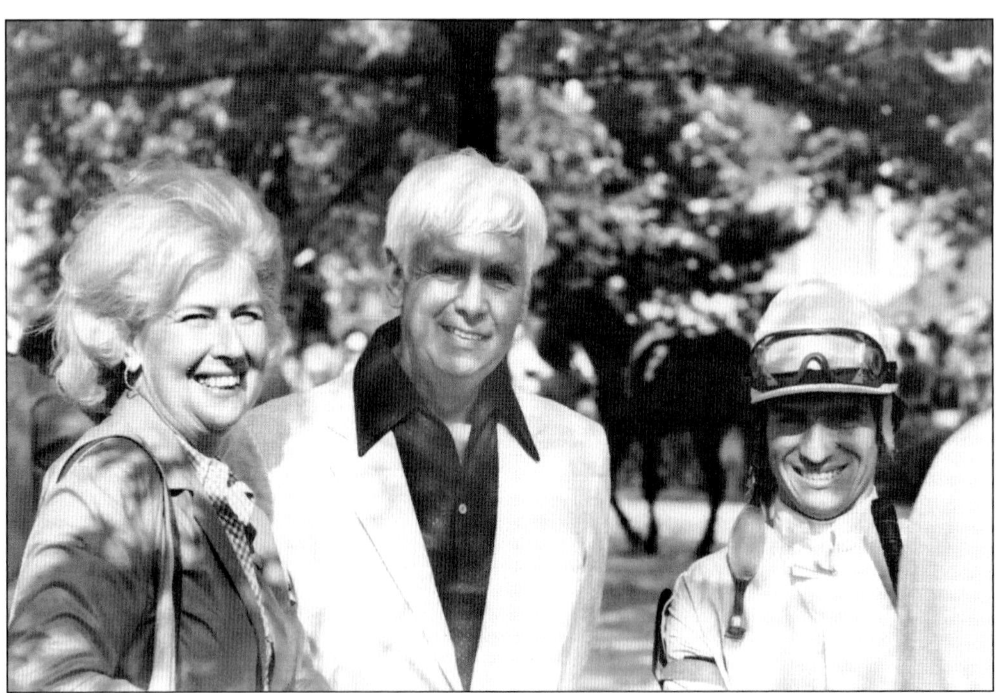

Carlos Silva (right) is in the Arlington paddock with breeders/owners Patricia and Robert Curran. Silva is Arlington's third-all-time leading rider and was a top 10 jockey there from 1990 to 2000. Silva and trainer Gene Cilio teamed up to capture numerous Chicago stakes and Silva later formed a successful partnership with leading trainer Richard Hazelton. Silva, a native of Chile, retired in 2010 with more than 3,500 career wins. (Courtesy of Midwest Outdoors.)

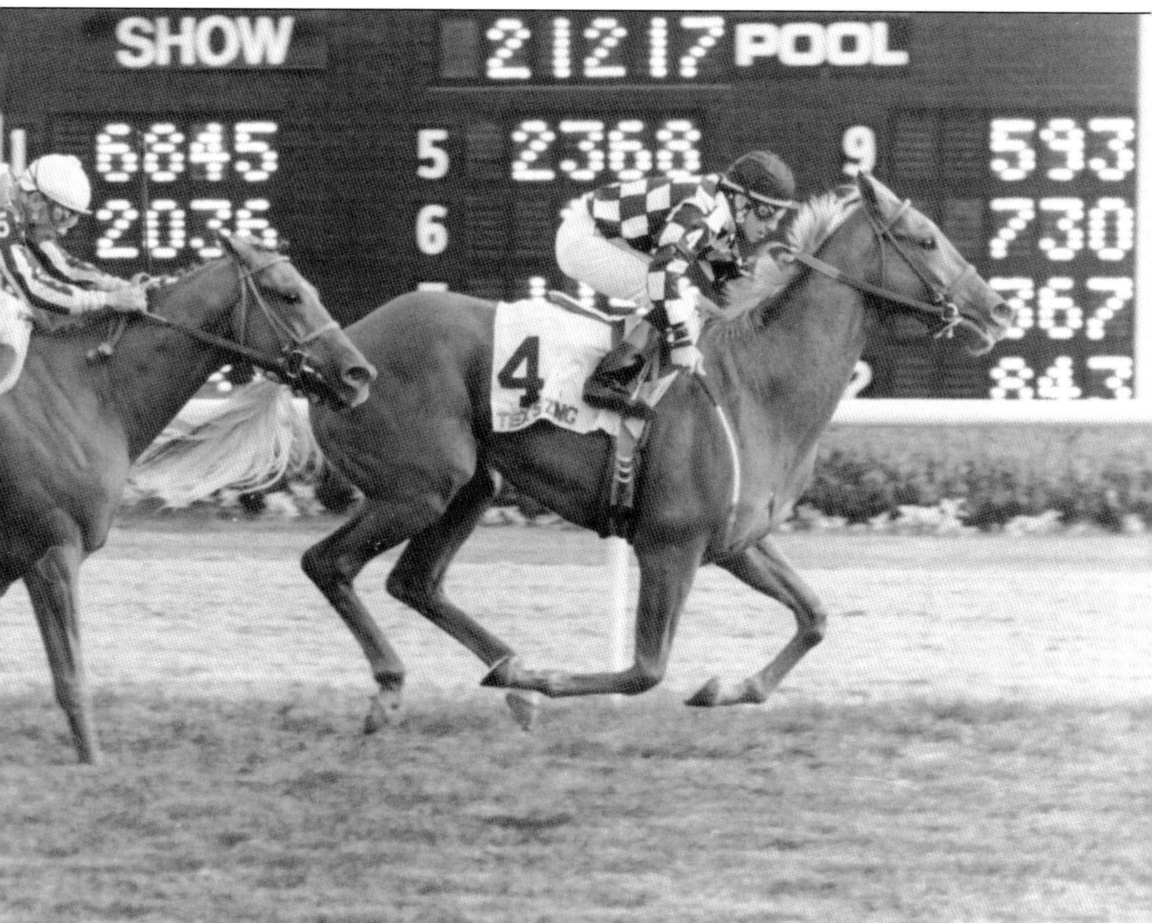

Tex's Zing gives jockey Earlie Fires career victory 5,000 by winning the Bishop Handicap on October 9, 1990. Tex's Zing was a front-running son of Text-Toot's Zing, by Zingalong, who was an extremely versatile Illinois-bred horse—being competitive on grass or the dirt. Foaled March 27, 1986, Tex's Zing was trained by Robert Byrne, a graded stakes–placed conditioner who trained 320 winners to $4,403,243 in career earnings. Tex's Zing was a striking chestnut colt, bred and owned by Loretta J. Clark, who earned $557,598 from 28 starts, with 17 wins, 5 seconds, and 3 thirds. A multiple-stakes winner, Tex's Zing captured the 1989 and 1990 W.H. Bishop Handicap and the 1990 Springfield Stakes at Arlington, and was also runner-up in the 1989 Hertz Stakes. He won multiple allowance and handicap events at Arlington during his three-year career from 1988 to 1990. (Author's collection.)

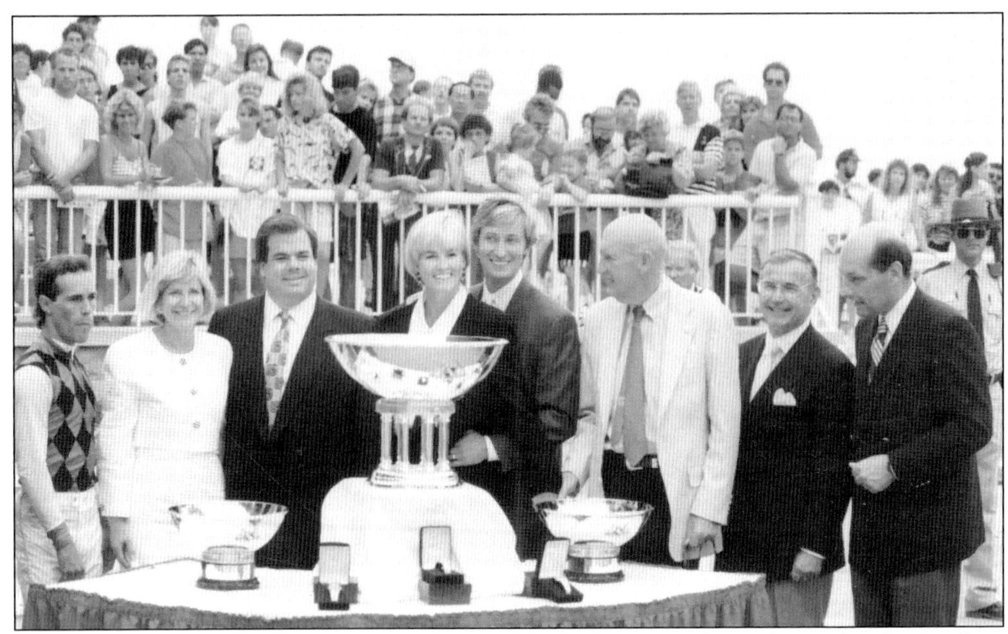

Co-owner Wayne Gretzky, rider Gary Stevens, and trainer Charlie Whittingham—his third million victory—celebrate Golden Pheasant's Arlington Million win on September 2, 1990. A $44,000 yearling, the Kentucky-bred roan son by Caro raced from 1989 to 1992, winning the Gr. I Japan Cup and Prix Neil (Gr. II) Stake at Longchamp and finishing third in the 1992 Million. From 22 starts, he scored 7 wins and earned $2,453,958. Pictured from left to right are jockey Gary Stevens, Jane McNall, Bruce McNall, Janet Gretsky, Wayne Gretsky, Charlie Whittingham, Richard Duchossois, and Ed Duffy. (Courtesy of Midwest Outdoors.)

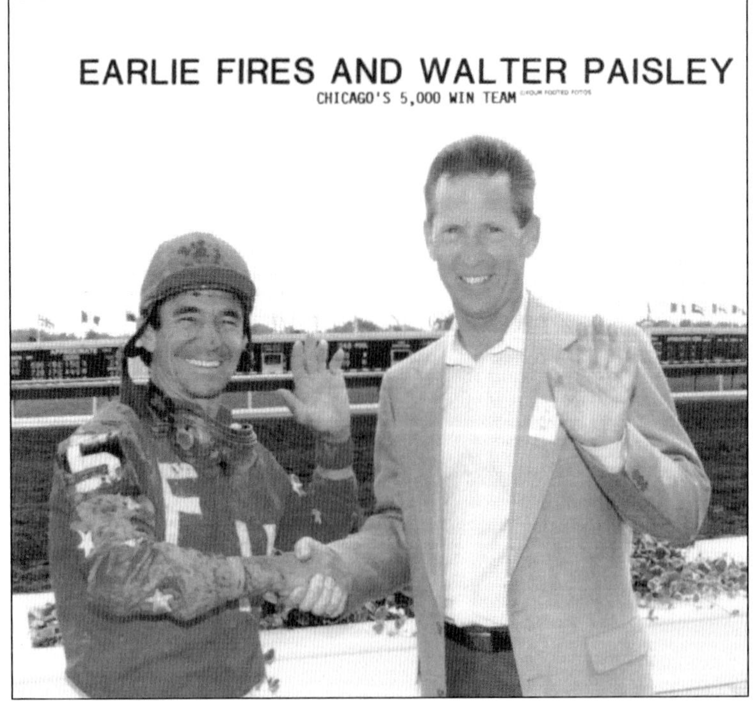

Jockey Earlie Fires and Standardbred driver Walter Paisley celebrate their membership in the 5,000-win club. Both of these talented horsemen achieved a milestone by winning 5,000 races in their respective industries. Fires began riding in 1964 and retired in 2008 with 6,470 victories. In 1983 and 1987, Fires set an Arlington record by winning seven races on a single card. He is Arlington's all-time leading rider, with 2,886 victories. (Author's collection.)

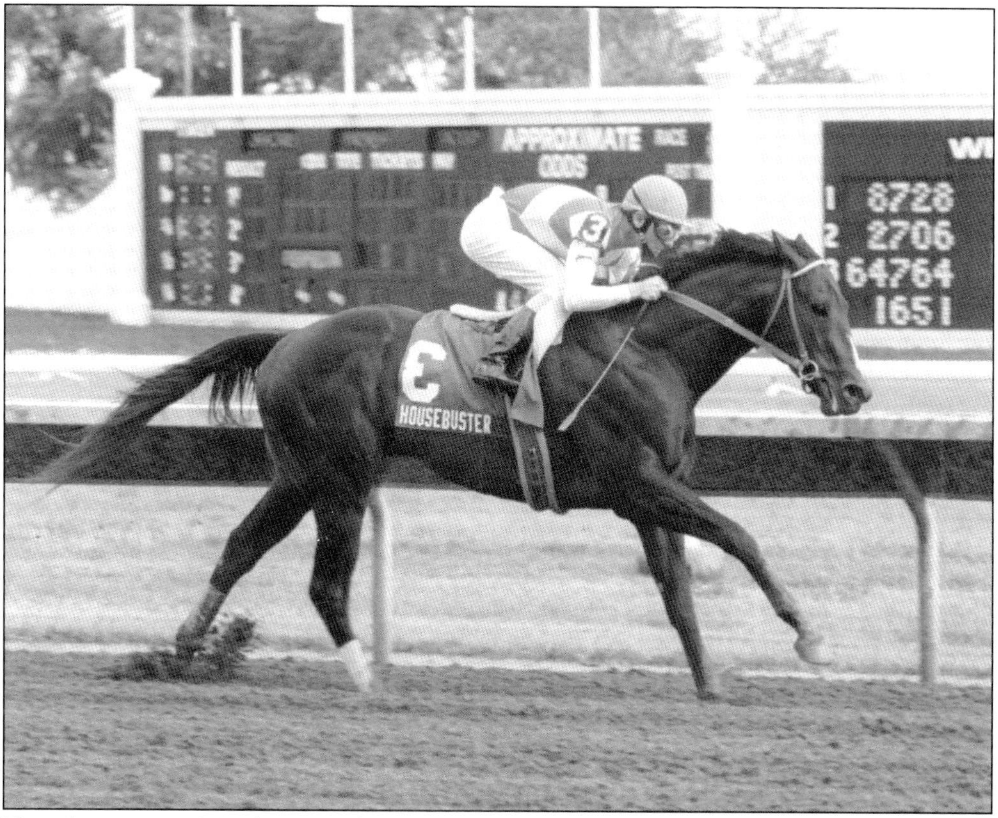

Housebuster was a March 7, 1987, homebred son by Mt. Livermore and was owned by Robert Levy and trained by Warren Croll Jr. He won Arlington's 1990 Sheridan Stakes (Gr. III) and 1990 Spectacular Bid Stakes. He was a multiple graded stakes winner of 15 of 22 starts and $1,229,696, the Eclipse Award–winning Champion Sprinter of 1990 and 1991, and a National Hall of Fame inductee in 2013. (Courtesy of Midwest Outdoors.)

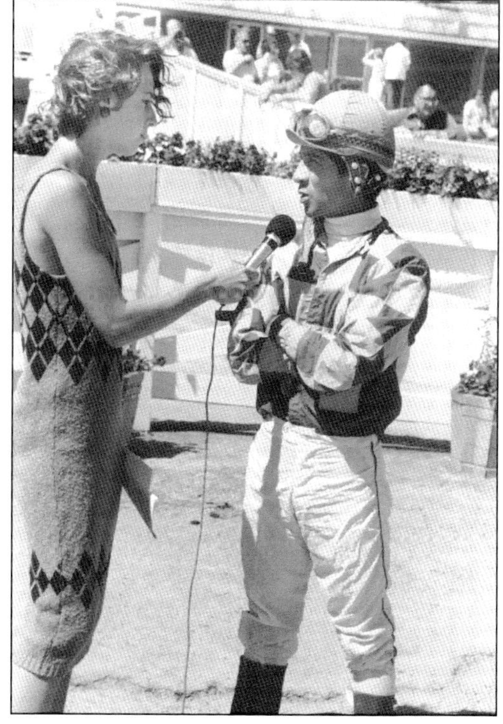

Arlington's Julie McEvoy interviews jockey Jorge Tejeira, who was born in 1948 in Panama. He is one of the few jockeys to win eight races in a single day, on June 16, 1976, when he won three at Philadelphia's Keystone Racetrack and five at New Jersey's Atlantic City Race Course. Tejeira won 3,419 races in his career, and won the Equipoise Mile (Gr. III) with Timeless Native in 1985 at Arlington. (Courtesy of Midwest Outdoors.)

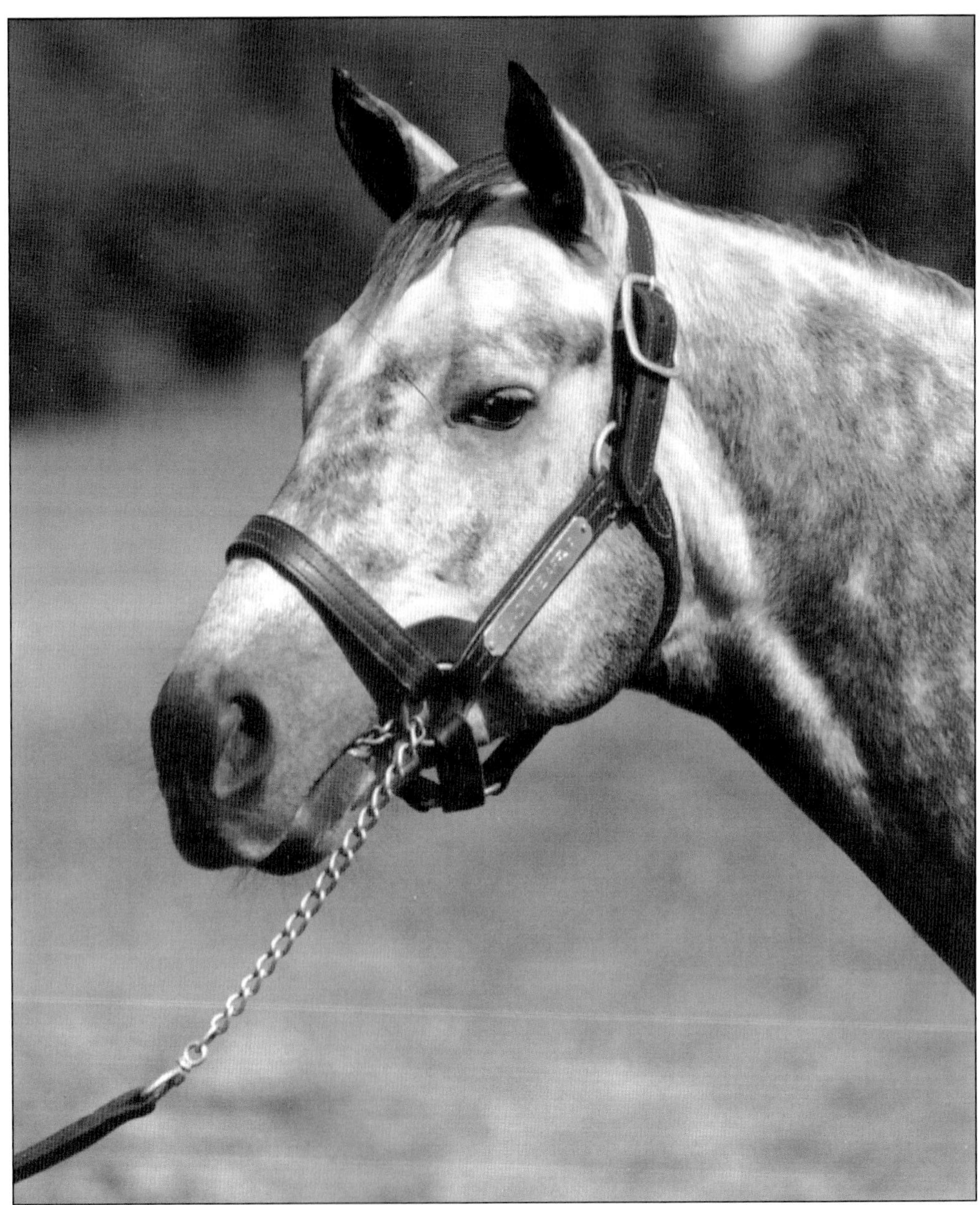

Black Tie Affair, a son of Miswaki, was foaled April 1, 1986. Owner Jeffrey Sullivan purchased him in 1989 for $125,000 as a three-year-old on the advice of trainer Ernie T. Poulos. Black Tie Affair was a grades stakes-race winner at two, three, four, and five—winning the 1990 Equipoise Mile, 1991 Michigan Mile, 1991 Washington Park Handicap, and 1991 Breeders' Cup Classic before being named 1991 Horse of the Year. He retired in 1992 with $3,370,694 from 18 wins in 45 starts, and was sent to Kentucky, then Japan in 1997 for stud duty. In 2003, Black Tie Affair's ex-trainer's wife, Dee Poulos, started a campaign to bring him back to the United States and he was retired to Old Friends Equine in Georgetown, Kentucky. He was humanely euthanized there on July 1, 2010, due to laminitis. Trainer Poulos, a Chicago native, started conditioning horses in 1952 and was greatly admired by his peers. When Poulos died on March 30, 1997, his funeral was held at Arlington Park. (Courtesy of Midwest Outdoors.)

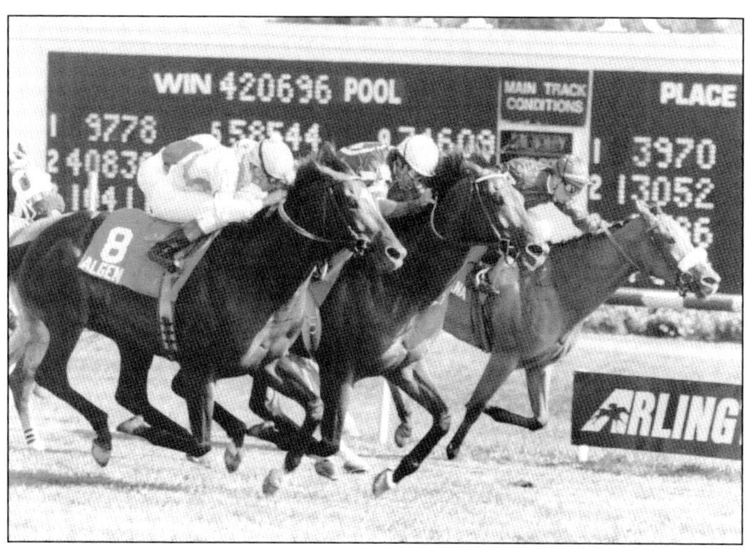

Tight Spot (center) captured the 11th edition of the Arlington Million on September 2, 1991, for jockey Laffit Pincay Jr., clocked in 1:59.2 for the one-and-a-quarter-mile turf test, the second-fastest in Million history. Tight Spot bested Argentine Horse of the Year Algenib by a head, with French filly Kartajana third. (Courtesy of Midwest Outdoors.)

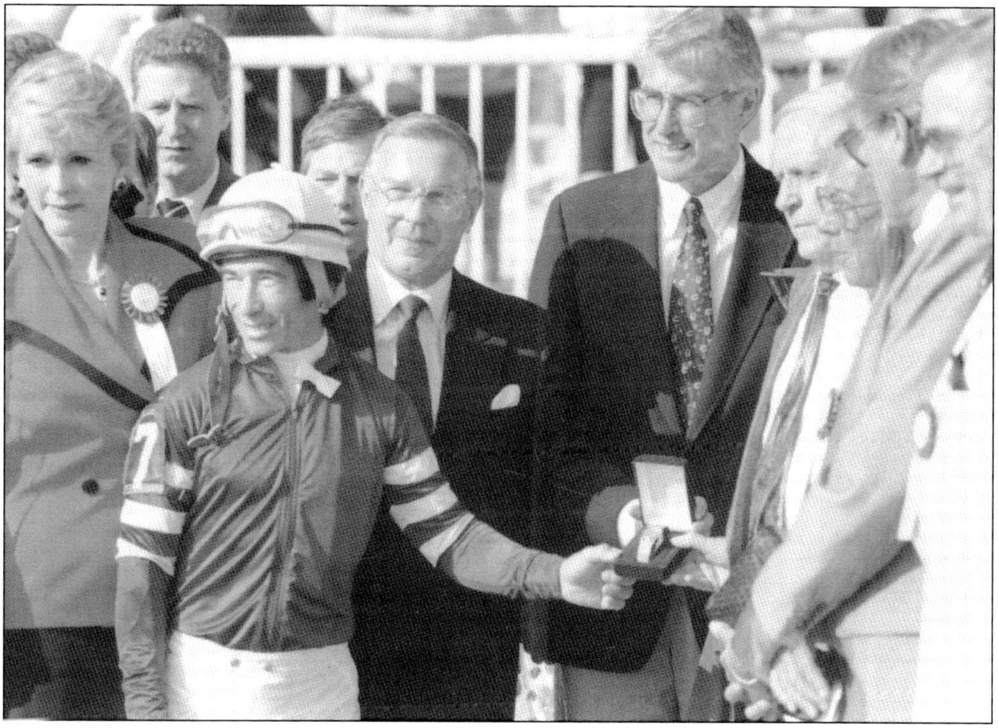

Tight Spot's winning jockey, Laffit Pincay Jr., stands with Arlington owner Richard Duchossois and Illinois governor James Edgar. The winning Tight Spot gave Ron McAnally his third Million victory—having won in 1981 and 1984 with John Henry and tying Charlie Whittingham for that honor. Tight Spot was the first supplemental entry to win the Million, as owner-breeder Verne Winchell plunked down $50,000 to enter the eventual winner. (Courtesy of Midwest Outdoors.)

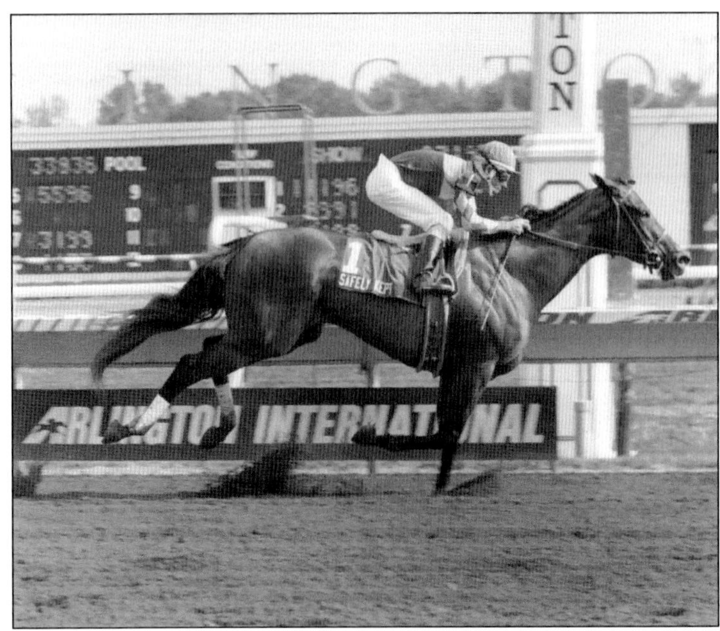

Safely Kept was a 1986 Maryland-bred daughter by Horatius, who won the 1990 Breeders' Cup Sprint (Gr. I) and the following year won the Chicago Budweiser Breeders' Cup at Arlington on June 30, 1991. Owned by Jayeff B Stable, trained by Alan Goldberg, and ridden in most of her races by Gary Stevens, this $2,194,206-winning mare won 24 of 31 stakes and rarely finished off the board. (Courtesy of Midwest Outdoors.)

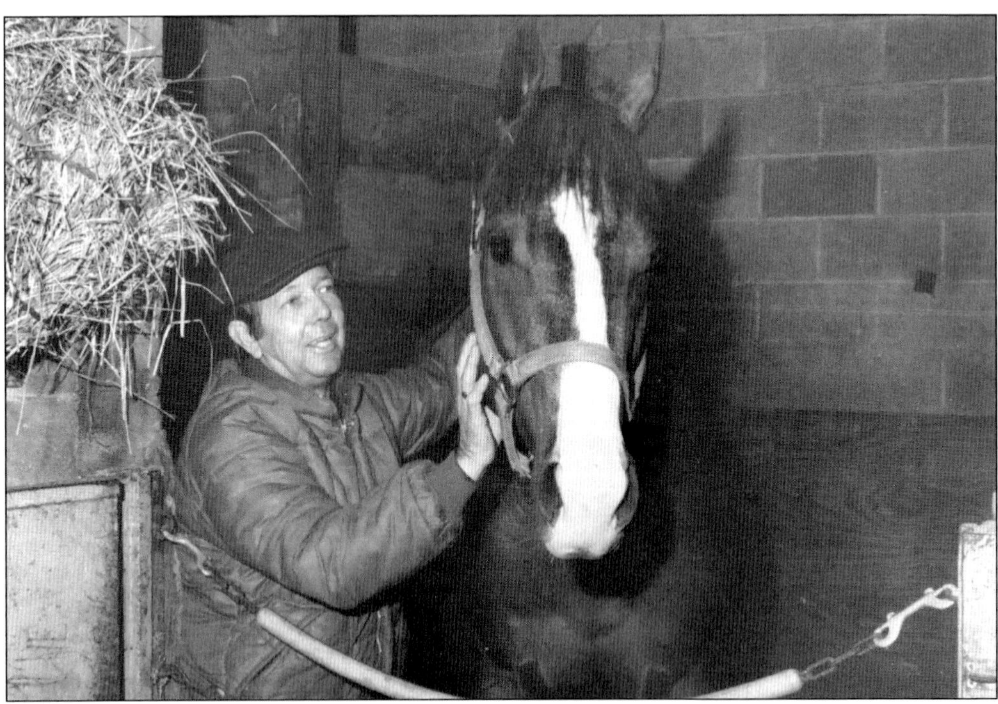

Trainer Eddie Cole was a graded stakes winning trainer, based in Chicago. He visited the winner's circle 1,691 times with 12,754 starters who earned $14,550,120. Cole's top horse was the filly Peach of It, who captured the 1992 Sixty Sails Handicap (Gr. III) with E.T. Baird in the saddle. (Courtesy of Midwest Outdoors.)

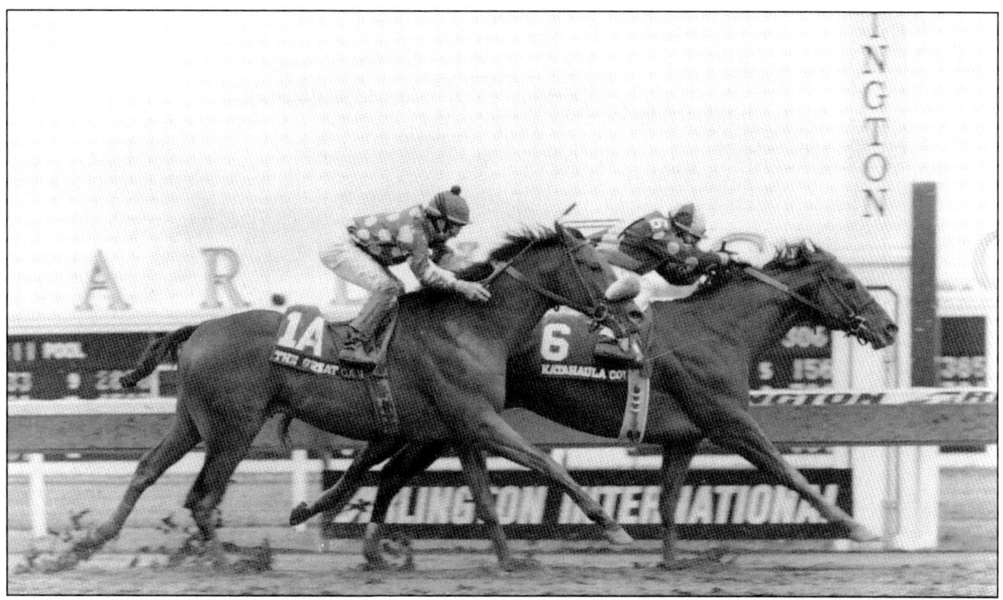

Katahaula County was a 1988 Ontario-bred son by Bold Ruckus, who was owned by Richard Duchossois and trained by David MacLean. This striking chestnut won the $75,000 Equipoise Mile Handicap (Gr. III) on May 24, 1992, on the dirt for jockey Curt Bourque and went on to earn $178,322 from 6 wins, 4 seconds, and 2 thirds in 17 starts. (Courtesy of Midwest Outdoors.)

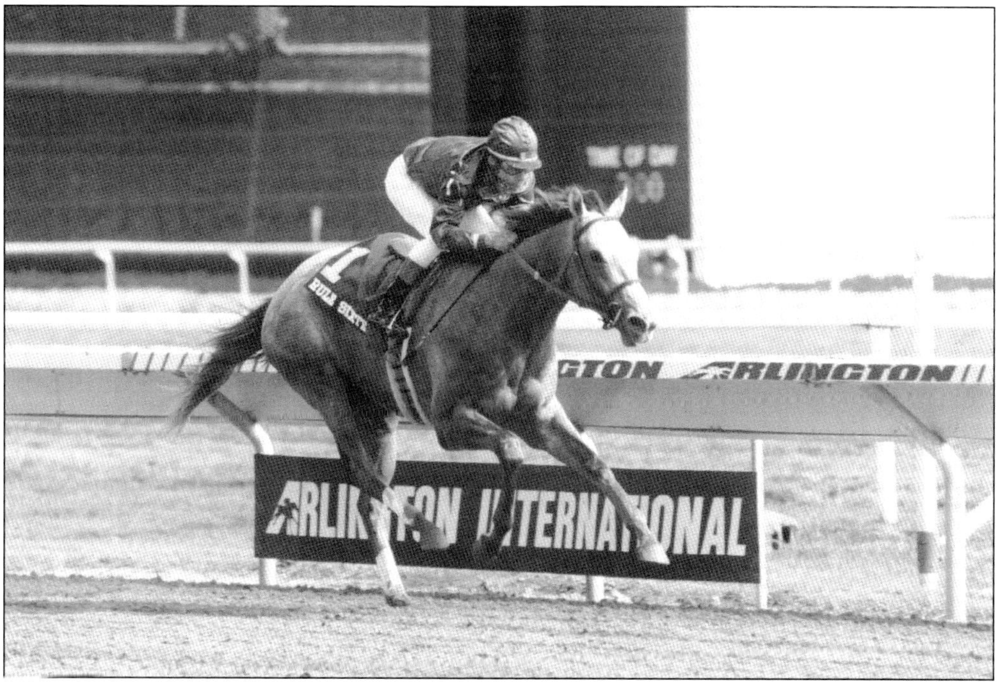

Here, Bruce Duchossois's Rule Sixteen captures the seven-furlong, 1992 Arch Ward Stakes at Arlington in 1:23.71. Foaled in 1990, Rule Sixteen was a multiple-stakes-winning son of Ogygian and retired with $266,133 from 18 wins, 11 seconds, and 6 third-place finishes in 65 starts. The Arch Ward Stakes began in 1956 at Washington Park but shifted to Arlington in 1959. (Courtesy of Midwest Outdoors.)

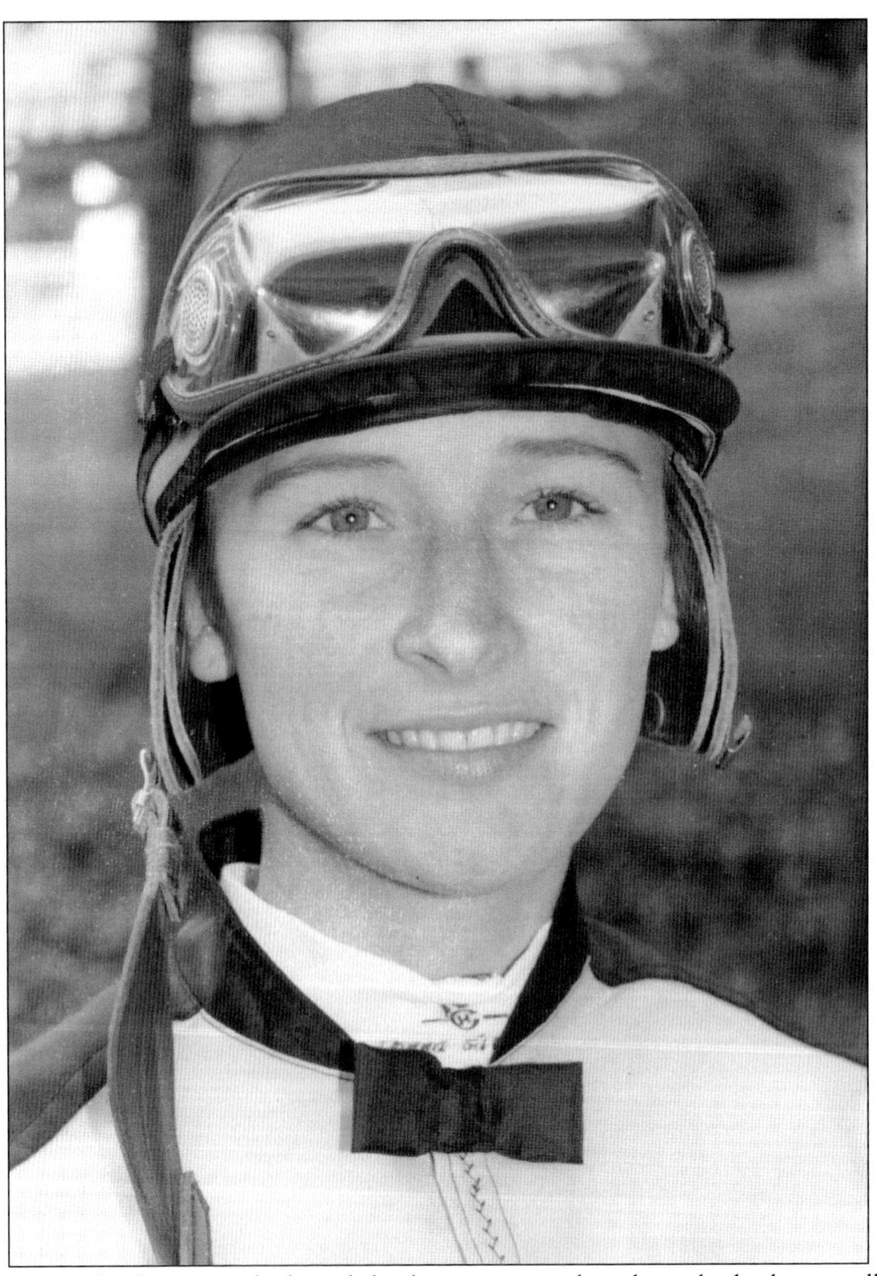

Donna Barton-Brothers is a multiple graded stakes–winning jockey who ranks third among all-time female winning riders in purses earned, with $18,658,028. Born April 20, 1966, in Alamogordo, New Mexico, Barton-Brothers followed her mother, jockey Patti Barton, along with a sister and brother who were also jockeys, into the Thoroughbred racing industry. She began riding professionally in 1987 and continued for 11 years, with her best season coming in 1996, when she scored 134 wins from 1,025 starts, for seasonal earnings of $4,091,474. Lifetime, she scored 1,130 winners, 1,083 second-place finishes, and 1,081 third-place finishes from 9,233 starts. She retired after marrying trainer Frank Brothers in 1998 and now works as a TV correspondent, covering some of racing's biggest events, such as the Triple Crown and Breeders' Cup, usually on horseback. (Courtesy of Midwest Outdoors.)

Cigar came to Arlington Park on July 13, 1996, for the $1,075,000 Arlington Citation Challenge, which he won by three and a half lengths. Arlington created the race for Cigar, who carried 130 pounds and became the first American horse to win 16 consecutive races since Citation did so in 1948 and 1950 (this streak was eclipsed by Zenyatta in 2010). Trained by Bill Mott and ridden by Jerry Bailey, the Maryland-bred son of Palace Music was foaled April 18, 1990, earning $9,999,815 from 19 wins in 33 starts for owner-breeder Allen E. Paulson. Cigar won the 1995 Breeders' Cup Classic and 1996 Dubai World Cup, and was the 1995 and 1996 Horse of the Year and Champion Older Horse of the Year, inducted into the Hall of Fame in 2002 and retired as the leading money-winning Thoroughbred at that time. Cigar passed away on October 7, 2014, at the Kentucky Horse Park in Lexington. (Courtesy of Midwest Outdoors.)

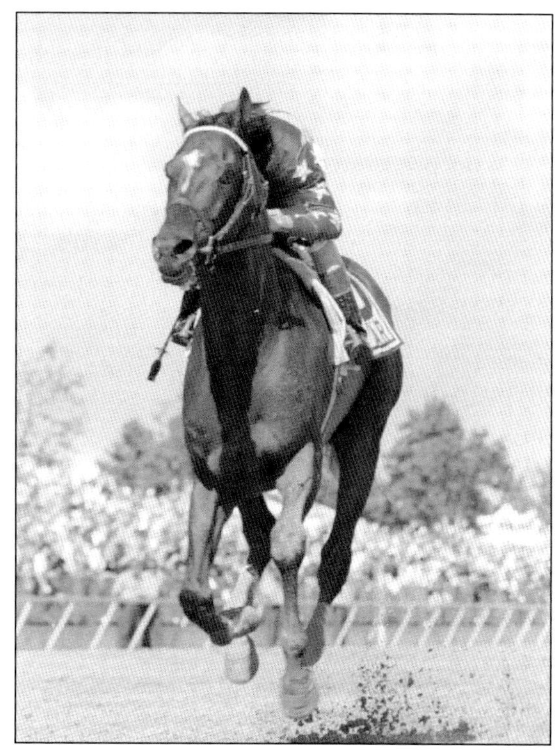

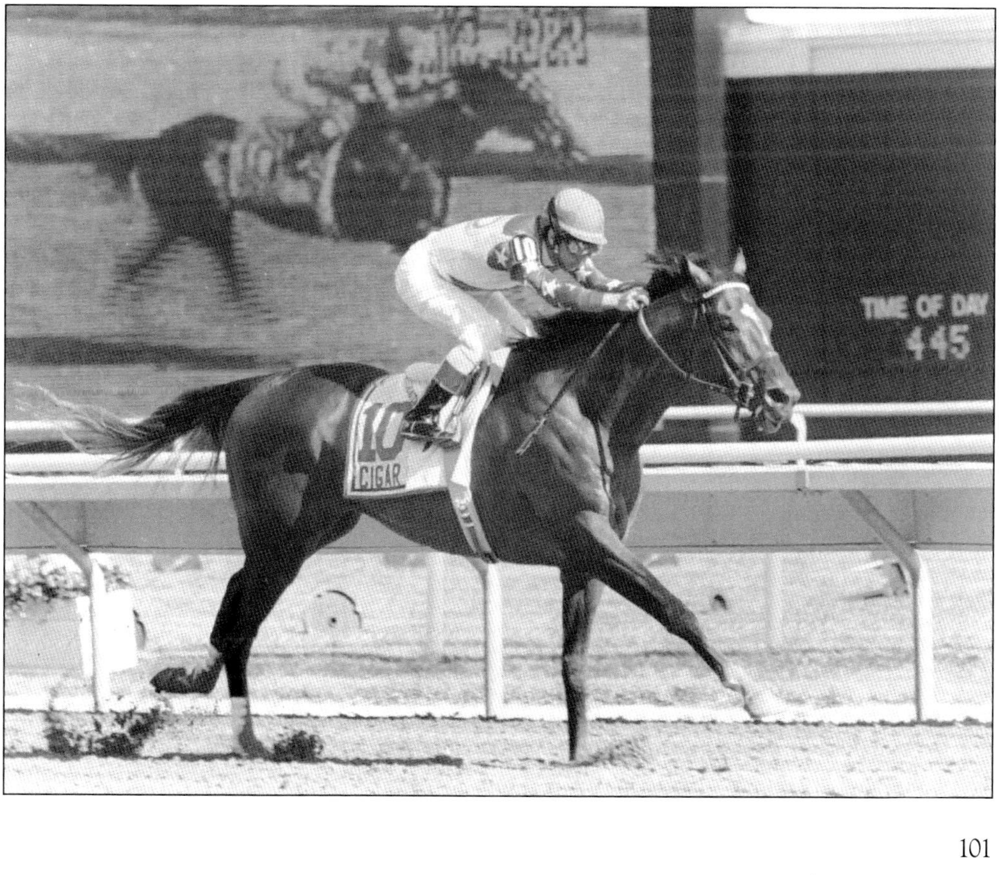

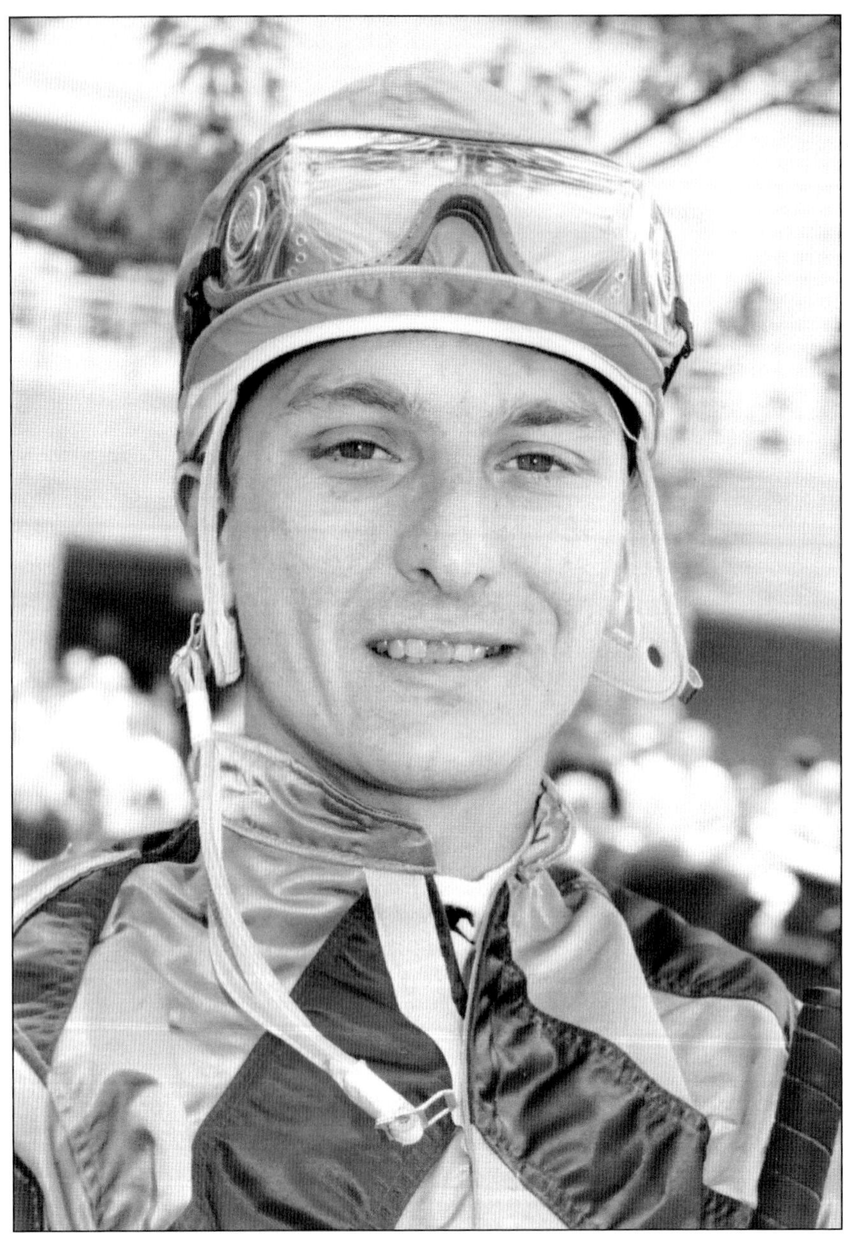

Curt Bourque was a multiple graded stakes–winning jockey who started riding in 1984 at Evangeline Downs before venturing to Chicago. Born August 22, 1967, in Erath, Louisiana, Bourque garnered riding titles at Fair Grounds, Hawthorne, and Sportsmans. He began riding in Chicago in 1992 and, though he never won an Arlington title, was always in the top 10 of the jockey standings and scored triumphs in numerous Arlington Stakes. Bourque won the 1992 Equipoise Mile with Katahaula County; the Grade III $125,000 Washington Futurity, a seven-furlong test over the Polytrack synthetic dirt track, with Polar Expedition for trainer Hugh Robertson in 1:39.28 and again in 1997 with Announce. He also won the 1993 Stars & Stripes Stakes with Little Bro Lantis, and the 1993 Breeders Futurity (Gr. II) with Polar Expedition, among others. When he retired in 2010, Bourque had ridden 3,536 winners, 2,957 seconds, and 2,771 thirds from 24,079 starters who had earned $46,713,861. (Courtesy of Midwest Outdoors.)

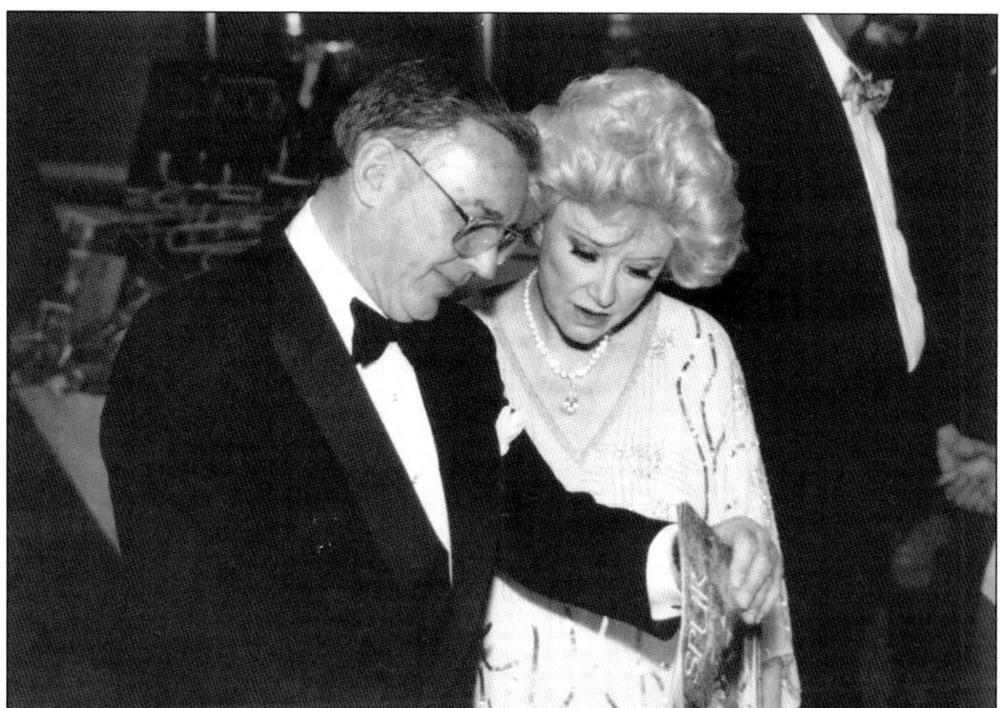

Richard Duchossois and Phyllis Diller were close friends, having met in 1955 at the Purple Onion nightclub in San Francisco. It was Diller who was with Duchossois, in fact, when he learned that Arlington was on fire in 1985. The two kept tabs on each other's family and children, with Diller sending the Duchossois family a small painting depicting children or animals, each Christmas. (Courtesy of Midwest Outdoors.)

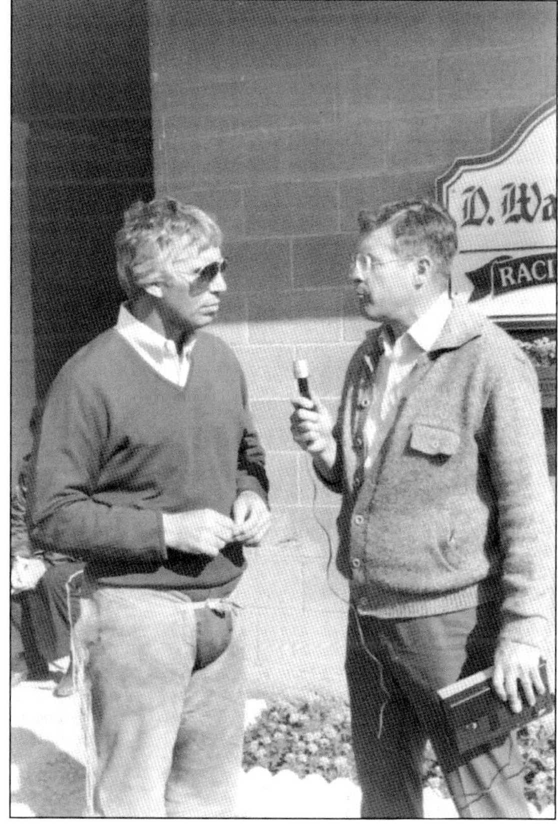

Illinois Thoroughbred Breeders & Owners Foundation (ITBOF) former executive director Dave Hooper (right) talks with D. Wayne Lukas (left) on the Arlington back side. Lukas, the first trainer to earn more than $100 million in purses, has been the sport's leading money-winning trainer 14 times. Born on September 2, 1935, in Antigo, Wisconsin, Lukas has 14 Triple Crown wins, 20 Breeders' Cup victories, and five Eclipse Awards, with his horses earning 25 year-end honors. (Courtesy of Midwest Outdoors.)

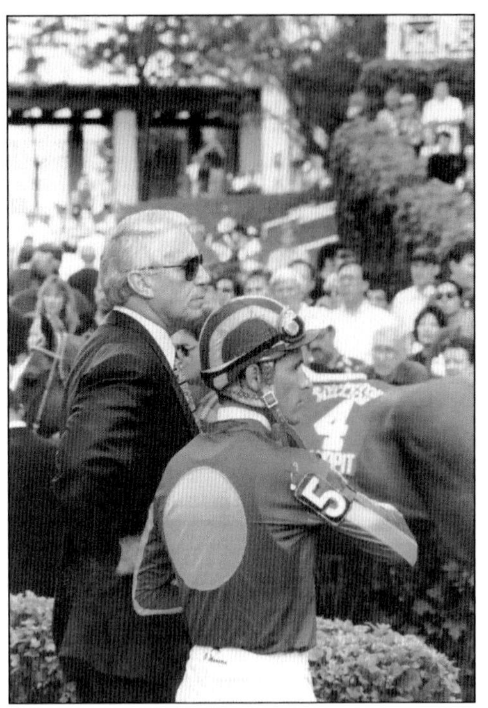

D. Wayne Lukas and jockey Gary Stevens share a moment prior to the 1997 Arlington Million. Stevens, born March 6, 1963, in Caldwell, Idaho, is one of the most successful jockeys of all time, with more than 5,100 victories to his credit. Stevens has retired twice and come back to riding twice, continuing in 2017. He has appeared in movies and as a TV racing analyst, among his other endeavors. (Courtesy of Midwest Outdoors.)

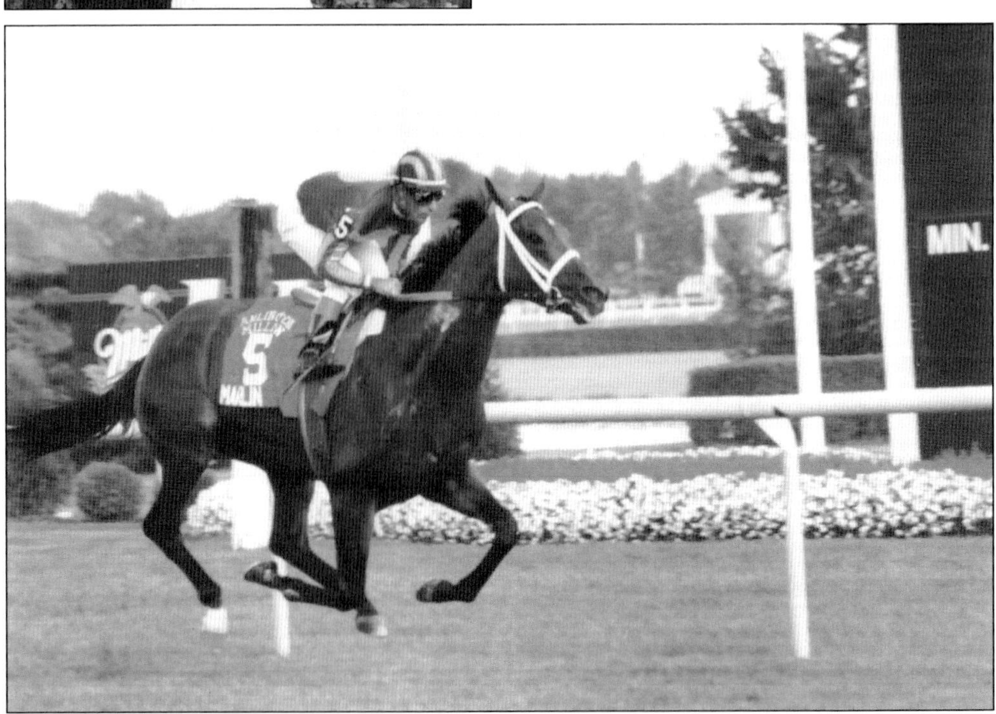

Marlin united with rider Gary Stevens, trainer D. Wayne Lukas, and owner Michael Tabor to capture the 1997 Arlington Million in 2:02.54 in a wire-to-wire effort. The Irish-bred Marlin earned $2,448,880, winning 9 of 26 starts, with 3 seconds and 5 thirds, and racing from 1995 through 1997. A $30,000 yearling, Marlin had also won the 1996 Secretariat stakes (Gr. I) in 1996. (Courtesy of Midwest Outdoors.)

On July 16, 1987, Hall of Fame trainer Jack Van Berg (shown here with champion Alysheba) became the first trainer in Thoroughbred history to win 5,000 races when he saddled Art's Chandelle to victory at Arlington. Pat Day was aboard the four-year-old gelding, who was in for a $10,000 claiming tag for the then 51-year-old conditioner. (Courtesy of Midwest Outdoors)

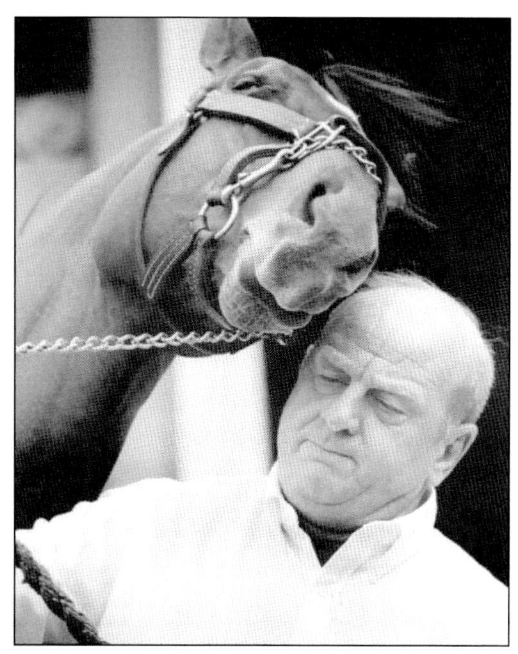

South Wilmington, Illinois, native Joe Bollero worked at Arlington for 67 years as a jockey and exercise rider before training Zenobia Empress, Buffalo Lark, Hurry Up Blue, and Big Steve. Bollero won Arlington training titles in 1979 and 1982 and trained 1,344 winners from 7,010 starts for $14,251,047. He died in 1991 at age 80. (Courtesy of Midwest Outdoors.)

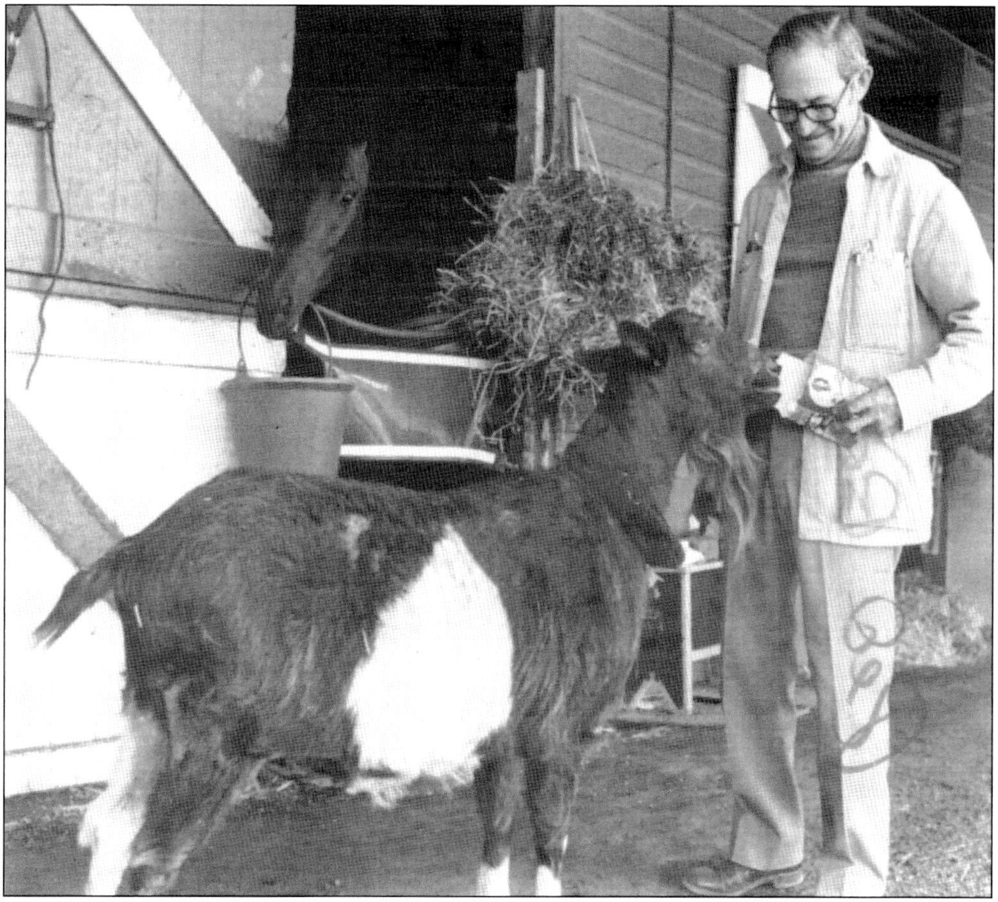

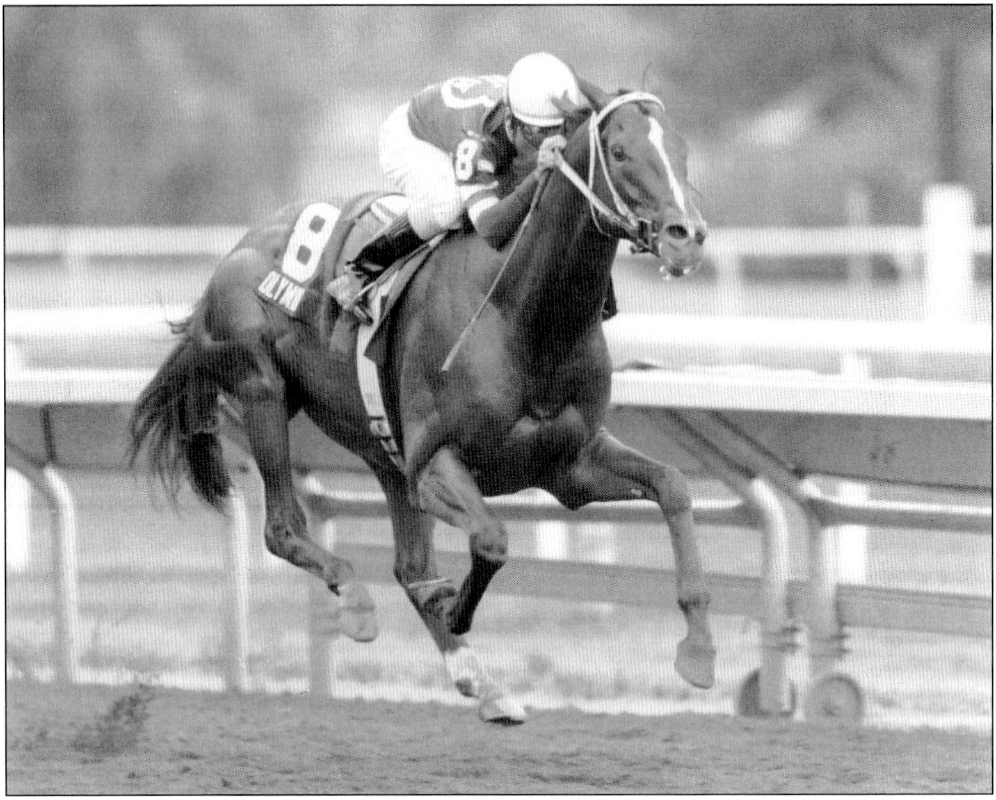

Olympio was a 1988 Kentucky-bred son of Naskra and was trained by Ron MacAnally for breeder Verne Winchell. Racing from 1990 to 1992, Olympio captured the American Derby (Gr. II) on August 3, 1991, and was second in the Secretariat Stakes (Gr. I) at Arlington one month later. A winner of $1,456,315, Olympio won 9 of 17 starts with 4 second-place finishes as well. (Courtesy of Midwest Outdoors.)

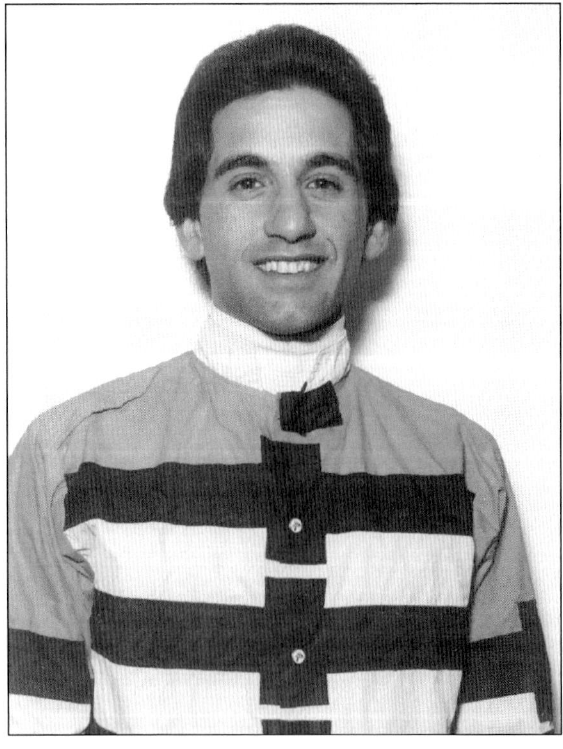

Vince Amato was a multiple-stakes-winning, Chicago-based jockey who raced from 1976 through 1995. From 2,111 mounts, he scored 206 wins, 215 seconds, and 234 thirds for $1,179,747 in career earnings. Amato, after retirement, became the clerk of scales for Arlington and other Chicago tracks. (Courtesy of Midwest Outdoors.)

Mark Guidry, born August 6, 1959, in Lafayette, Louisiana, was Chicago's dominant jockey for 10 years, winning 1992 and 2000 Arlington titles. He won the Arlington Handicap (1996, 1997); Arlington-Washington Futurity (1996, 2002, 2005, 2006); Washington Park Handicap (1996, 2005); Arlington Classic (2001, 2015), and Modesty Stakes (2001), and retired with 5,022 career triumphs. (Courtesy of Midwest Outdoors.)

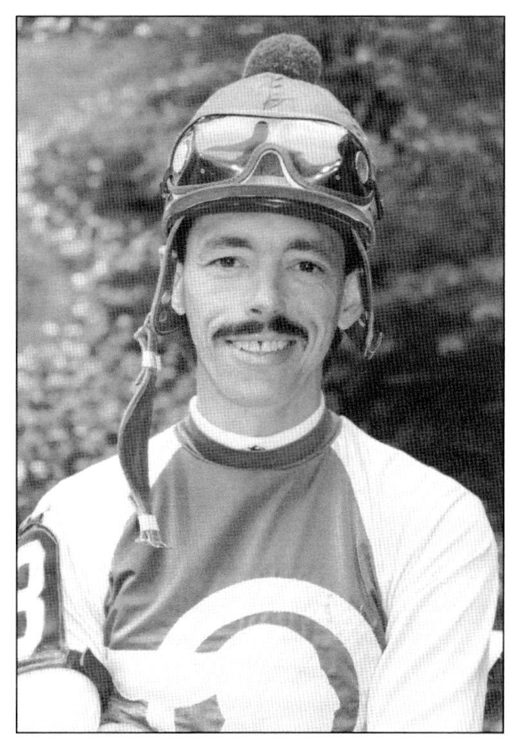

Filago was a 1987 foaled son of Foolish Pleasure, out of the French mare Derly, by Lyphard. Trained by Bobby Frankel for Edmund Gunn, this winner of $911,645 scored 6 wins in 18 starts, racing from 1989 through 1991. On August 11, 1991, Filago captured the Arlington Handicap (Gr. II), after spending his first two years racing in France and England. (Courtesy of Midwest Outdoors.)

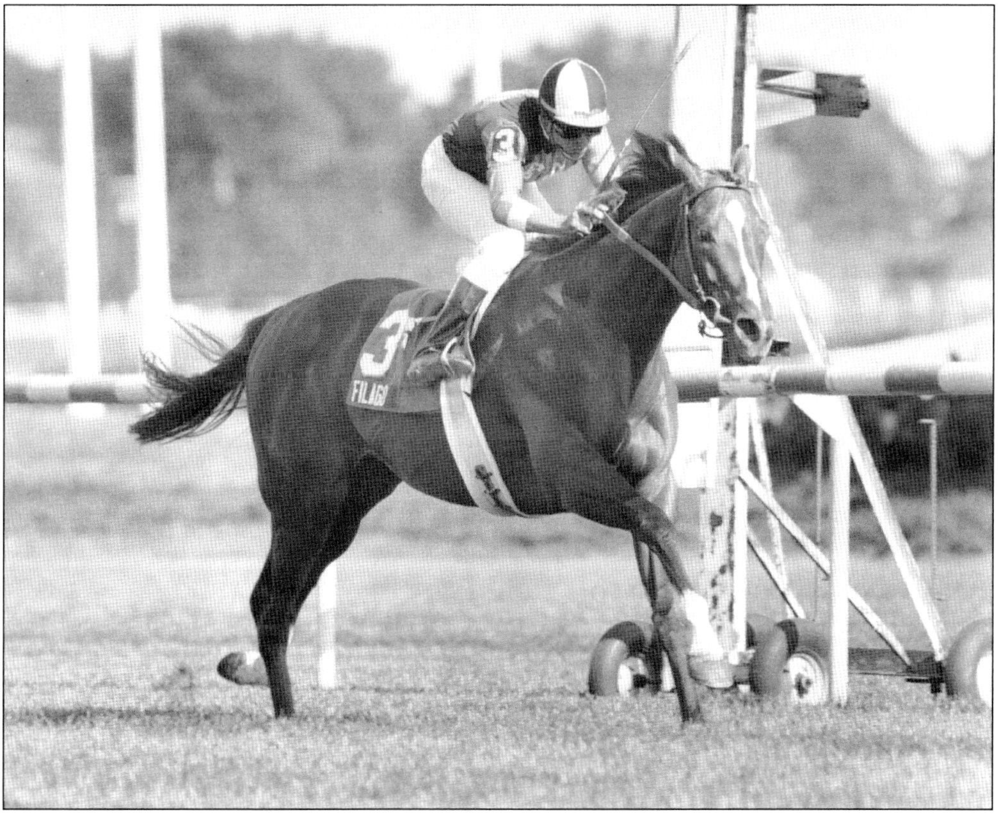

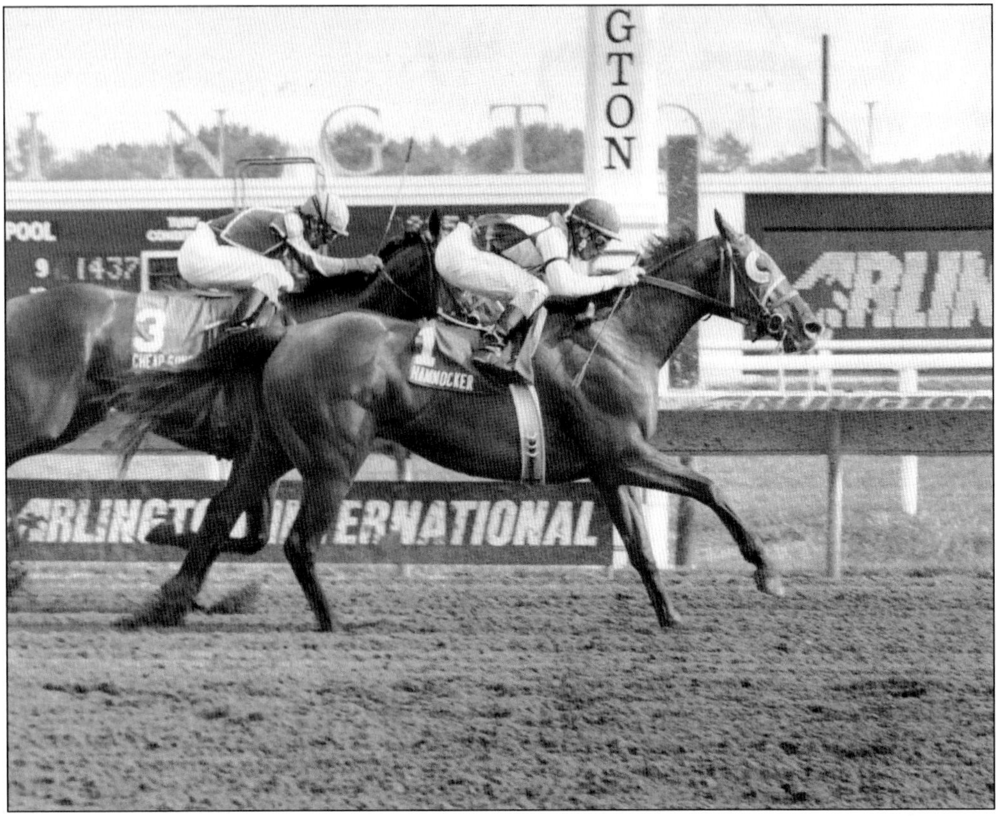

Hammocker was an Illinois-bred son of Bushido, foaled March 25, 1984, who earned $435,293 from 18 wins in 61 starts for breeders, owners, and trainers Harvey and Nancy Vanier. The grey gelding won numerous allowance and handicap events racing on the Chicago circuit and also captured the 1990 Arlington Sprint Championship Handicap and the 1991 Explosive Darling Handicap at Arlington. (Courtesy of Midwest Outdoors.)

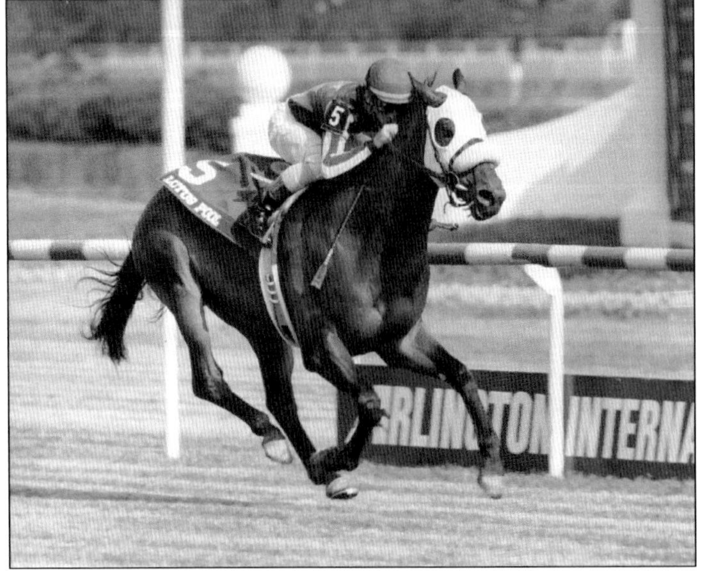

Lotus Pool was a Virginia-bred, 1987 son of Spectacular Bid and was trained by Burt Kessinger Jr. for the New Phoenix Stable. He captured the Sea O' Erin Handicap (Gr. III) at Arlington on May 30, 1992—among his many achievements—and retired with $694,543 in earnings from 11 wins, 7 seconds, and 3 third-place finishes from 43 starts. (Courtesy of Midwest Outdoors.)

John "Jumbo" Gural visits with Joseph Gjondla Jr., Arlington Park's jockey silk's attendant. The multiple-stakes-winning trainer was known for his storytelling around the racetrack, and was nicknamed "Jumbo" for his elephant-like memory and ability to recall horses and colorful racetrack characters from the past. Gural passed away on September 14, 1997, after training 212 winners to $2,576,149 in career earnings. (Courtesy of Midwest Outdoors.)

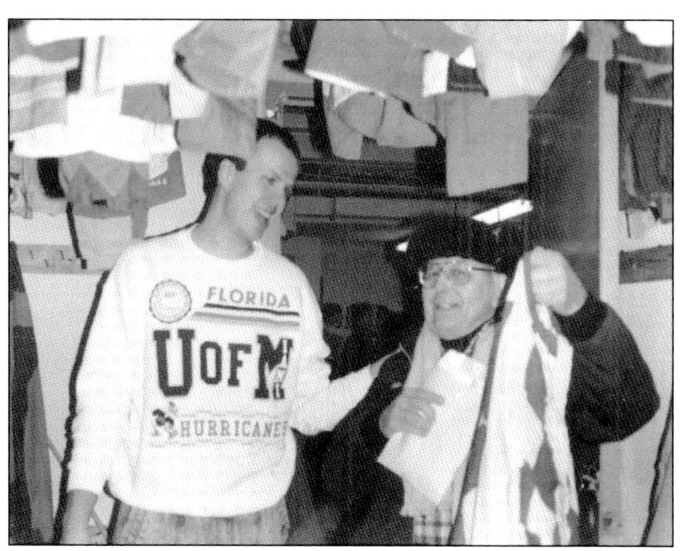

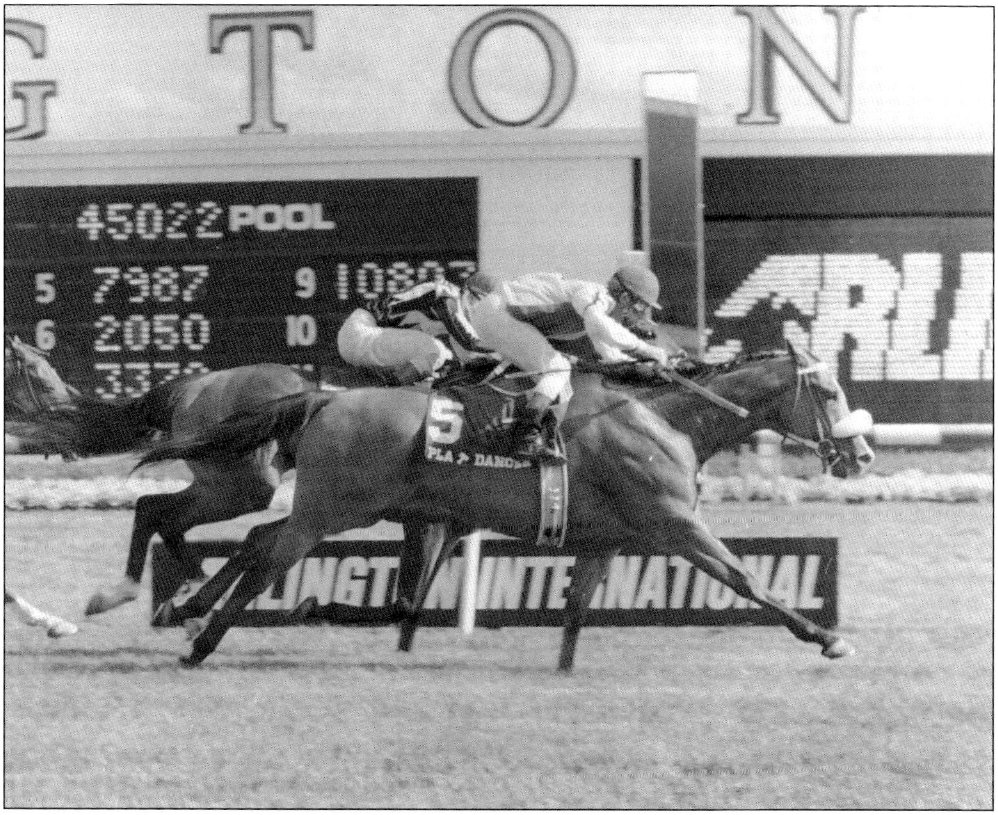

Plate Dancer was an Ontario-bred, 1985 son of Bucksplasher and was owned by Irish Acres Farm and trained by Noel Hickey. Plate Dancer earned $618,106 from 16 wins in 69 career starts. He won three 1991 Arlington stakes—the Mister Gus Stakes, the General Casimir Pulaski Invitational Handicap, and Oil Capitol Stakes—and the 1992 Stars and Stripes Handicap (Gr. III). (Courtesy of Midwest Outdoors.)

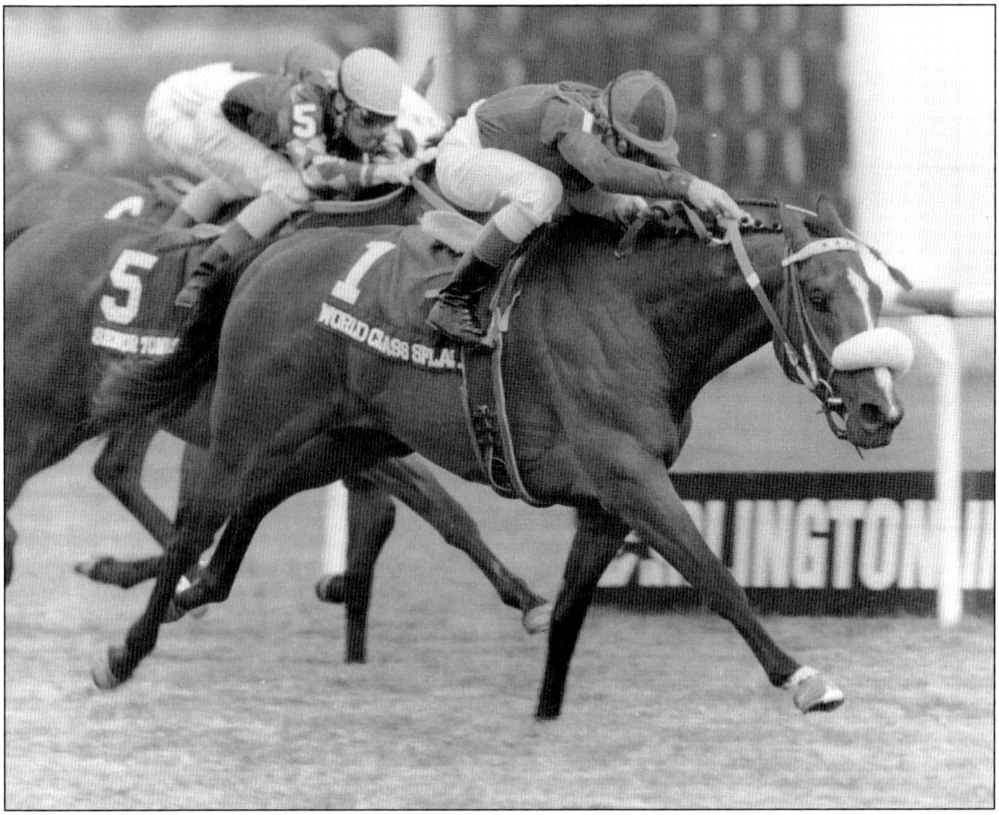

World Class Splash was a 1989 Illinois-bred son of Bucksplasher trained by Jere R. Smith for Richard Trebat, and won the 1992 Round Table Stakes (Gr. III). Inaugurated in 1961, the Round Table was named for the 1958 Horse of the Year and was last contested at Arlington in 2007, when it was won by the Todd Pletcher–trained Pavarotti in a track record 1:49.75. (Courtesy of Midwest Outdoors.)

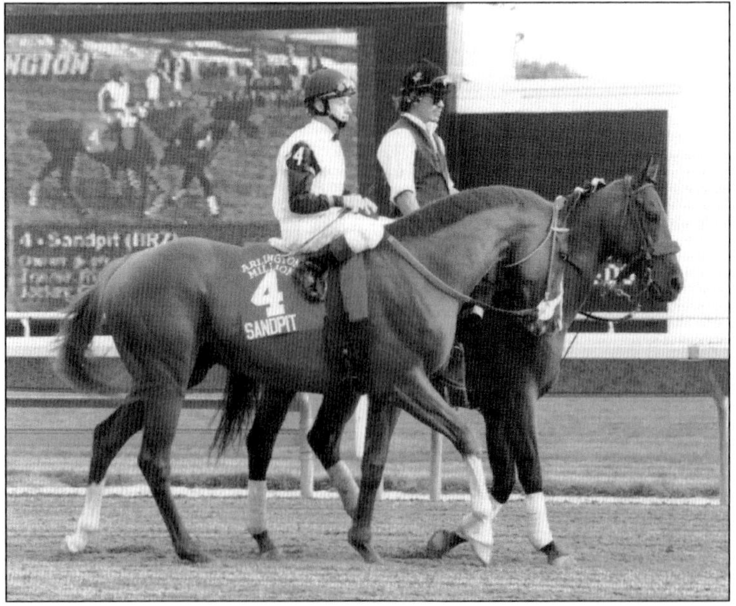

Sandpit began his career in Brazil in 1991 and raced through 1997. The 1989 foal was owned by Sierra Thoroughbreds and trained by Richard Mandella. He was second in the 1995 Arlington Million to Award; third in the 1996 Million to Mecke; and second in the 1997 Million to Marlin. Sandpit retired with 14 wins from 40 starts and $3,812,597 in earnings. (Courtesy of Midwest Outdoors.)

Six

In the Spotlight 2000–2006

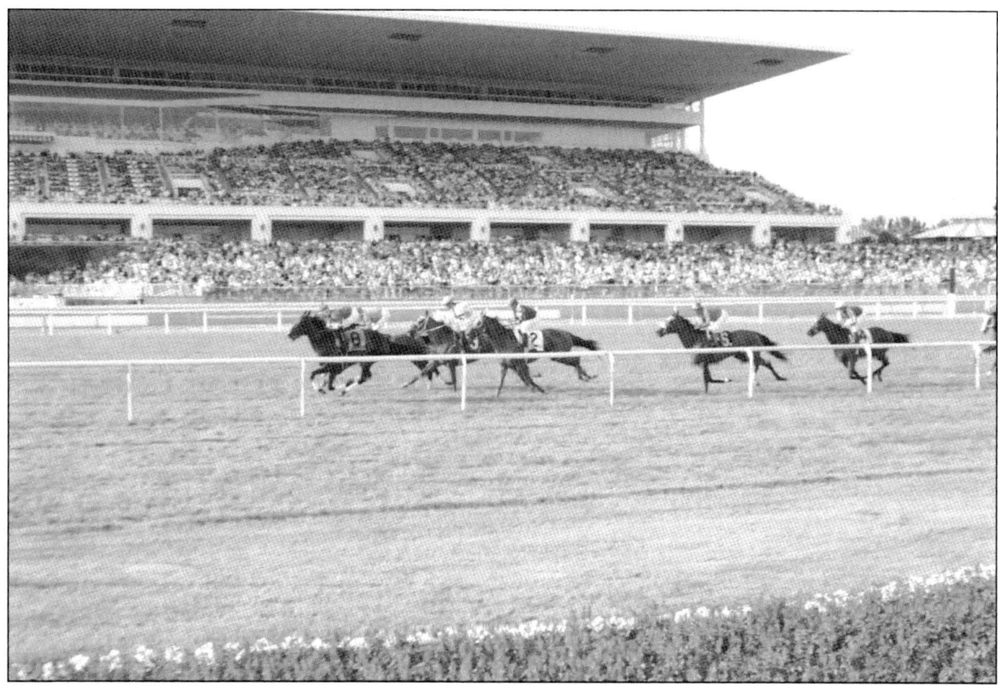

In 1998 and 1999, Arlington ceased operating when owner Richard Duchossois became frustrated with the Illinois legislature's refusal to pass a pro-slot bill that would allow the track to be on an even playing field with the Prairie State's riverboat industry. The boats offered stiff competition to Illinois tracks for wagering dollars. (Courtesy of Midwest Outdoors.)

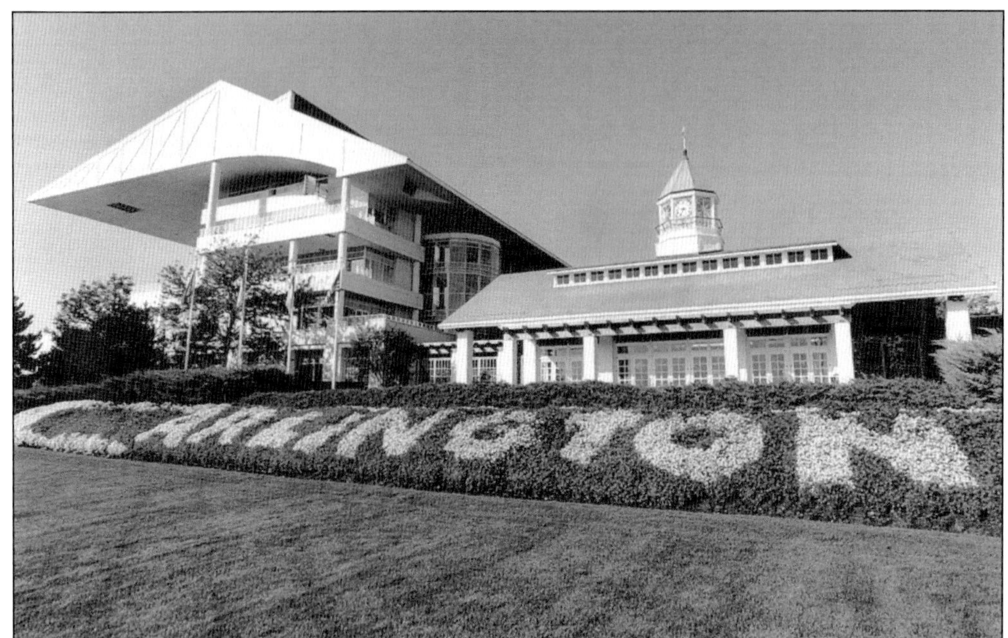

In 2000, Arlington International merged with Churchill Downs, Inc., and was renamed Arlington Park. Churchill had purchased or merged with four other tracks during the late 1990s and 2000s to thwart declines in wagering and attendance that had affected many of the sport's top venues. The 2000 Arlington meet ran from May 14 through September 30. (Courtesy of Midwest Outdoors.)

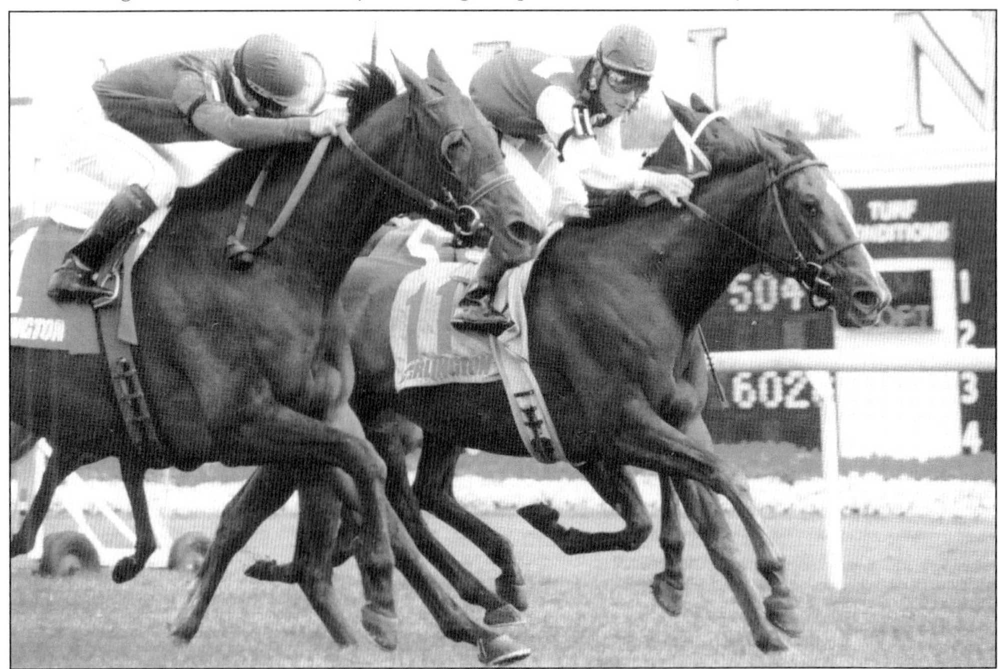

Wade for Me, a 1995 daughter by Western Playboy, was a chestnut mare trained, owned, and bred by Harvey and Nancy Vanier. Racing from 1997 to 2000, Wade for Me had 11 wins from 31 starts, earning $429,080. This graded stakes winner is shown here capturing the Modest Stakes (Gr. III) at Arlington in 2000 with jockey Jose Valdivia in the irons. (Courtesy of Midwest Outdoors.)

Jockey Jose Valdivia is a multiple graded stakes–winning jockey with more than $70 million in earnings. Born December 8, 1974, in Lima, Peru, Valdivia began riding in 1994 and has not stopped. He won the 2011 Belmont Stakes with Ruler on Ice and 2016 and 2017 Arlington jockey titles. Valdivia won the $700,000 Beverly D. (Gr. I) with Heat Haze on August 16, 2003. (Courtesy of Midwest Outdoors.)

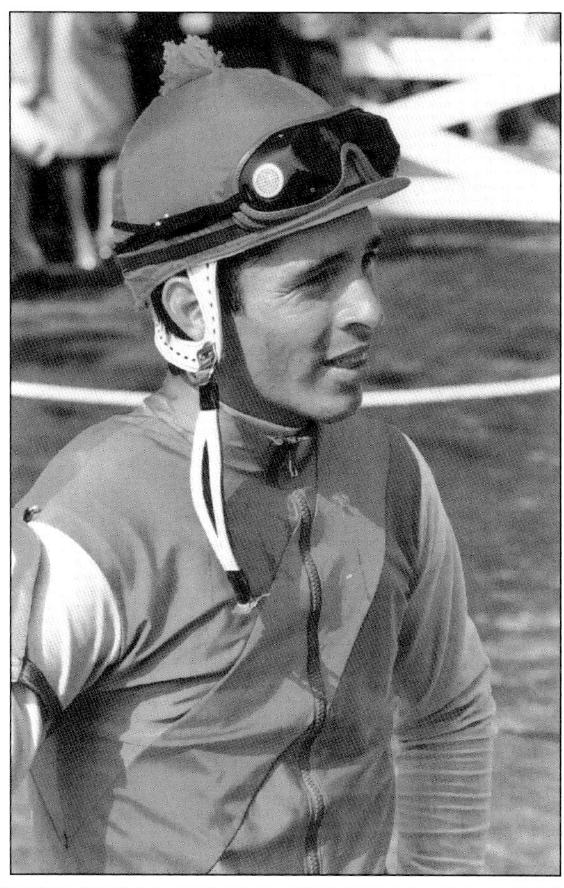

Kicken Kris, a 2000-foaled Kentucky-bred son by Kris S, was sold as a yearling for $400,000 to Brushwood Stable. This multiple graded stakes winner was trained by Michael Matz and ridden regularly by Javier Castellano. From 19 starts, he had 6 wins and $1,326,600 in career earnings. Kicken Kris won the 2003 Secretariat Stakes (Gr. I) and the 2004 Arlington Million (Gr. I). (Courtesy of Midwest Outdoors.)

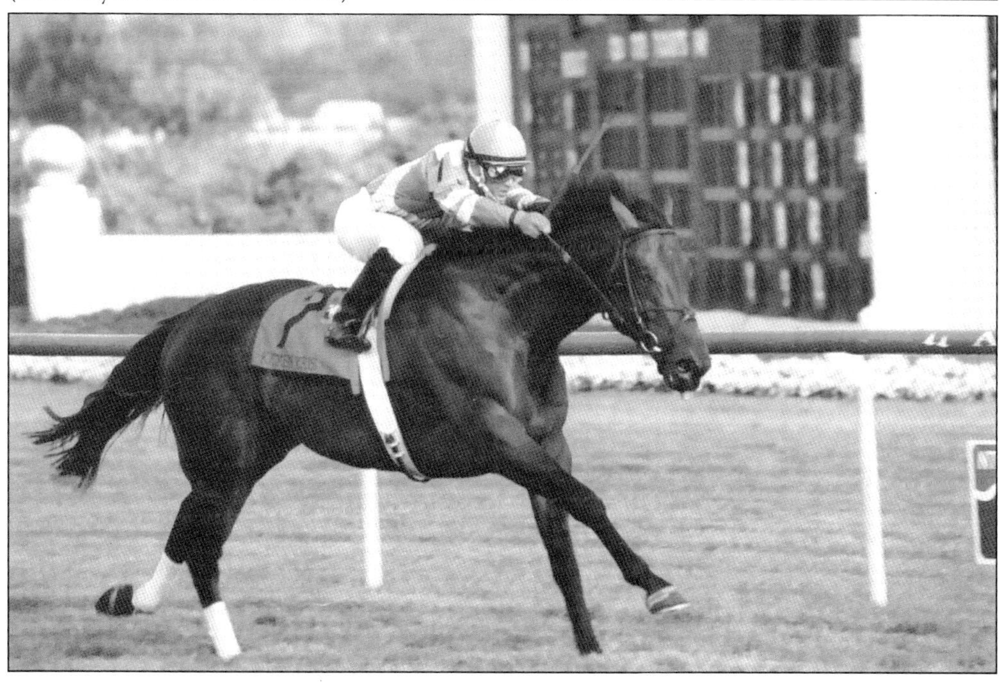

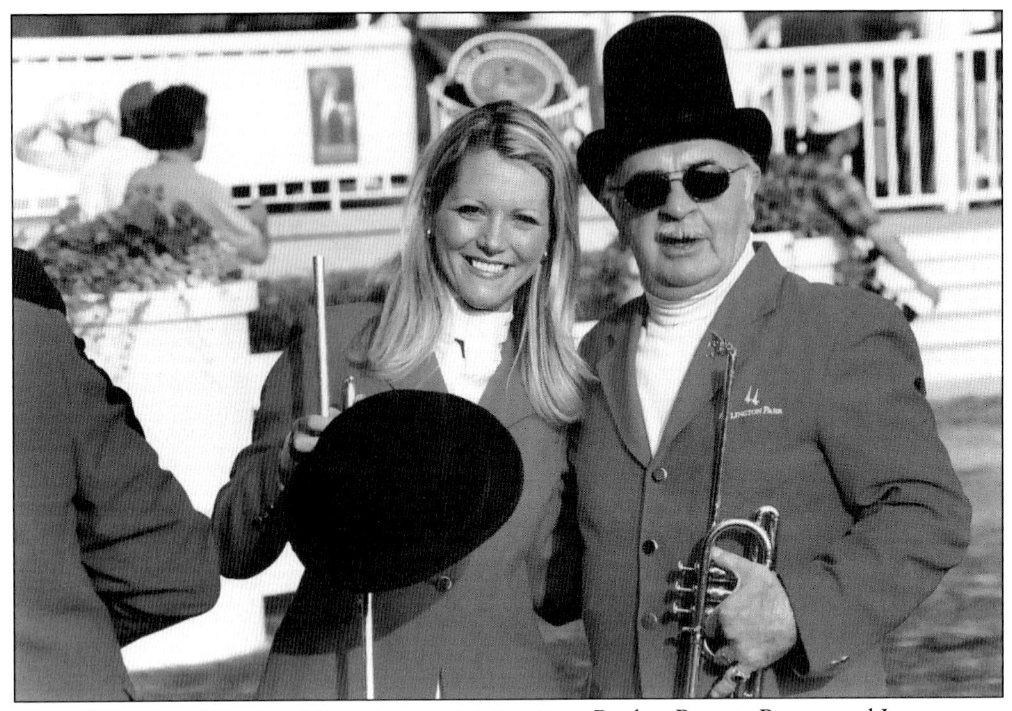

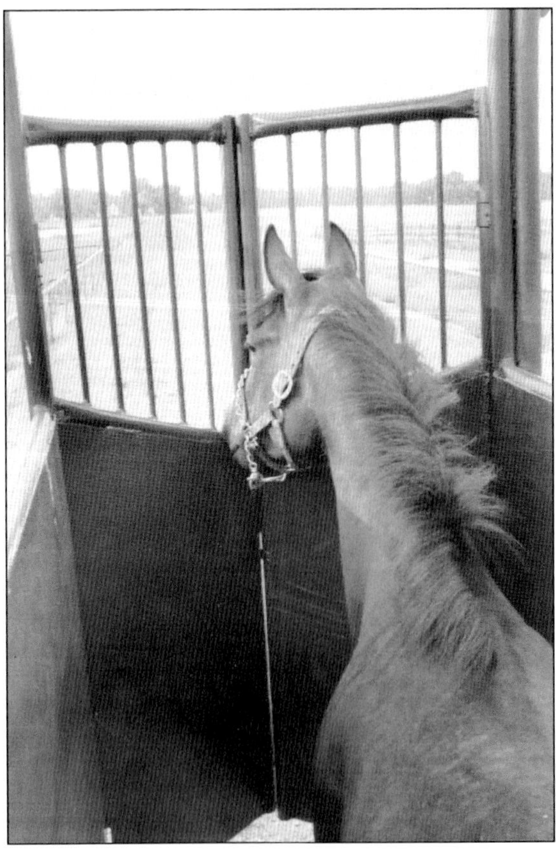

Buglers Bonnie Brown and Joe Kelley prepare to sound the call to the post for the 2002 Breeders' Cup races at Arlington—the first and only time they were contested in Chicago. Wagering on the cup program set a Breeders' Cup record of $115,523,156, eclipsing the old record of $108,603,040 from Churchill Downs in 2000. The Arlington on-track crowd of 46,118 wagered $13,568,233. (Courtesy of Midwest Outdoors.)

A Thoroughbred youngster peers out the starting for the first time on Arlington's training track. Many trainers introduce their young colts and fillies to a starting gate as yearlings, to acclimatize the neophyte racehorses to their futures. If training is begun early, most horses will learn to readily move into the close confines of the starting gate without issue. (Courtesy of Midwest Outdoors.)

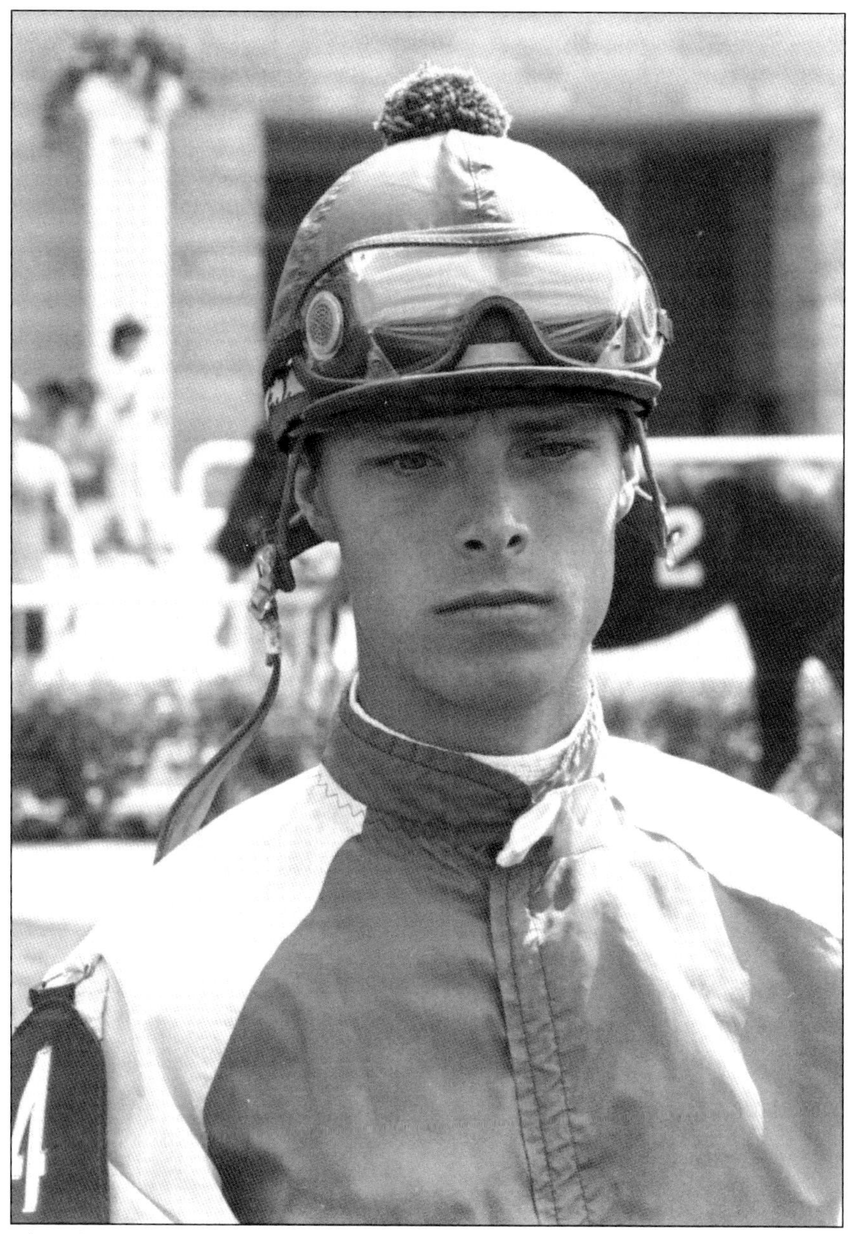

Jockey Edward Thomas "E.T." Baird, grew up in Rolling Meadows, Illinois, near Arlington Park, and followed in the footsteps of his father, jockey Robert L. "Bobby" Baird. E.T. began riding in 1985, with 3 winners from 34 starts and $14,928 in earnings. One year later, he scored 171 wins from 1,054 starts, earning $2,130,764. He won numerous stakes at Arlington and scored seven $2 million seasons and 27 different $1 million seasons, with 2009 as his best year, when he piloted 114 winners to $3,138,606. Among his top horses were Recapturetheglory ($402,462), an Illinois Derby winner, and Just As Well ($355,349), with whom Baird won the Arlington Park Handicap. Baird won the Arlington Park Sprint Handicap three years in a row (2012, 2013, 2014) for the Michele Boyce–trained Saint Leon, and won that same five-and-a-half-furlong test in 2009 with Yankee Injunuity. Baird retired in 2016 with 2,399 wins, 2,136 seconds, and 2,148 thirds from 18,401 starts and $48,454,755. (Courtesy of Midwest Outdoors.)

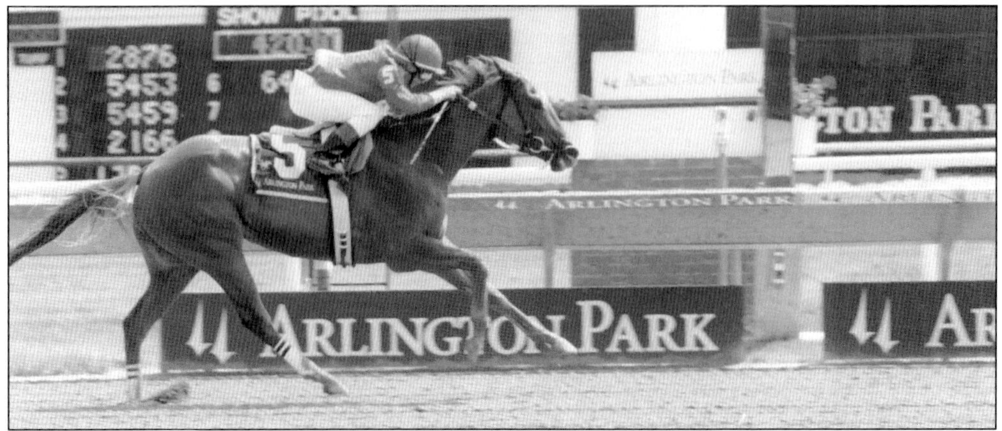

Coach Jimi Lee, a 2000-foaled son of Roar–Princess Lili, by My Gallant, holds the Illinois record for six furlongs, set December 12, 2003, at Hawthorne in 1:07.27. Trained and co-owned by Jimmy Divito and Lee Battaglia, the gelding scored 18 wins and $1,007,693, winning the 2003 Shecky Greene Handicap and Forward Pass Stakes at Arlington. (Courtesy of James Divito.)

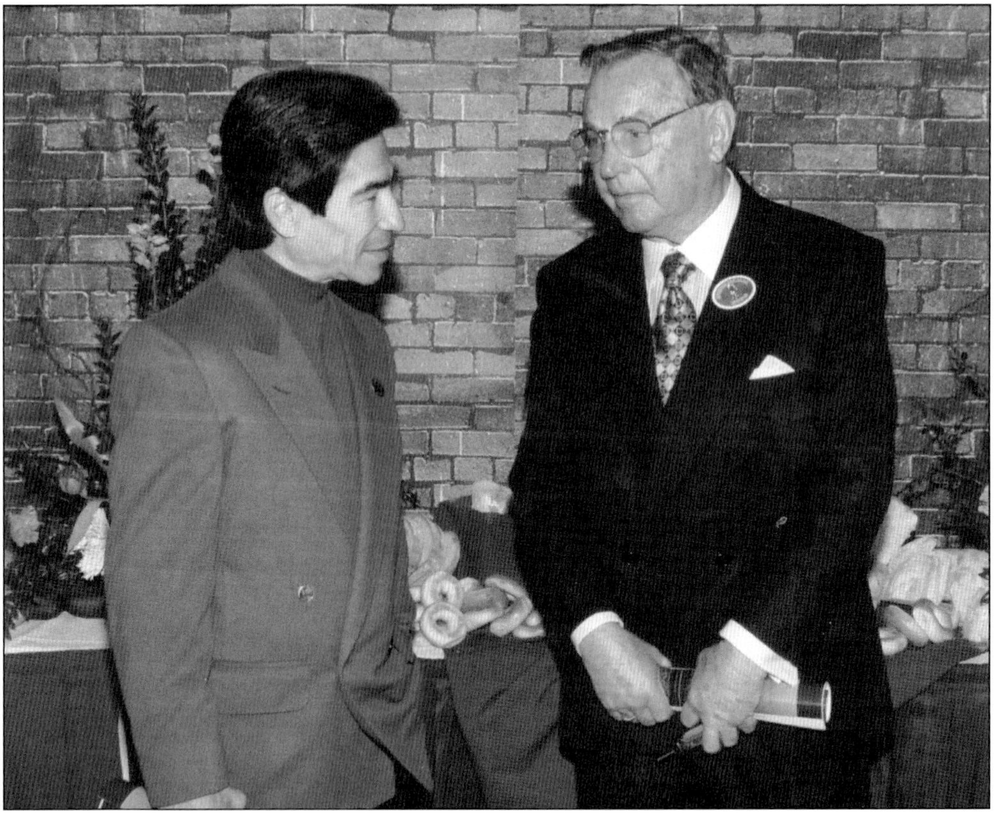

Arlington owner Richard Duchossois, shown here with Laffit Pincay Jr., received his third Eclipse Award in 2004. The Eclipse Award of Merit was presented by representatives from the *Daily Racing Form*, National Turf Writers & Broadcasters, and National Thoroughbred Racing Association. Duchossois had previously received the Jockey Club's Gold Medal (1986); Canada's Special Sovereign Award (1988); and Britain's Lord Derby Award (1988). (Courtesy of Midwest Outdoors.)

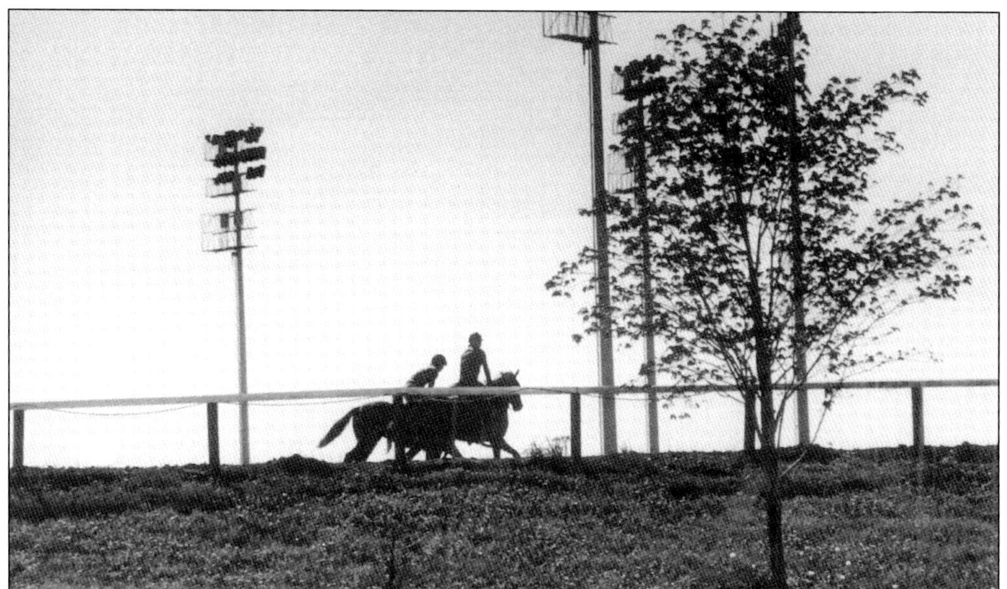

In 2004, Arlington Park began the process of building two new dormitories for the racetrack's backstretch workers, at a cost of $4 million, which included 96 new housing facilities. The racetrack is home to some 2,000 workers and their families, which include caretakers, hot-walkers, exercise riders, and blacksmiths. (Courtesy of Midwest Outdoors.)

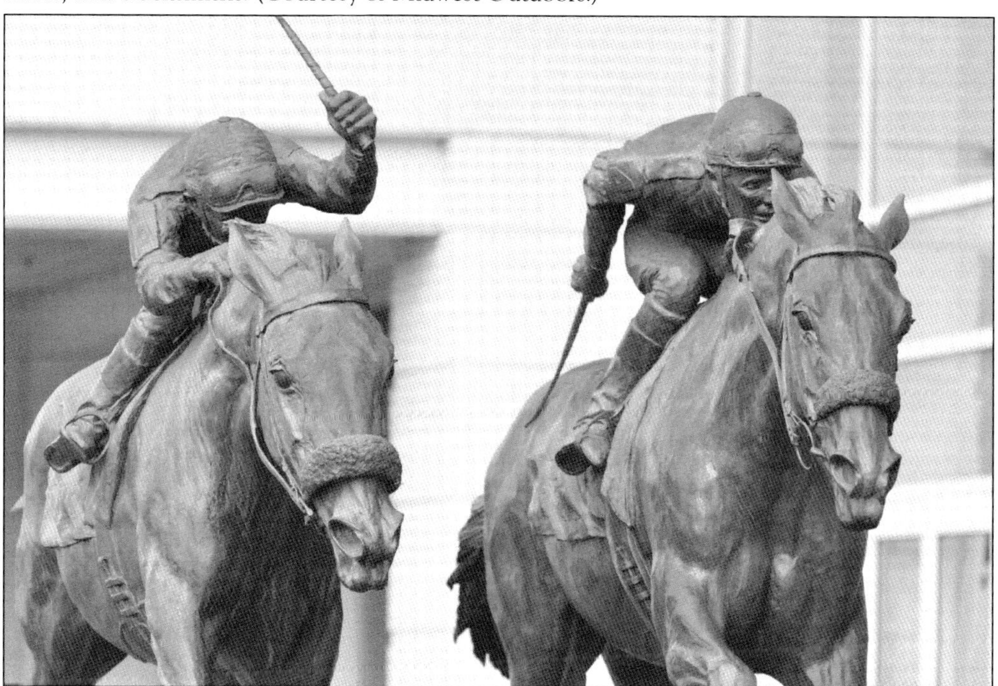

Against All Odds is a bronze statue that commemorates the 1981 Arlington Million when John Henry bested The Bart by a nose at the finish wire. It sits atop the paddock, over the tunnel leading to the racetrack. Sculptor Edwin Bogucki's statue is extraordinarily detailed, right down to the shoes worn by both horses, and was unveiled in 1989 during Arlington's reopening ceremonies. (Author's collection.)

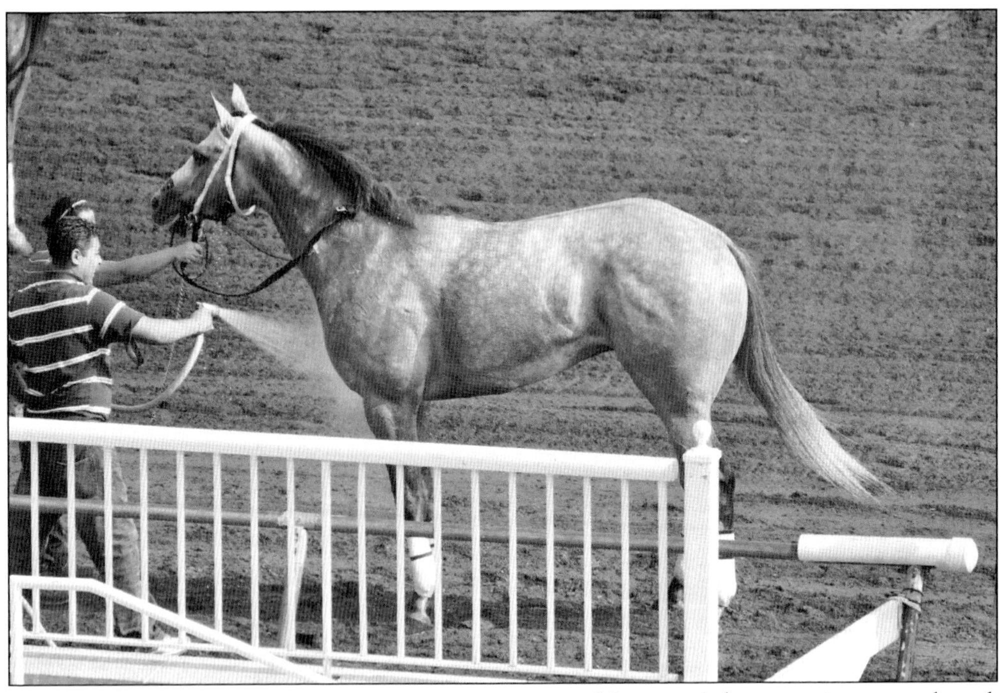

Here, an Arlington winner gets hosed down outside the winner's circle on a 96-degree afternoon. Thoroughbreds need to be well-hydrated to compete during high-heat days and a cold water spray helps to bring their temperatures down. After they walk back to their stables, they are then given a proper soap and water bath and walked until they are completely "cooled out." (Author's collection.)

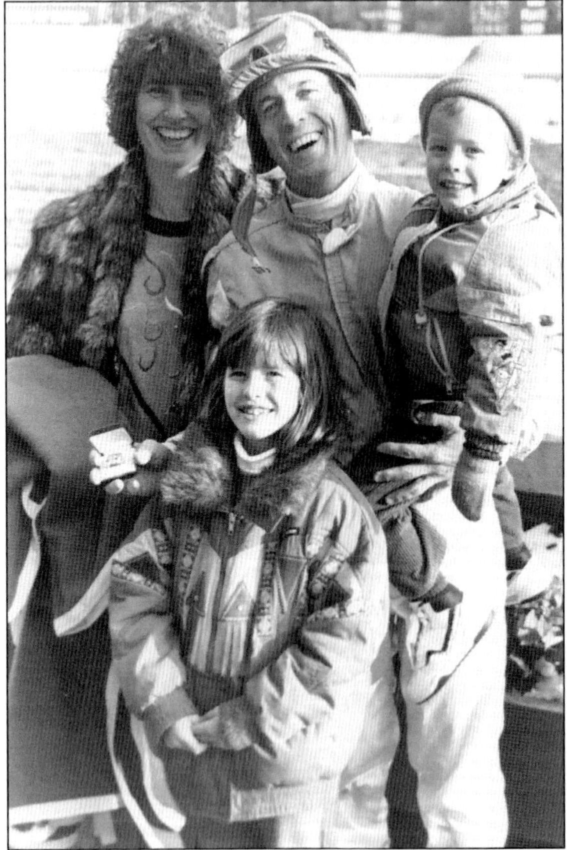

Randy Meier, shown here with his family, was a graded stakes winning jockey and top rider in Chicago. He was aboard 33,238 starters, winning 4,106 races, with 3,975 seconds and 3,856 third-place finishers who earned $58,529,925. Meier rode for four decades, winning numerous stakes at Arlington, including the $256,800 American Derby (Gr. II) with Fan Club's Mister. (Courtesy of Midwest Outdoors.)

Seven

THE NINTH DECADE 2007–2017

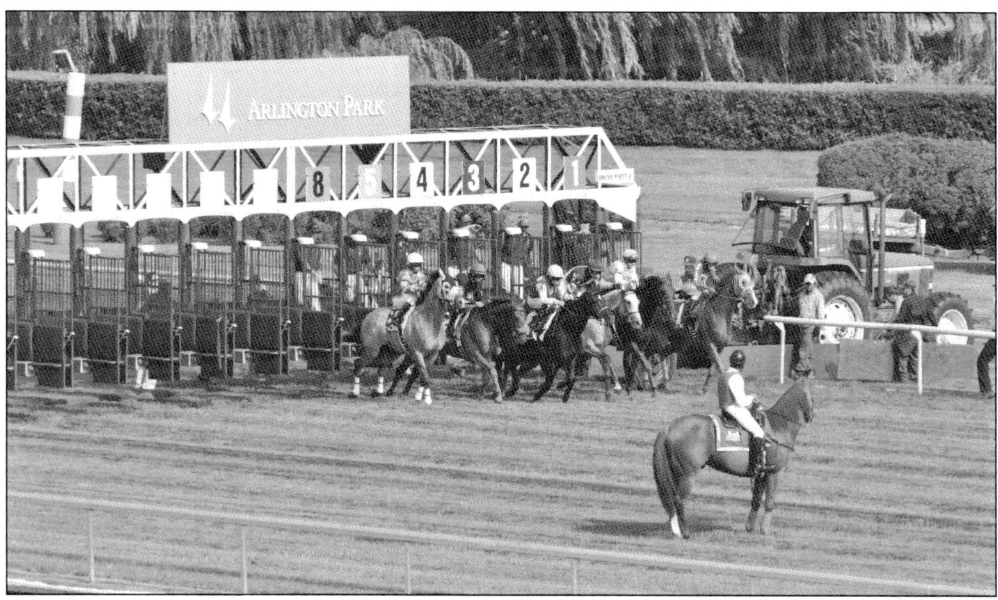

In March 2007, Arlington was resurfaced with Polytrack, costing $11 million, in preparation for the 94-day meeting. Made up of high-grade silica sand, spandex fibers, rubber, and ground-up jelly cable, Polytrack does not hold water, thus eliminating the chance of horses shying or jumping over puddles, and provides a more uniform surface than a traditional track. (Author's collection.)

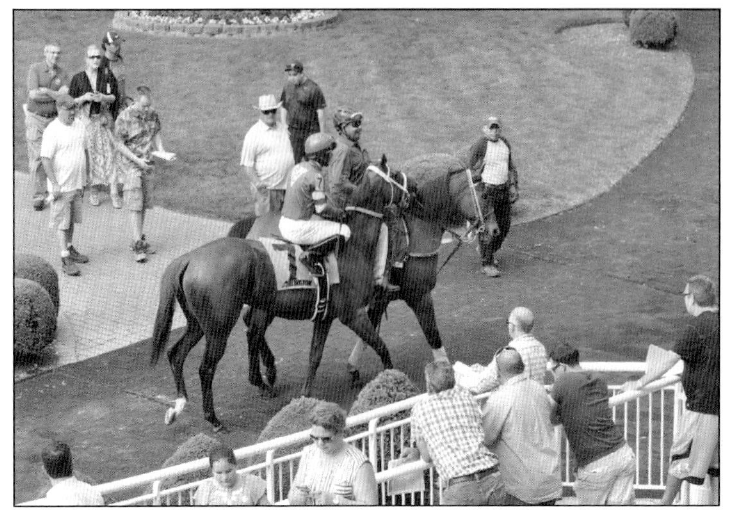

Arlington's walking ring and saddling area allows fans to watch the horses prior to racing. Forever innovative, Arlington became one of the first tracks to allow patrons to purchase and print Arlington tickets via the Internet, and was featured on the CBS series *Undercover Boss*, with the show following Churchill Downs CEO Bill Carstanjen working undercover at the track. (Author's collection.)

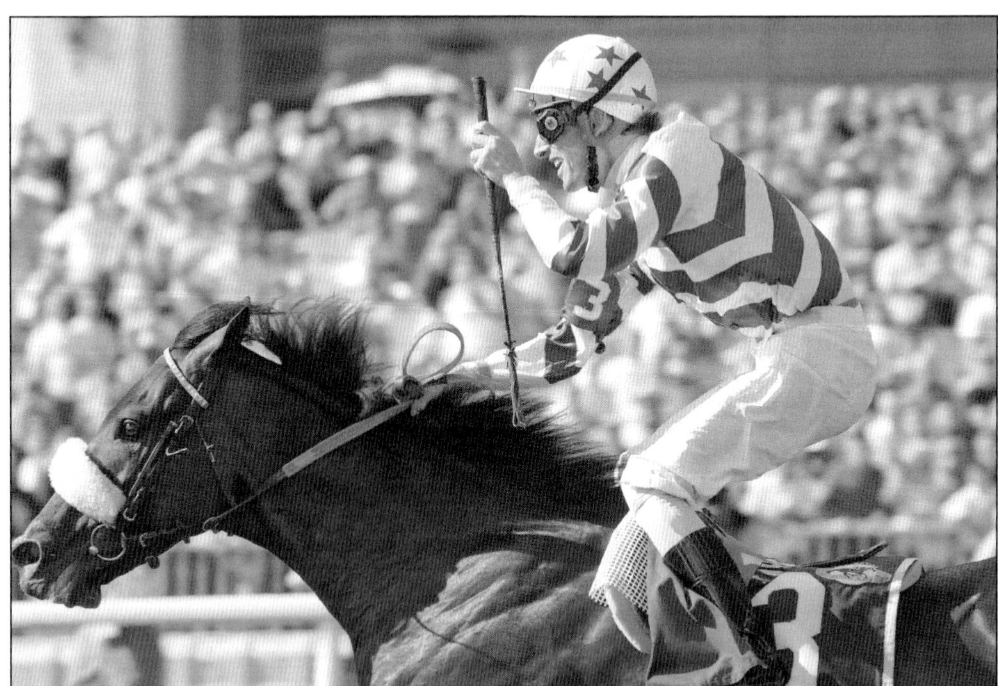

Spirit One posted a wire-to-wire triumph in the 26th running of the Arlington Million on August 9, 2008. Ridden by Ioritz Mendizabal, Spirit One finished three-quarters of a length ahead of Archipenko, with Mount Nelson third. Spirit One was a four-year-old colt owned by Kamel Chehboub and trained by Philippe Demercastel, and his Million victory boosted his career earnings to $1.1 million. (Courtesy of Midwest Outdoors.)

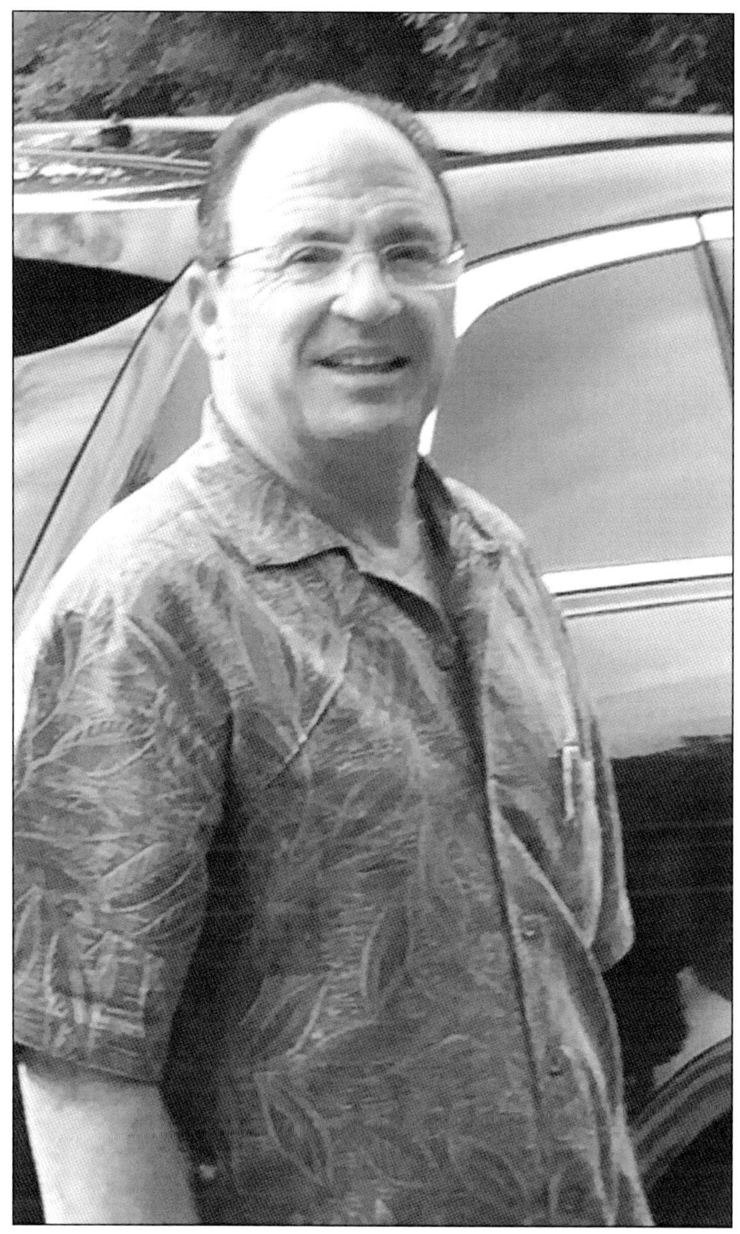

Wayne Catalano, born July 24, 1956, in New Orleans, Louisiana, is a former jockey who morphed into one of Arlington's leading trainers. Catalano has trained three Breeders' Cup winners, two Eclipse winners, and a plethora of stakes victors during his five decades in horse racing. In 1977, he was the second-leading jockey in the nation, and by 1983, after 1,792 wins, he hung up his tack, began training, and scored his first career win at Arlington with Dreamin' of You. To date, Catalano has won nine Arlington Park training titles. Some of his top horses include Little Sucker, Cuzzy Bear, Crypto Star, and Dreaming Of Anna, who won the 2006 Breeders' Cup Juvenile Fillies, and She Be Wild, with whom he won the 2008 edition—both fillies being named Two-Year-Old Filly Champions. In 2011, Catalano won his third Breeders' Cup, capturing the Juvenile Fillies Turf with Stephanie's Kitten. He has 2,742 wins from 13,463 starters and $62 million in earnings. (Courtesy of Renee Catalano.)

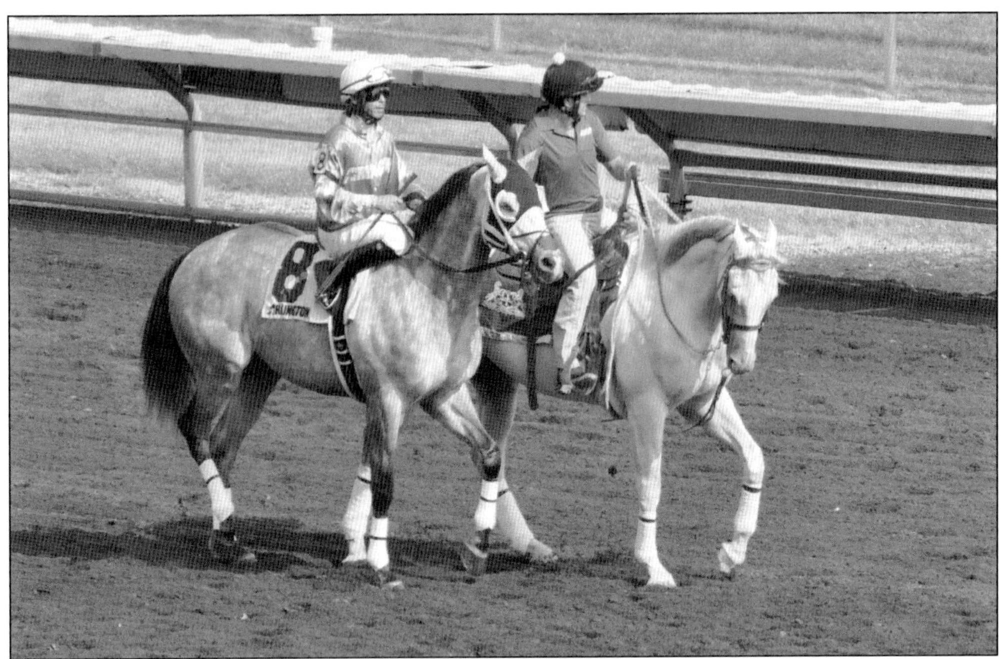

A lead pony assists a jockey and his steed in an Arlington post parade, which consists of Thoroughbreds parading in front of the grandstand, and then trotting or cantering off to the starting gate. The pony riders often have a leather strap attached to the runner's bridle for control. (Author's collection.)

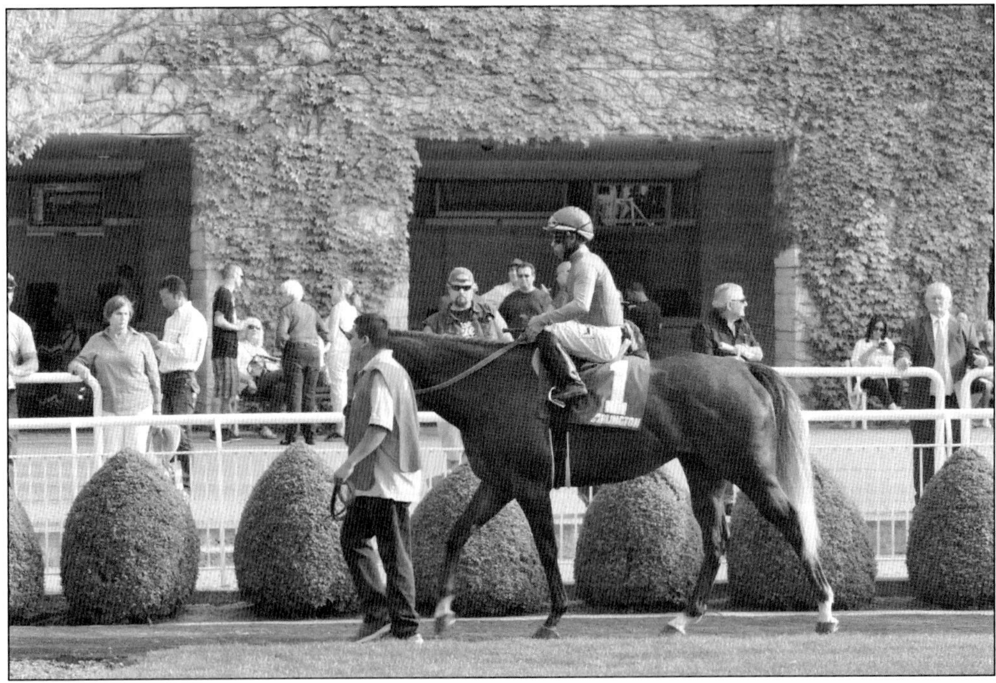

Arlington Park's tree-lined walking ring is overseen by fans above and on the ground. As the horses make their way to the tunnel, they pass underneath the life-sized statue of John Henry and The Bart battling it out in the 1981 Million. (Author's collection.)

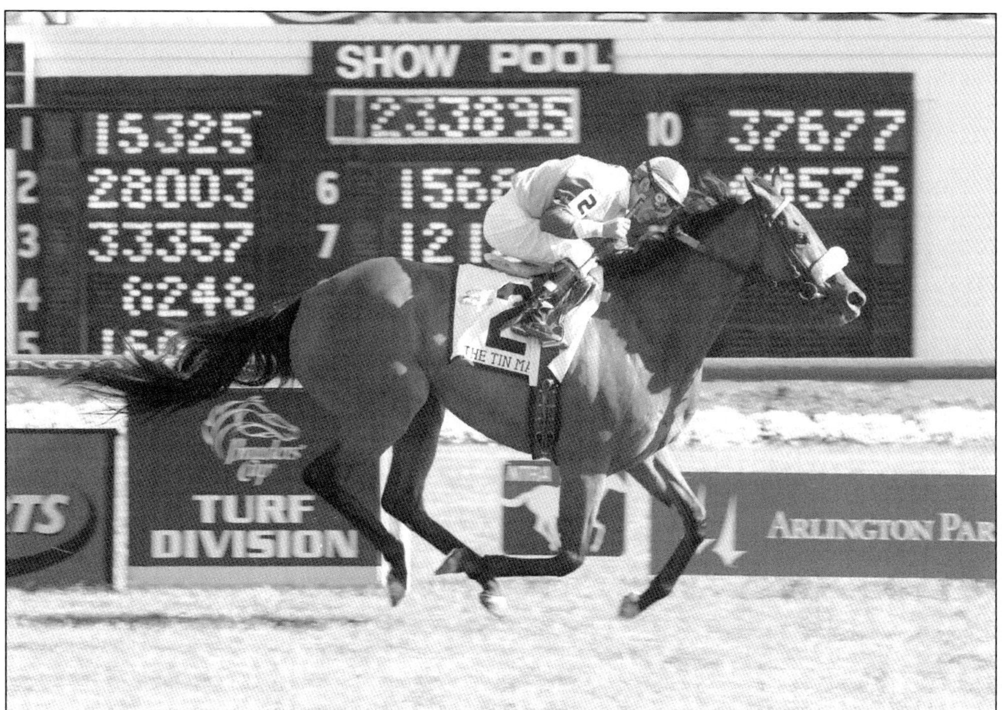

The Tin Man, an eight-year-old gelded son of Triple Crown winner Affirmed, captured the 2006 Arlington Million with Victor Espinoza in the irons for trainer Richard Mandella and owners-breeders Ralph and Aury Todd. Time for the one-and-a-quarter-mile course was 2:01.1. Cacique (Edgar Prado) was second, with Soldier Hollow (Rene Douglas) third. The victory gave The Tin Man his 11th victory in 26 starts and upped his earnings to $2.9 million. He was the second-oldest horse, behind John Henry, to win the Million, and was also one of three horses to win the Million with a wire-to-wire effort, following in the footsteps of Teleprompter (1985) and Marlin (1997). The Tin Man earned $3,663,780, winning 13 of 31 races. He passed away on April 29, 2015, at age 17. (Courtesy of Arlington Park.)

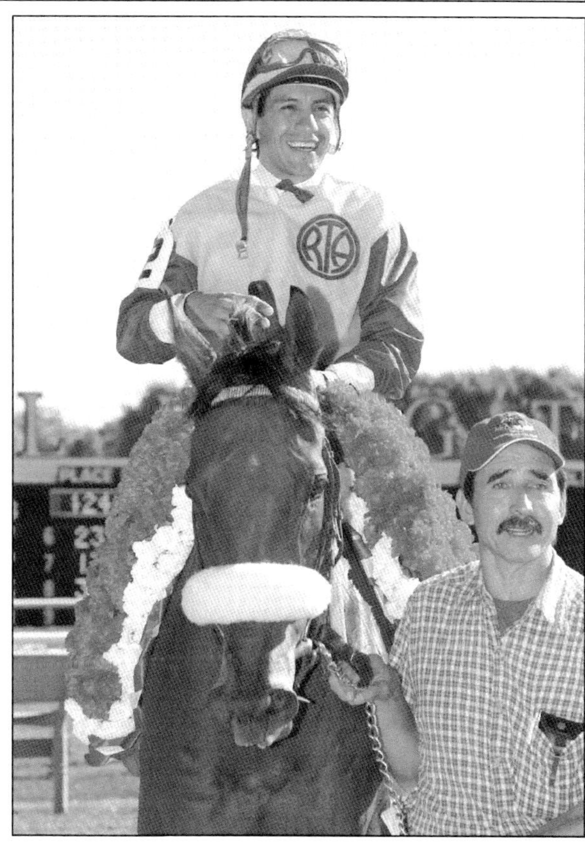

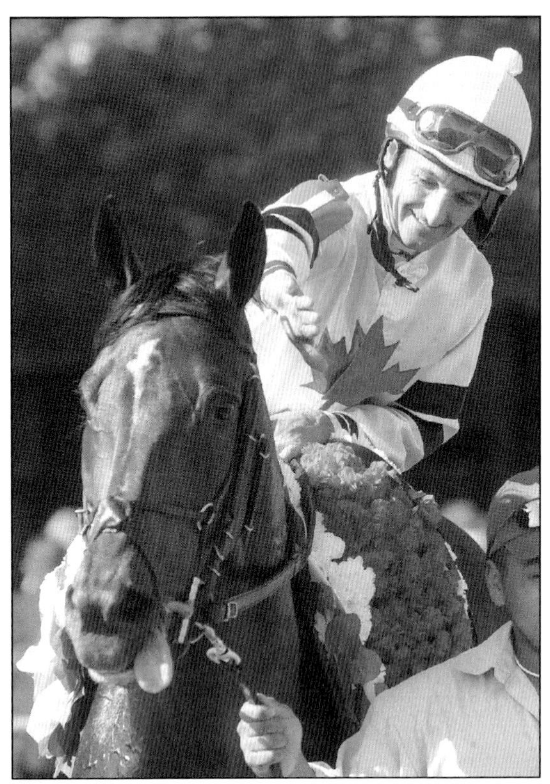

Jambalaya and Robbie Albarado celebrate after winning the 25th Arlington Million on August 11, 2007. The Canadian-bred son by Langfuhr covered the one-and-a-quarter-mile turf in 2:04.76. Trainer Catherine Day Phillips and husband Todd purchased Jambalaya for $2,500 at the 2003 Keeneland sale, and he rewarded them by earning $1,588,214. Phillips became the first female trainer to wear the Million crown. (Courtesy of Midwest Outdoors.)

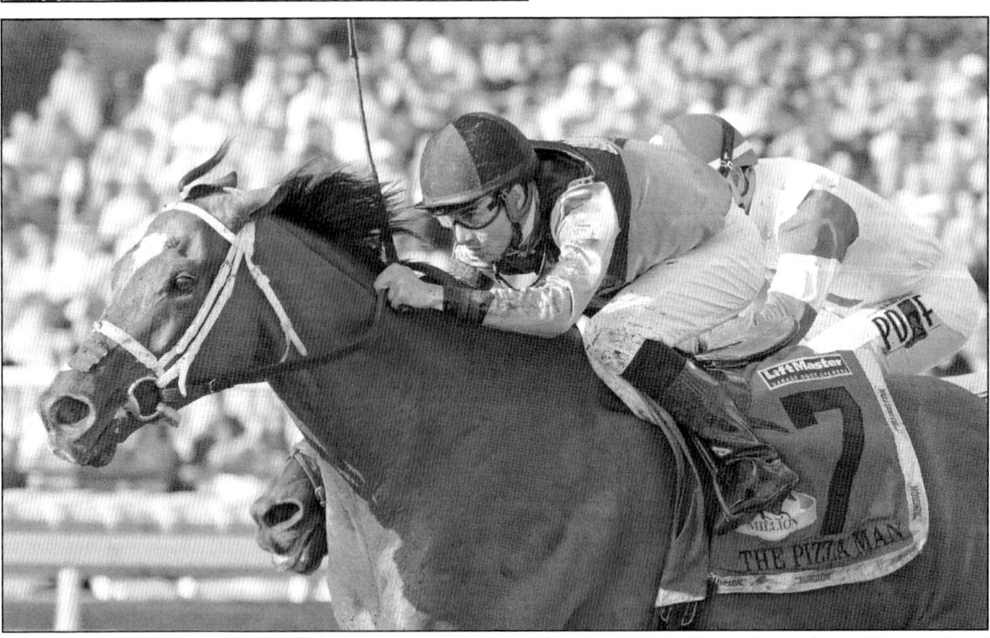

The Pizza Man won the 2015 Arlington Million and retired in 2017 as the richest Illinois-bred ever, with $2,158,941. The 2009 gelded son of English Channel—owned and bred by Midwest Thoroughbreds—scored 10 triumphs over Arlington's turf course. Trained by Roger Brueggemann and winning 17 of 36 starts, The Pizza Man won five graded stakes and was a three-time Million contestant. (Courtesy of Arlington Park.)

Chris Emigh recorded his 1,000th Arlington victory riding Baltic Star on July 2, 2017. Emigh, 46, earned his first Arlington title in 2006 with 110 wins, and scored his 3,500th career triumph in the 2014 Washington Park Handicap (Gr. III) with Avanzare. He is the fifth rider to win 1,000 races at Arlington, joining Earlie Fires, Pat Day, Carlos Silva, and Mark Guidry. (Author's collection.)

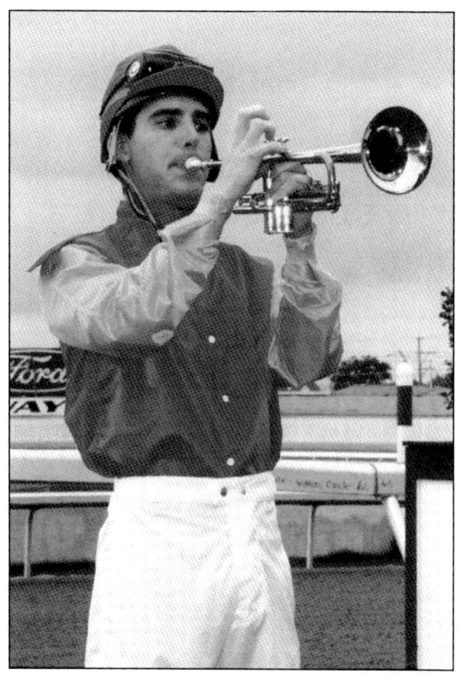

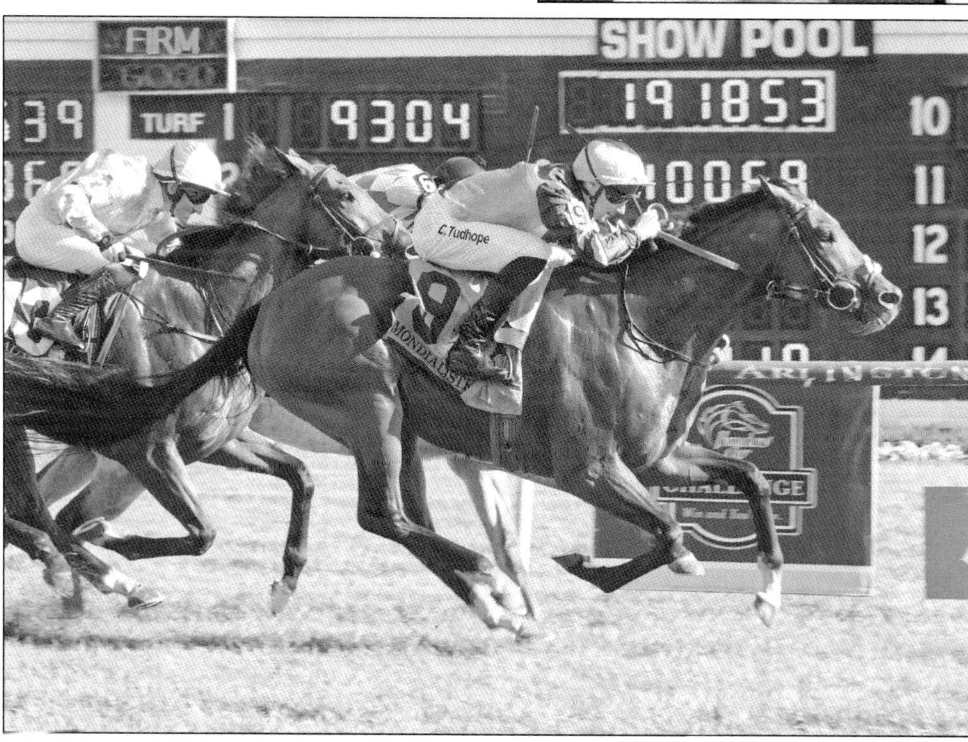

Mondialiste, a 2010 Irish-bred son of Galileo, captured the 34th edition of the Arlington Million on August 13, 2016. Daniel Tudhope rode the colt, whose name means "Globalist." Mondialiste was a true globalist, racing in Europe, Canada, Dubai, and Hong Kong. From 31 starts, he scored 5 wins, amassing $1,830,660 for owners Geoff and Sandra Turnbull and trainer David O'Meara. (Courtesy of Arlington Park.)

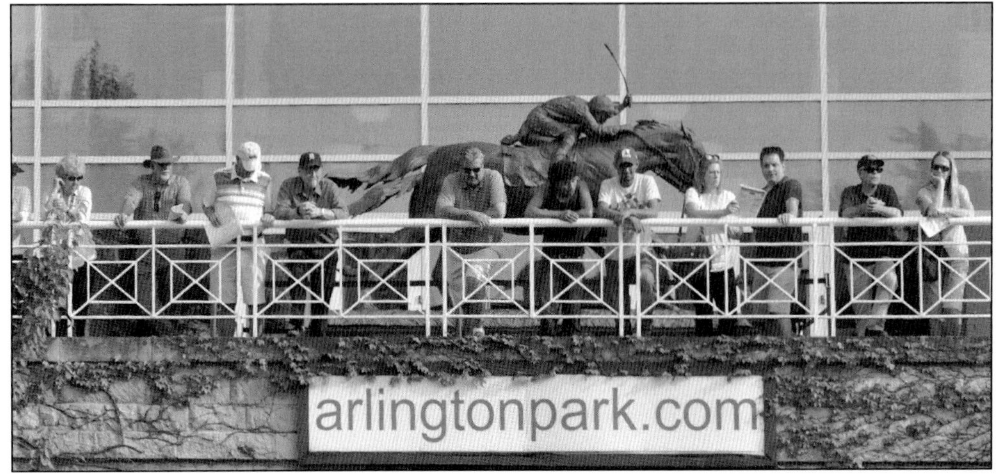

Fans are the lifeblood of Arlington Park, and on September 29, 2013, fourteen lucky patrons each cashed winning tickets in excess of $75,000 when the 10-cent Jackpot Pick 9's mandatory distribution was paid out. The jackpot pool had $759,941 in its bankroll, with another $700,000 added at the end of that season's meeting. (Author's collection.)

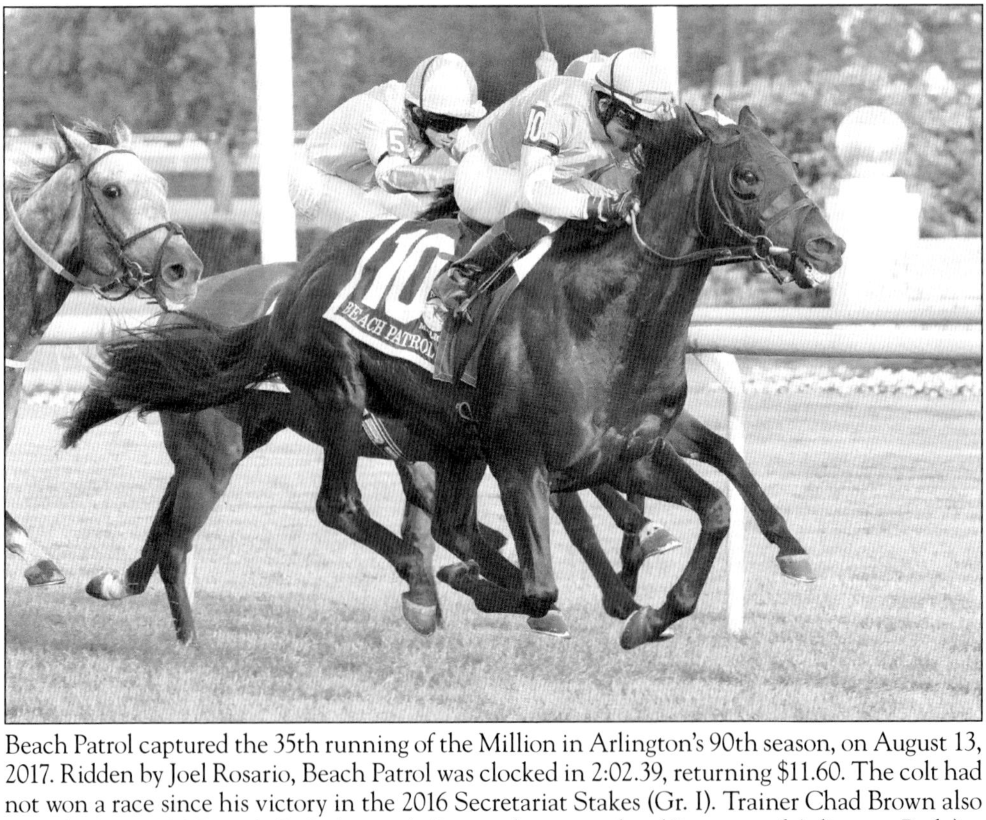

Beach Patrol captured the 35th running of the Million in Arlington's 90th season, on August 13, 2017. Ridden by Joel Rosario, Beach Patrol was clocked in 2:02.39, returning $11.60. The colt had not won a race since his victory in the 2016 Secretariat Stakes (Gr. I). Trainer Chad Brown also won the $600,000 Beverly D Stakes with Dacita that same day. (Courtesy of Arlington Park.)

Two longtime Arlington Park fans, Judy Davis-Wilson (left) and Dr. Bill Cassidy (right) share a laugh on Arlington's paddock area balcony in 2014, with *Against All Odds* looming in the background. Cassidy, an avid handicapper, is a former *Daily Racing Form* writer and now a journalism professor at Northern Illinois University, while Davis-Wilson works for the Delaware horse racing program. (Author's collection.)

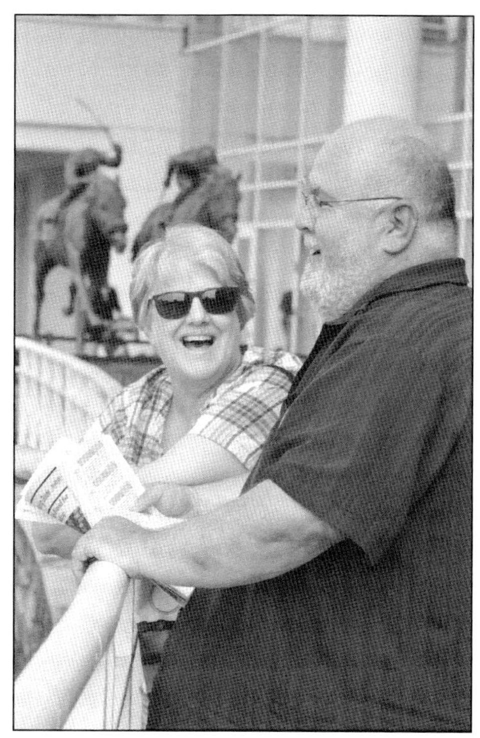

Arlington Park celebrated its 90th season in 2017. The green-and-white awnings near the saddling area are a testament to the longevity of this storied track, which has hosted many of the sport's greatest horses, jockeys, and trainers. Arlington Park has attracted starters from nearly every continent, and fans are hopeful that future champions will continue to grace its surface for generations to come. (Courtesy of Arlington Park.)

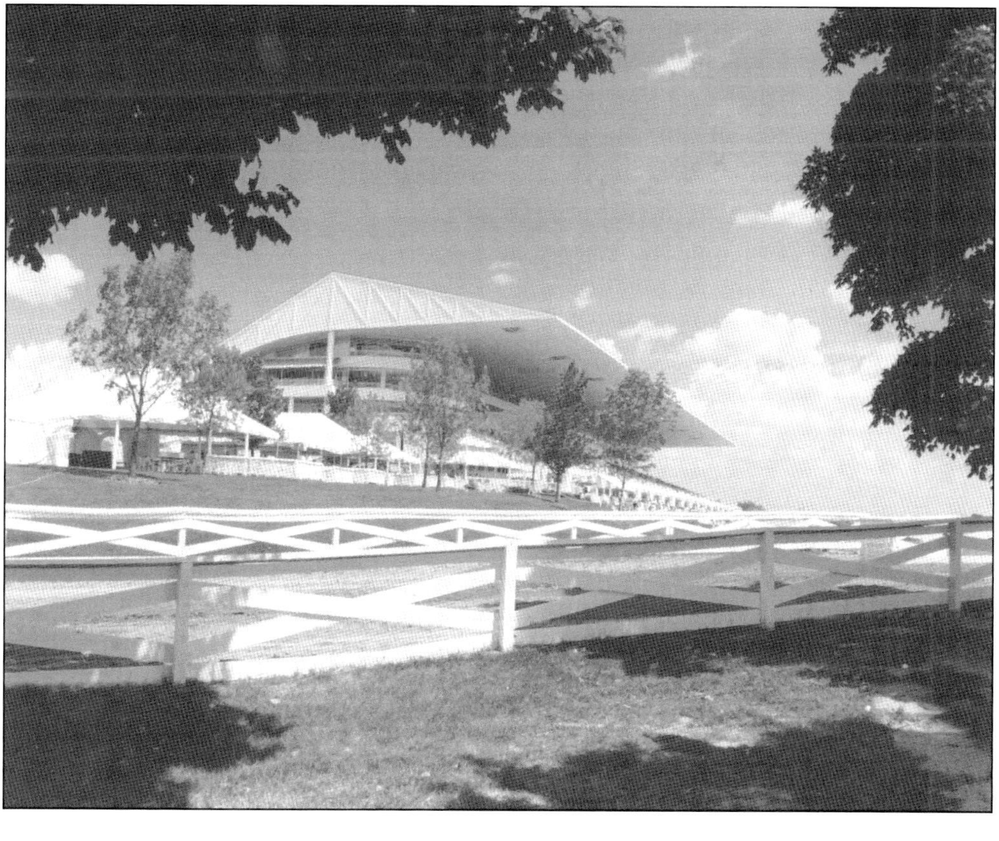

Discover Thousands of Local History Books Featuring Millions of Vintage Images

Arcadia Publishing, the leading local history publisher in the United States, is committed to making history accessible and meaningful through publishing books that celebrate and preserve the heritage of America's people and places.

Find more books like this at
www.arcadiapublishing.com

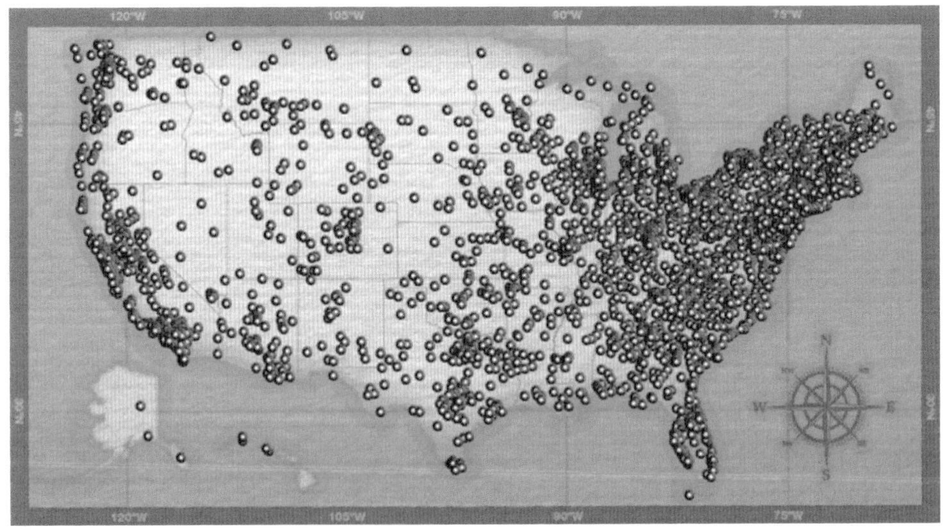

Search for your hometown history, your old stomping grounds, and even your favorite sports team.

Consistent with our mission to preserve history on a local level, this book was printed in South Carolina on American-made paper and manufactured entirely in the United States. Products carrying the accredited Forest Stewardship Council (FSC) label are printed on 100 percent FSC-certified paper.

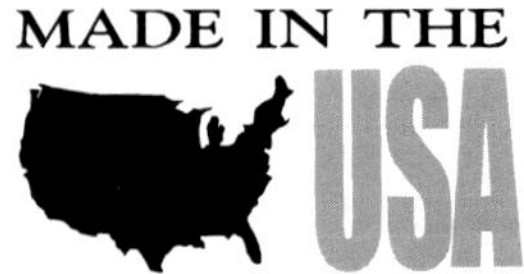